MW00625728

This book examines the developmer ⟨…⟩ school from its beginnings in Vienna in the 1870s to the present. The modern Austrian school is generally known for holding rigorous but heterodox views on a variety of issues: subjectivism, entrepreneurship, market processes, and the use of mathematics in economic theory. Professor Vaughn traces the origin of these views and shows how they form aspects of a largely coherent theoretical perspective organized around the problem of time and ignorance in human affairs. She demonstrates how concern for the notions of time and ignorance permeates Carl Menger's original works, primarily in his descriptions of market processes and in his linking of economic growth to the generation and dissemination of knowledge in society. The recognition of the importance of time and ignorance was the key that permitted other Austrians such as Ludwig von Mises and Friedrich Hayek to recognize the fatal flaws in central economic planning, evidenced as early as the 1930s, brought about by limited knowledge and time lags.

Despite current controversy, Professor Vaughn suggests that modern Austrian economics has begun to articulate a promising alternative research program that examines the implications of real time and ineradicable ignorance to economic theory and methodology. For anyone who is skeptical of the increasing formalism of modern economic theory, this cogent account of the Austrian approach should prove a refreshing change.

Historical Perspectives on Modern Economics

Austrian economics in America

Historical Perspectives on Modern Economics

General Editor: Professor Craufurd D. Goodwin, Duke University

This series contains original works that challenge and enlighten historians of economics. For the profession as a whole it promotes better understanding of the origin and content of modern economics.

Other books in the series:

Austrian economics in America
The migration of a tradition

Karen I. Vaughn
George Mason University

CAMBRIDGE
UNIVERSITY PRESS

PUBLISHED BY THE PRESS SYNDICATE OF THE UNIVERSITY OF CAMBRIDGE
The Pitt Building, Trumpington Street, Cambridge CB2 1RP

CAMBRIDGE UNIVERSITY PRESS
The Edinburgh Building, Cambridge CB2 2RU, United Kingdom
40 West 20th Street, New York, NY 10011-4211, USA
10 Stamford Road, Oakleigh, Melbourne 3166, Australia

First published 1994
Reprinted 1998
First paperback edition 1998

Library of Congress Cataloging-in-Publication Data is available.

A catalog record for this book is available from the British Library.

ISBN 0-521-44552-3 hardback
ISBN 0-521-63765-1 paperback

Transferred to digital printing 2003

To Garry and Jessica, who make everything matter

Contents

Preface

Twenty years have gone by since I first became seriously interested in Austrian economics. Although as an undergraduate in the early sixties I had read some books by Ludwig von Mises and had met Murray Rothbard and various New York Austrians and libertarians, my real attraction in those days was to the politics of the Austrians and not so much to their economics, of which I knew little. My real initiation into the economics of the Austrian tradition did not take place until 1974 at a conference on Austrian economics held in South Royalton, Vermont. Unbeknownst to me at the time, that conference was a decisive event in bringing about a revival of interest in the Austrian school among contemporary economists. For me, however, it was primarily an experience that raised a number of questions in my mind about economics in general and Austrian economics in particular that were not easily answered.

I found Austrian arguments intriguing, but elusive. I agreed with many of the sentiments expressed, but I could not quite figure out why I found them so appealing. I had first fallen in love with microeconomic theory as an undergraduate and had an abiding faith that it was sufficient to answer all important questions about the market (indeed, about life itself!), yet I also found Austrian critiques of parts of the corpus of microeconomics compelling. What was Austrian economics really about? How did it fit with the economics I had been taught? Could I believe both at once?

The question, "What is Austrian economics?" continued to haunt me long after the conference at South Royalton was over. I made my first attempt to answer that question more than a decade ago when my colleague Laurence Moss and I attempted to write a review article on Austrian economics for the *Journal of Economic Literature*. Despite the fact that we had the blessings of the editor and all good intentions, our project never came to completion largely because we could not agree on how to delimit the literature we were supposed to survey. Was Austrian economics simply the sum total of all the writings of everyone who was an Austrian? But there was such heterogeneity in this group that one could hardly find convincing links between, say, Morgenstern's game theory and Kirzner's theory of entrepreneurship to place them in the same camp. Was Austrian economics a particular set of ideas that challenged mainstream economics? In that case the ideas the Austrians claimed as their own were often espoused by other, non-Austrian economists. My coauthor and I gave up in confusion and went on to other things.

I never forgot the project, however, and for the past decade, as a side issue to my other pursuits, I continued my search for the real Austrian economics. I taught a course in Austrian economics for five straight years where one of the overriding aims, besides getting students to think critically about economics – any economics – was to help me answer my unanswered question. I read avidly in the contemporary Austrian literature, I wrote essays on Menger and on Hayek, I attended seminars in Austrian economics, and I even helped to establish an Austrian presence at George Mason University through participation in the Center for the Study of Market Processes.

During all this time, although I taught the subject and worked in the area, I resisted calling myself an "Austrian," because I could not give myself a label I did not fully understand. I found myself, as I often do, arguing both sides of the fence, depending on the nature of the adversary. In neoclassical circles, I defended the Austrian position, but with Austrians I pushed them to consider neoclassical arguments. This behavior did not necessarily win me many friends and, not surprisingly, kept me perpetually on the fringes of Austrian economics despite my obvious sympathies with those who did call themselves Austrians.

This book is finally my systematic attempt to answer that question that first plagued me almost two decades ago. I think I have finally arrived at a satisfying answer to my question by acknowledging that there really is as yet no "Austrian economics" where that means a fully articulated and importantly distinct economics apart from the neoclassical paradigm. There are Austrian insights and theories that supplement contemporary economics, and there are Austrian insights and theories that tend to undercut it. At its best, Austrian economics contains rumblings of a revolution that would in fact establish a new and different Austrian paradigm, but the ideas and their implications are still in flux.

The current flux in Austrian debate largely dictated an indirect approach to unraveling its subtleties. Instead of trying to lay out all the propositions of Austrian economics in a systematic manner, I have attempted to explain the essence of Austrian economics by recounting its history. More to the point, I try to explain modern Austrian economics by retelling the history of the modern Austrian school from the perspective of its current debates. Because of this specific focus, this book is not meant to be an exhaustive history of the development and impact of Austrian ideas from 1871 to the present. Such a book would be several times the length of this one and unnecessary for my specific purpose, which is to understand how a very small, very vocal, feisty and dedicated subset of the economics profession that currently identify with the Austrian school came to be where they are and to argue as they do.

Some may question the relevance of examining the origins of a controversy in order to either understand it or resolve it. As a toiler in the vineyards of a subdiscipline that has probably the lowest prestige rating in economics – the history of economic thought – I am all too familiar with this attitude. Who cares what Menger, or even Mises or Hayek said? All we should care about is whether the ideas currently under debate are right or wrong. My answer to that is twofold.

First, I examine the history of the debate because it is interesting for its own sake. The history of economic thought is interesting because it is the history of what is particularly human about us – our ideas, our beliefs, our ways of structuring the world around us. Economists are not generally impressed by claims that something is done just for the fun of it, however. They want to know what the underlying payoff is. In this case studying the history of the modern Austrian school has enormous instrumental value. In fact, it would be impossible fully to understand current Austrian ideas and debates without delving deep into the history of the Austrian tradition for the simple reason that current Austrians far more than their neoclassical contemporaries look to the whole one-hundred-year-long tradition for inspiration and enlightenment.

Most modern Austrians read Menger not as a historical curiosity the way a modern neoclassical economist might read Jevons, for example, but as a source of theoretical inspiration and enlightenment. Although separated by over a century, Menger, Hayek, Mises, Lachmann, and Kirzner are all part of the contemporary conversation about the meaning and substance of Austrian economics. They are all part of what Mises called the "real present," the span of time relevant for formulating a plan and carrying out the plan. We can define the intellectual real present as the time in which all participants are thought to contribute to the solving of some intellectual problem. For modern economists, the intellectual real present may be no more than a year or two. For Austrians, it is over a century in length.

For Austrians, the reason that the real present is so much longer than for other contemporary economists is that they do not believe, as Stigler once argued (1969), that all the insights of their chronological predecessors have been fully appreciated or incorporated into current discussion. In fact, they generally argue that neoclassical economics almost from its very inception traveled down the wrong track and left out important theoretical considerations that were part of the Austrian tradition. By studying Menger, Wieser, Mises, Hayek, and all the other stars in the Austrian firmament, modern Austrians believe they can find insights into the construction of a better economics than is currently practiced by the "mainstream." Hence the need to examine the origin, progress, discovery, and rediscovery of the ideas that form the leitmotif of the Austrian tradition.

I examine the history of the modern Austrian school, then, because the history is also the current literature from which modern Austrians draw. But the purpose of looking backward is to get our bearings on how to proceed forward. In trying to establish what the special contributions of the Austrian tradition have been we get glimmers of what it also could be.

In the writing of this book, I have come to believe that the issues raised by Austrians and the critiques of contemporary economics that have come from Austrian pens may well have within them the seeds of a genuine scientific revolution. The full nature of this revolution is but dimly perceived right now, but all the necessary elements are there: An unwillingness to abstract from time and ignorance, an insistence on the centrality of market processes, a renewed appreciation of economic institutions in market orders, and an increased willingness to understand man as both an individual and a social creature are all elements in contemporary Austrian debate that both build on the full sweep of the Austrian tradition and point the way forward to a new way of organizing economic theory. This book is an attempt to clear away the underbrush so that the hoped-for revolution can have more hospitable soil in which to take root.

Acknowledgments

I am grateful for the generous financial support I received from the Earhart Foundation, which allowed me to devote myself full time for two summers and part time for an academic year to this project. I also wish to thank the Krieble Foundation for support that enabled me to get relief from teaching responsibilities to devote myself to this project.

The broad outline of the story told here first appeared in *History of Political Economy* (Vaughn, 1990). An earlier version of chapter 7 was published in *Review of Political Economy* (Vaughn, 1992).

Although the writing of this book took less than two years, the thinking and planning are the product of a decade. During that time, I profited from innumerable conversations, seminars, and conferences, many of which my conscious (if not my unconscious) mind has forgotten. Of the many colleagues and friends whose ideas have inspired and influenced me along the way, I can name only a few.

First, I thank Laurence Moss, my erstwhile coauthor on a project on Austrian economics now long forgotten, whose many disagreements with me as well as his agreements helped me to see the problem I wanted to address.

I owe a debt as well to James Buchanan, whose own subjectivist inclinations, coupled with both his interest in Austrian economics and his reservations about the Austrian project, provided the basis for many fruitful conversations during the past ten years.

I am also greatly indebted to the many students who have passed through the Center for the Study of Market Processes in their pursuit of a Ph.D. in economics at George Mason University. Both in class and in the Market Process weekly colloquium, I learned as much from listening to them as, I hope, they learned from listening to me. I wish to single out for special acknowledgment the following students, two of whom are now launched on their own academic careers, whose ideas I have found especially stimulating and thought-provoking as I ruminated over the mysteries of Austrian economics: Peter Boettke, Steven Horwitz, and William Tulloh. Whether they knew it or not, all three helped me to think through crucial parts of this work. I am especially grateful to Peter

Boettke, who provided invaluable help by giving me detailed comments on my manuscript.

I also wish to acknowledge the contribution of two colleagues neither of whom would probably think of himself as a great contributor to this volume. First, Richard Wagner helped me immensely by listening to far too many monologues on my part that were masquerading as conversations, and by reading earlier drafts of each chapter. His unflagging interest in my project, as well as his own deep searching into the Austrian tradition, was an unceasing source of support for the past two years.

Second, my thanks go to my long-time colleague, Don Lavoie, who during his time in the Economics Department always seemed to me the person who most shared the odd wavelength on which I function. Not only has he helped me by reading and commenting upon chapters of this book, he has been a major source of the enthusiasm I now have come to feel for many Austrian ideas.

Finally, I wish to acknowledge a person who has been more than a colleague and more than a friend to me for almost all of my adult life, my husband, Garry. All through the years, through thick and (sometimes very) thin, Garry has been my one-man cheering section, my constant emotional support, the one person who has always believed in me and had confidence in me no matter what the problem and no matter what the odds. I started this book at a particularly bad time in my life. That I am finishing it full of hope is in no small measure due to his presence in my life.

CHAPTER 1

Introduction

It has now become commonplace to point out that Austrian economics has undergone something of a revival in the past twenty years. Certainly, the number of books and articles that take an Austrian view of some issue or another or that make reference to the views of some well-known Austrian economist have grown dramatically since the early 1970s. There are Austrian graduate programs at two universities, New York University and George Mason University, a Ludwig von Mises Institute at Auburn University, and innumerable undergraduate courses in Austrian economics taught at colleges and universities around the United States. Sessions on Austrian themes at professional meetings always draw a respectably sized crowd, and in a few areas such as banking theory and methodology, Austrian ideas are on the cutting edge of the profession. And since the collapse of communism in Eastern Europe and the former USSR, there are few economists who have not heard that the Austrians were right after all about the economic impossibility of socialism.

Although the number of self-identified Austrian economists is still quite small as a percentage of the economics profession as a whole, a marked increase in interest in Austrian ideas – even among those who disagree with most of them – cannot be denied. Yet, despite a greater professional presence of Austrian ideas and Austrian economists now, there is still little general understanding as to what Austrian economics is all about. Austrians say interesting things about the economy that often seem to be true, but how these all relate to contemporary economic theory and practice is still something of a mystery to the profession at large.

Those outside modern Austrian circles are often puzzled by many Austrian claims. Some economists are prone to dismiss Austrian economics as nothing more than conventional economics with a mystifying and wholly anachronistic aversion to mathematics and econometric modeling: As one of my colleagues rather unsympathetically put it, Austrian economics is simply neoclassical economics in words. Others see little more than free market advocacy in Austrian writings. These are people who perhaps have read only Hayek's *Road to Serfdom* (1944), or dabbled in Mises' later writings, or read some of Rothbard's defenses of libertarian politics. Such judgments are not wholly without justification. Austrians do

1

avoid expressing their ideas in mathematical symbols and most do defend free markets, although this latter activity is hardly unique to Austrians. It is even becoming a rather fashionable activity among intellectuals as the benefits of free markets are increasingly extolled by policy makers from formerly communist countries.

Aversion to mathematics and free market advocacy are distinctively Austrian traits, but they are also superficial identifying characteristics. Those who look a bit deeper often find in the Austrian literature, especially as produced by Ludwig von Mises and Friedrich Hayek, by Israel Kirzner and Ludwig Lachmann, an understanding of market processes that they find enlightening and convincing. Austrians write about the role of entrepreneurship in competitive markets; they describe competition as rivalry, highlight the heterogeneity of products and production techniques that one finds in a market process, and emphasize the role of competition in bringing about new products and new discoveries.

Unlike conventional economists, Austrians are more intrigued by the dynamic and unpredictable change inherent in markets than by the stability that makes equilibrium models appealing tools of analysis. As a consequence, for many economists, especially those who teach introductory courses, who study law and economics, who do public policy analysis and in particular antitrust work, or who have been interested in the contrasts between planned and market economies, the Austrians have touched chords that have resonated with their own intuitive understanding of the economic world, if not always with their theoretical models. Austrian economics seems to be saying something true about the world, something that economists can recognize without being able fully to articulate in the language in which they have been trained.

Indeed, some economists have been so taken with what they call the Austrian "intuitions" that they have felt called to "formalize" them using standard economics modeling techniques. This was the fate, for example, of Hayek's discussion of incentives during the socialist calculation debate when, a decade later, economists such as Oscar Lange (1962) and Leonid Hurwicz (1973) began modeling incentive compatible systems. Or, we might point to the economics of information that was in part motivated by Hayek's essays on knowledge. We also note that Sir John Hicks developed a formal theory of capital he called Austrian (1973) and inspired a cottage industry in modeling time-consuming capital processes (Burmeister, 1974). More recently, Ron Heiner (1983) has attempted to model Austrian insights into the link between uncertainty and institutions in a highly formal manner. Hence, Austrian ideas are sometimes thought to be absorbed into the mainstream. Yet, rather than being grateful for having their fuzzy notions systematized, Austrian are more likely to complain that the formal models miss the point of what they are trying to say. Where formalization means mathematical models of equilibrium states of the world, Austrians would just as soon pass.

To the uninitiated, this is in many respects the most puzzling aspect of Austrian attitudes. Austrians do not seem to want to play the game by the same rules as the rest of the economics profession, but the rest of the profession is not quite sure what rules they do want to follow. However, here we encounter a catch-22. When Austrians try to talk about the rules – why they do not like the rules of the mainstream of the economics profession or why they think they have better rules – they are accused of concentrating too much on "mere methodology." Methodology is generally believed to be what you do when you cannot do real economics. The cry is often heard: If those Austrians would just forget about methodology and actually do some economic analysis, they would have more credibility. Yet, how do you do convincing economic analysis when your methods are misunderstood or dismissed by those in the dominant game?

The modern Austrian literature reflects this dilemma first by consisting of a disproportionate amount of criticism of mainstream economics and second by containing an unusual amount of methodological writings. Instead of being a source of weakness, however, it is an inescapable consequence of the nature of the Austrian tradition. Austrian writings, as they have emerged since the mid-1970s, present no less than a fundamental challenge to how economists look at the world and do their work. At the very least, Austrian economics is a complete reinterpretation of the methods, substance, and limitations of contemporary economics. At most, it is a radical, perhaps even revolutionary restructuring of economics.

That I describe the Austrian relationship to neoclassical economics as a range rather than a point, however, reflects a deep, divisive, and largely unreconciled debate within the Austrian literature itself. Although current Austrians all acknowledge the same ancestors and emphasize the same principles, the interpretation they place on the relationship of their doctrines to conventional neoclassical analysis divides Austrians broadly into two camps. By exploring the nature of the division between these two camps, we will be in a position both to be clear about what Austrian economics is and is not, and to understand why the answer has been so elusive for so long. But before we describe what it is that Austrian economists disagree about, we should first understand what they have in common.

All modern-day Austrians agree to a few basic propositions: Most fundamentally, they agree that economics should make the world intelligible in terms of human action. This seems to be shorthand for two related ideas. The first is that a social science should devise explanations about social phenomena that are traceable to the ideas and actions of individual human beings. In more familiar language, economics should subscribe to methodological individualism. The second implication is that since individuals only experience the world through the filter of their own subjective intelligence, economics must explain human action as the responses people make to their subjective interpretations of their internal and external environment. Austrians call this either "thorough-going" or "radical" subjectivism to differentiate it from the more limited subjectivism of neoclassical economics that is content to posit subjective preferences with little attention to other manifestations of human subjectivism in its theories. Such other manifestations include the subjectivism of expectations and of knowledge itself.

Austrians also agree that all human action takes place in time and always under conditions of limited knowledge; this requires that economics not abstract from either time or ignorance in developing its theories. From this, Austrians infer that economics should be about how humans pursue their projects and plans over time, and with limited knowledge of present conditions and with pervasive uncertainty about the future. One prominent area of investigation for Austrians is the institutional remedies humans create to reduce the consequences of uncertainty and ignorance. To paraphrase Hayek, Austrians believe the crucial question economics needs to answer is not why people might be wrong from time to time in their economic decisions, but given the nature of the world they face, why they should ever be right (Hayek, 1978a:86–88).

Although neoclassical economists could also argue that they are theorizing about the human pursuit of projects and plans within the known environment when they model choice as constrained maximization, Austrians are likely to claim that constrained maximization is too narrow a framework to capture the kinds of action that they take to be distinctly human. Human action involves typical economizing behavior, to be sure, but it also involves breaking out of known constraints and discovering new ways of doing things and new wants to satisfy. In fact, the whole Austrian emphasis on uncertainty is linked to a concern with the limitations of knowledge and the way human beings overcome those limitations. To an Austrian, the fact that knowledge is a multifaceted, heterogeneous, disaggregated, often private or tacit and imperfect phenomenon is one of the driving features of the market process. Further, this view of knowledge leads to questions about communication and learning in market processes that take us beyond usual neoclassical concerns.

In sum, all Austrians agree that the market process is best understood as the concatenation of all the actions and interactions of heterogeneous individuals with differential knowledge and different expectations about the future who pursue their projects and plans through exchange with one another. Following Hayek (1976:108), they are likely to refer to this phenomenon as a "catallaxy" rather than an economy. An economy, they argue, presumes some single intelligence that wishes to "economize" on resources to fulfill an articulable set of objectives. A catallaxy implies a set of procedures within which heterogeneous individuals pursue their own plans in cooperation and competition with one another; a structure where there is no one articulable goal but only many often conflicting individual goals. Further, the interaction of all these purposeful individuals leads to unintended consequences that can never be foreseen in their entirety and always lead to new knowledge as a by-product. This action, interaction, and their unintended consequences is a never-ending process that is not fully captured in contemporary models of economic equilibrium.

Although all Austrians agree with these propositions, not all agree on what follows from them. In fact, two sharply different views of how Austrians should go about constructing economic theories of human action have emerged.

In the current debate, one side of the divide believes that Austrian insights into time and ignorance, subjectivity and processes serve as a vital supplement to neoclassical economics. This side of the argument, most clearly articulated by Israel Kirzner but subscribed to by many others, accepts much of the basic corpus of conventional economics but wishes to change the emphasis in economic explanation away from equilibrium states to the economic processes that lead to their achievement. Kirzner and those who agree with him argue that in economics, equilibrium does no more than describe an end state in a market process, whereas it is the process itself that is of interest. Hence, while accepting the basic legitimacy of the equilibrium construct for theorizing about economic action, these Austrians see their role as one of providing a theoretical supplement to show how equilibrium is in principle capable of being achieved. For Kirzner, as well as for others, the inclusion of an entrepreneurial function in standard economics goes a long way to providing the necessary supplement.

The other side of the debate takes a far more radical view. This side, taking its inspiration from Ludwig Lachmann, believes that taking time and ignorance seriously requires abandoning conventional concepts of equilibrium and developing a whole new paradigm for Austrian economics. This side would argue that all of the disparate threads of Austrian literature can only be woven into whole cloth by abandoning static equilibrium theory entirely and embracing some form of evolutionary process theory that does not have a static state as an end point. For this group, constant, endogenously driven change is the hallmark of a market process. Interestingly, both sides look for doctrinal support to the same Austrian ancestors – Mises, Hayek, and ultimately Menger. Even more interestingly, both sides are correct in their appeals to the same legitimating ancestry.

In the following pages, I argue that this current controversy, fully articulated only during the 1980s, has roots that go back to the original work by the founder of the Austrian school, Carl Menger's *Principles of Economics*. Both sides claim the same founding ancestor with complete confidence because the same ideas and conflicts that we find in modern debate are present in the pages of Menger's writing. Menger, so often hailed as one of the originators of modern neoclassical economics because of the central role demand played in his theory of value and because of his independent discovery of the principle of diminishing marginal utility, is also the originator of ideas and theories that are not generally captured in conventional neoclassical economics. Although the substance of many Mengerian ideas were easily melded into a neoclassical orthodoxy, the entire organizing principle of Menger's view of the economy, the metaphor that he used to understand economic order, was different from that of his neoclassical contemporaries.

Philip Mirowski (1989) has shown at great length that early neoclassical economics borrowed its method of theorizing from nineteenth-century physics. Mirowski also argues that Menger, unlike his contemporaries, was not at all influenced by nineteenth-century physics and was, in fact, quite innocent of its substance. Mirowski counts this as an inadequacy and accuses Menger of borrowing the mantle of science for his work without the least idea of what science was about (260–261). What Mirowski counts as a shortcoming in Menger, however, I regard as a lucky, perhaps even accidental strength. Menger's innocence of nineteenth-century physics means that he was never completely captured by the methodology of physics that was to lead to the theoretical dead end of modern neoclassical economics that Mirowski so eloquently describes.

On the other hand, Menger did not completely escape allusions to physics; mentions of equilibrium do lightly pepper his prose. Even more, some of his statements about long-run prices can only be understood within the context of general equilibrium states. But equilibrium terminology notwithstanding, physics was not Menger's analogue for scientific economics. Max Alter (1990) has shown that Menger had more acquaintance with evolutionary biology, at least as he understood it, than with physics. Although he had some objections to a slavish borrowing of biological analogies to illuminate economics, the biological analogy was nevertheless an underlying theme of his work (Menger, [1883] 1985:129–138). Hence, Menger's casual indifference to the characteristics and determination of equilibrium states, but his profound concern with the causes and consequences of economic growth and with questions of increasing knowledge, technological capacity, and increasing economic complexity – all issues that would more naturally be analyzed in an evolutionary context.

At the time of Menger's writing, the discordance between Menger's organizing vision and that of his neoclassical contemporaries was not widely recognized. Menger's successors understandably developed those aspects of Menger's theory that most closely linked up with the emerging neoclassical consensus: his theory of value, opportunity cost, and capital. The side of Menger concerned with processes and change was taken for granted and served no more than as a background assumption to a basically neoclassical program. It was only after 1920 – when first Ludwig von Mises and then, a decade later, Friedrich Hayek engaged in a long and frustrating debate over the economic feasibility of centrally planned economies – that the suppressed Mengerian vision began to be rediscovered.

This debate has justly been described as a turning point both for Austrian economics and for Friedrich Hayek in particular (Caldwell, 1988; Kirzner, 1988; Vaughn, 1990). It kindled a searching if somewhat delayed reexamination of the underlying theoretical presumptions of economic theory and the way in which these presumptions were translated into economic policy. It eventually was to serve not only as a critique of naive applications of neoclassical economics to real-world situations, but, decades later, it was to provide a new set of questions around which to organize Austrian debate.

During the socialism debate, the Austrians increasingly perceived that the reason socialism seemed plausible to neoclassical economists was that they began with a static equilibrium model in which discovery, innovation, changing preferences, and disparate knowledge were ignored. These were the very issues that sixty years earlier had concerned Menger as well. Yet, despite their seminal importance, even Hayek's antisocialism essays – essays that were replete with insights into the nature and use of knowledge in economies, that repeatedly emphasized the dynamic nature of real markets, and that cried to economists to pay attention to the details of market processes rather than stopping short with broad generalization – were not sufficient to engender an immediate revival of Mengerian economics. It would take thirty more years for the insights that Mises and Hayek drew from Menger and applied to the real problem of an alternative economic order to enflame academic debate.

These thirty years were years partly of Austrian assimilation into the mainstream of the academy and partly of Austrian diaspora. Those who assimilated (and they were eminent economists who had left Austria during the 1920s or 1930s, men like Joseph Schumpeter, Fritz Machlup, Oskar Morgenstern, and Gottfried Haberler) carried on inquiry into Austrian themes using accepted neoclassical language and techniques. Those who did not assimilate (Ludwig von Mises was the most prominent example here, although a case can be made that this was Friedrich Hayek's fate as well) existed on the sidelines of academia, marking time and despairing for the future. The perceived triumph of the theory of socialism over its critics had robbed any potential Austrian economics research program of professional credentials.

In the early 1970s, for a variety of reasons both academic and political, the time of Austrian quietude gave way to an awakening of renewed interest in the Austrian tradition. Taking place mostly in the United States, but also in England, Germany, and, to a lesser extent, Austria itself, a new generation of budding economists became attracted to Austrian ideas and Austrian policy views. They were perhaps as much driven by their criticism of the reigning orthodoxy in economics as they were attracted by Austrian ideas. Whatever the motivating force, they once again took up the mantle of Menger and reopened the issues of process, change, growth, and complexity that Menger had begun in his *Principles of Economics*.

The twenty-year period from the early 1970s to the early 1990s has seen a flowering of new Austrian literature. It began with a small, often beleaguered group of people, intrigued with the economics of Ludwig von Mises and talking mainly to each other about his work and the Austrian economics it represented to them. Eventually, the small group grew larger (and older) and opened up their conversation to include friendly voices closer to the mainstream who could help them better understand the relationship between the Austrian tradition and the orthodoxy against which they were rebelling. The conversation continued to widen as others within the profession – such as post-Keynesians, Shackelean radical subjectivists, and institutionalists who have rebelled at some of the same static, equilibrium theorizing that the Austrians criticize, and who have made the same criticisms of the institutionless, ahistorical nature of contemporary theory that characterize Austrian writing – have entered in.[1]

---

[1] The conversations have not always been free of acrimony. Especially where groups view themselves on opposite sides of the political fence, the language has gotten heated. See for example, William Dugger's intemperate diatribe against Austrian economics (1989:115–124), in a volume of *Researches in the History of Economic Thought* that was intended to present a friendly exchange of views between institutionalists and Austrians.

Out of this conversation has come a self-conscious reflection on what Austrian economics is or might be, after all. (One of my students once quipped that the most accurate definition of a modern Austrian economist is one who asks the question, "What is Austrian economics?") And as we noted above, what has been discovered is that there is no one clear and uncontroversial version of what modern Austrian economics is all about. Some see the strength of the Austrian tradition in its ability to supplement current equilibrium theories with stories of adjustment processes that call upon all the Austrian stock of insights into knowledge, expectations, and creative choice. Others see the only possible resolution of all the tenets of Austrian doctrine to be a recasting of Austrian ideas in an entirely different paradigm. These two positions, exemplified by Israel Kirzner on one hand and Ludwig Lachmann on the other, at the very least seem likely to continue to engender vigorous debate. Clearly, the debate illustrates my contention that not all the important questions in Austrian economics are answered. More important, it marks Austrian economics as a vibrant intellectual endeavor.

In the concluding chapters of this book, I examine the reasons offered by those on each side for their vision of what Austrian economics is all about and offer my own suggestions for the future of Austrian economics. Despite the daunting nature of the task, I ultimately side with the Lachmannians, who argue that if Austrian economics is to have a future, it must lead to a complete recasting of the organizing principle of economic theory. Otherwise, it seems inevitable that the ideas of the new Austrians will either fade from view or be absorbed into the neoclassical orthodoxy in ways that Austrians will claim still miss the point.

A word is in order here about terminology. I use the terms "neoclassical economics" and "mainstream economics" frequently and interchangeably in the following pages. I realize that such a blanket term covers many uncomfortable and perhaps incompatible bedfellows. I suppose one could argue that I am using the terms to mean anyone who is not Austrian and does not also call himself something else (i.e., institutionalist, post-Keynesian, radical political economist, etc.). Such a charge is only partly fair. In fact, I think there is one defining feature of "mainstream" and "neoclassical" economics that warrants the lumping together of many different theoretical approaches. That is a program that explains all human action as variations on constrained maximization where preferences are considered to be given, well-ordered, and stable, and where there is widespread knowledge of constraints. In such a program, the solution to any economic problem is inherent in the data of the preferences and constraints as a matter of "blueprint logic," as Schumpeter might have said (see [1942] 1962:196). This constrained maximization paradigm may be formalized in mathematical terms, but even if it is not,

the logic of neoclassical economics always suggests that such formalization is possible.

What I mean by Austrian economics is not quite so easily stated. Indeed,
the rest of this book is an exercise in answering that question. The old
Austrian school presents no problems of definition. Austrian economics
from 1871 until the 1930s was economics developed by Austrians in
Austria. It was not even clear that the national distinction reflected any
sharp doctrinal differences with neoclassical economics. However, clearly
by the late 1960s in the United States, Austrian economics was regarded
by its practitioners as an alternative form of economics analysis from the
mainstream, and the set of Austrian economists in this sense was dominated by Americans. How this transition took place is, of course, one of
the central topics of this book.

By "new-Austrians," then, I mean those economists who, from some-
where in the 1960s on, residing mostly in the United States, saw themselves as participating in a tradition of economics that began with Menger
but was carried forth and modified by Ludwig von Mises. The new
Austrians, then, were Austrians by adoption, not by birth, and their
allegiance originally was primarily to Mises and only secondarily to the
rest of the older Austrian school. For these new Austrians, Mises set the
terms of discussion and the topics of debate. We will see that the progress
of the new Austrians since the late 1960s has largely been a function of
their willingness to go beyond Mises in their exploration of the Austrian
paradigm.[2]

My primary goal in this book is to tell the story of the new Austrians and to
trace the genesis of the modern debate. That is interesting enough in
itself to justify the writing and the reading. The story naturally has a plot,
setting, fascinating characters, and intriguing ideas. Even if one does not
find much common ground between himself and the conclusions of the
modern Austrian school, the genesis and development of the new Austrians illuminate much of twentieth-century economic thought.

There are deeper reasons, however, for coming to understand what the
new Austrians are all about. Whether one is an Austrian or not, whether
one is sympathetic or not, the new Austrians generally have interesting

[2] Unfortunately, I use the term "paradigm" frequently throughout this work. I am sorry
and apologize to the reader immediately, but I simply could not think of another word
to capture the idea of an organizing principle or set of ideas. I also use "research
program" from time to time. Again, the overused term does convey important meaning
as a set of problems to investigate and so is indispensable. I do not hereby mean to
suggest that I subscribe to or am offering any accounts of the applicability of either
Kuhn's (1970) or Lakatos's (1970) (or anybody else's for that matter) theories of
scientific progress.

things to say about human action and interactions that can throw new light on economics. Moreover, the contemporary debate among the new Austrians is well worth our attention. The debate is not simply about some arcane, long defunct set of ideas; it is about the very core of economic analysis. The debate within Austrian circles about the relationship between Austrian economics and the neoclassical orthodoxy is really a debate about the nature of equilibrium constructs in economic analysis itself: about the appropriateness and usefulness of the assumptions and organizing principles of neoclassical economics. Surely, a debate over such fundamental and deeply planted pillars of economic theory is worth some attention whichever side one finally takes.

CHAPTER 2

Carl Menger and the foundations of Austrian economics

Modern Austrians of all stripes uniformly trace their beginnings back to the writings of Carl Menger (1840–1921), and especially to his *Principles of Economics* (1981), first published in 1871. Yet in many respects, Menger is an enigmatic ancestor whose work is only now beginning to be fully understood. And the more that we know of Menger's writings, the more it becomes obvious that Menger was a complex thinker whose unresolved theoretical problems are parent to at least two different modern Austrian views.

That this is the case is underlined by the contrasting ways in which Menger's writings have been interpreted in the twentieth century. He can and has been interpreted both as an unproblematic founder of neoclassical economics and as the originator of an alternative style of economic reasoning that challenges the neoclassical orthodoxy.[1] Both interpretations can be supported by good textual evidence. Although ultimately I think the interpretation that stresses Menger's differences from neoclassical economics is the more convincing one, it is by no means decisively so.

The textual ambiguities that account for much of the disagreement over the real Mengerian message will constitute the heart of this chapter. But first it is important to note another reason for the existence of starkly contrasting interpretations of Menger's place in the development of economic thought: the relative inaccessibility of Menger's text even within his own lifetime and certainly for years after his death.

Never a prolific writer, Menger was nonetheless a fastidious one, and he spent the last several decades of his life working fruitlessly on a second edition of his *Principles of Economics* that remained unfinished at his death.[2] In the meanwhile, he refused to allow the first edition to be

---

[1] To limit the field to two interpretations may be too modest. Modern economists as diverse as Friedrich Hayek, Israel Kirzner, Ludwig Lachmann, Sir John Hicks, Vivian Walsh, and Eric Streissler have all claimed with good justification to be following up on Mengerian themes in their work.

[2] A posthumous second edition of the *Principles* was published in 1923, edited by Menger's son, Karl Menger. Considerably longer than the first edition, it had to be assembled from assorted notes left by Carl Menger, Sr. While there is some debate as to how well the new edition represents Menger's thinking, the fact remains that because it was not available until 1923, a whole generation of economists before that date had limited access to his writings. And it is not clear that the second edition had much

reprinted, thereby depriving the next generation of economists of the opportunity to profit from a direct confrontation with his written statement. Hence, although economists with varying levels of allegiance to the Austrian school have actively and continuously participated in scholarly debate since the founding of the Austrian school, until recently, the works of Menger, the founder, have been relatively unknown. His ideas were presented to the mainstream of professional economics through the filter of his most famous students, Friedrich von Wieser and Eugen von Bohm-Bawerk, who each developed their own interpretation of Menger's message. Relatively few economists outside of Austria, even in Menger's lifetime, actually read Menger's most important work, his *Principles of Economics.*

Because the *Principles* was largely unread, Menger himself was known outside of Austria not so much for his important theoretical economics as for his later, more passionate writings on methodology. At the beginning of the twentieth century, Menger's name was most famous as one of the protagonists in the *methodenstreit,* the battle over methods between the Austrian school and the German historical school that many economists later judged to be a waste of professional energy (Schumpeter, 1954:814).

Hence it was that as far as contributions to theoretical economics are concerned, for nearly one hundred years, Carl Menger was regarded almost exclusively as simply one of the three revolutionaries who "discovered" modern neoclassical economics. Textbook after textbook in the history of economic thought throughout the twentieth century has credited Menger with being a codiscoverer along with William Stanley Jevons and Leon Walras, of subjective value theory and especially of the theory of diminishing marginal utility (see, e.g., Spiegel, 1964; Hutchison, 1966; Roll, 1974; Rima, 1986). In such textbooks, Menger is usually presented as a less scientifically minded founder than the other two because his version of value theory was written in words rather than mathematics (Knight, 1950:12). His apparent lack of mathematical skill is blamed for the supposed lack of rigor in his presentation of his theory.[3] Nevertheless, a founder he was, and his reliance on words rather than on mathematics did not reduce his claim in the eyes of the profession to have independently discovered the central core of neoclassical economic analysis (Stigler, 1941).

impact on contemporary economic thought. The second edition was also never translated into English.

[3] Jaffe argues that Menger's failure to use mathematics to develop his theory of value was a matter of principle and not of ignorance. He refers to correspondence between Menger and Walras in which Menger acknowledged mathematics as an expository device only and argued for the necessity instead of employing his "analytic-compositive method" (1975:521).

Menger is credited with a further claim to originality in the conventional textbook literature. He is generally praised for presenting a theoretical
structure that permitted his disciple, Friedrich von Wieser, to develop the
notion of opportunity costs as the logical extension of Menger's theory of
diminishing marginal utility, and in addition, an imputation theory of
factor pricing that derived from Menger's theory of goods of a higher
order. For most of the twentieth century, these were regarded as the major
positive contributions of the early Austrian school to economic thought.

Of course, assessments of the implications of these contributions
differed. Whereas mainstream economists approvingly regarded Menger's theories as forerunners to their more formal incorporation into
conventional economics, earlier Austrians tended to see them as fully
developed cornerstones of their particular brand of economic analysis.
Hence it was that mainstream economists could regard Menger's theory
of marginal use, for example, as an imperfect statement of a mathe-
matically precise theory of diminishing marginal utility while some latter-
day Austrians would regard it as a complete statement of the principles of
individual rational choice. Or, alternatively, neoclassical economists
could come to regard Menger's theory of higher-order goods as a blind
theoretical alley, while Austrians could see it as an important forerunner
to the Austrian theory of the business cycle.

In general, the textbooks in the history of economic thought reflected
professional consensus and treated the Austrian school as an episode in
the development of neoclassical economics whose major insights were
quickly and painlessly absorbed into the mainstream, an assessment that
was surprisingly shared by Austrians themselves in the 1920s and 1930s
(Mises, 1984:41; Hayek, 1992:62). By the fourth quarter of the twentieth
century, however, the neat classification system that characterized most
textbooks (and by implication, also characterized the way most economists understood the history of their profession) started to break down.

Menger's *Principles* was belatedly translated into English in 1950. However, it was not until the 1970s that a serious reevaluation of Menger's
contributions to economics began. In 1972, in commemoration of the
one-hundredth anniversary of the marginal revolution, Erich Streissler
published an article that asked, "To What Extent Was the Austrian School
Marginalist?" and concluded that the answer was "not very much at all "[4]
This article was followed in 1973 by a volume of essays edited by Sir John
Hicks along with W. Weber, *Carl Menger and the Austrian School of Economics*,
which was largely dedicated to a reassessment of Menger's capital theory,

---

[4] Streissler argued that Menger's *Principles* was a "conscious complement to Adam
Smith's *Wealth of Nations* and for this reason it is not static, but concerned with
economic progress" (1972:427). I find Streissler's argument wholly convincing.

and in 1975 by William Jaffe's essay, "Menger, Jevons and Walras Dehomogenized," in which he argued that the differences among the three heroes of the marginal revolution were far more important in assessing their ideas than were the similarities. In 1978, in an issue of the *Atlantic Economic Journal* devoted to essays on Carl Menger and his relevance to contemporary economics theory, Ludwig Lachmann published a short article that was to prove especially important to the modern reinterpretation of Menger, "Carl Menger and the Revolution of Subjectivism" (1978c). The upshot of all this was that it was no longer easy to regard Menger as simply a neoclassical economist in embryo.

Although each of these reassessments of Menger centered on a different problem, they all had one theme in common: Menger had been misrepresented by those economists who thought of him only as a marginal utility theorist who used words instead of mathematics. One argued that Menger's *Principles* was really more a treatise on economic development than on marginal utility theory. Another showed the importance of ignorance and error in Menger's theory (Jaffe, 1975:521), and still another argued that Menger's contribution was more to begin a subjectivist revolution than to carry it out in full (Lachmann 1978c:59). For one hundred years, these writers argued, Menger had been misunderstood. Far from being one of a homogeneous set of scientists all engaged in the same research program, or a case of Merton's "multiples" in scientific discovery, Menger was running on a completely separate track.[5] As a consequence of this breakthrough literature, the next twenty years was to see a continuing reevaluation of Menger that emphasized his differences from, rather than his similarities to, orthodox neoclassical economic theory (see, e.g., Vaughn, 1987a; Caldwell, 1990).

Despite the convincing nature of much of the new Menger scholarship, one cannot help but wonder, could the old interpretation of Menger be completely wrong? Was it simply a case of learning about Menger secondhand, and then only through neoclassically colored glasses? Or is this new interpretation of Menger the iconoclast a wishful exaggeration, an attempt to find a legitimate ancestor for a largely original late twentieth-century research program? Who is the real Carl Menger? Was he a naive neoclassical economist who, despite his brilliant insights into economic phenomena, was limited by his use of verbal analysis? Or was he the founder of a truly revolutionary way of theorizing about human social action that started from different assumptions and asked different questions from his neoclassical contemporaries?

[5] Not only has Mirowski (1989) recently made the same claim about Menger (see chapter 1), so has Max Alter, who emphasizes the importance of evolutionary biology to Menger's concept of social reality (1990).

Upon close scrutiny of Menger's texts, it seems that the simple answer to both questions is – yes. Both these Mengers spring forth from the pages of the *Principles* and from his methodological work, *Investigations into the Method of the Social Sciences with Special Reference to Economics* ([1883] 1985). The Menger the reader notices is the one that most conforms to his interests and background assumptions in economic science. Because both of these Mengers can be found in the pages of his *Principles of Economics,* neither interpretation can fully reconcile the disparate parts of Menger's writings.

But if both interpretations can find support from the text, which interpretation is truer to Menger's intentions? This is, of course, a tricky question that some would argue is irrelevant to our reading of his text. One can never get inside someone's mind to know what he intended to write, only what he actually wrote. Yet, at the risk of slipping into various interpretive traps, I do think a case can be made that the "new" Menger holds together as a theoretical structure better than the "old" Menger and fits more comfortably within Menger's context. One has to ignore too much of the text to accept the old interpretation, or at least more than one has to ignore to accept the new interpretation. Further, although we can never settle issues of intent, we can examine the questions Menger was trying to answer with his text, and that can give us important clues to his meaning.

Menger wrote to a specific audience to fulfill two main purposes. The audience was the German historical school, and the purposes were (a) to refute the despised labor theory of value and replace it with a theory of value centered around the choices of valuing individuals and (b) to show how this better theory of value could serve as an organizing principle for historical investigation. Although the first goal is consistent with the similar goals of Jevons and to a lesser extent Walras, the second goal opened up a different way of reasoning about processes than was typical of the other members of the holy trinity of economics. Despite the impression left by the acrimony of the *methodenstreit,* the verbal "war over methods" Menger fought with Gustav Schmoller during the closing decades of the nineteenth century, Menger respected historical research and attempted to develop a theory of economic growth and development to inform the research of the German historical school. The economic theory that he espoused, however, began with a theory of individual action that was very similar to, but not identical with, neoclassical economics. That he never completely managed to put all the pieces together explains many of the conflicts in Menger scholarship. It also helps to explain some of the major conflicts and future possibilities confronting the modern Austrian school.

Menger as incomplete neoclassicalist

The primary reason that Menger was first considered solely a marginal revolutionary was, of course, that an individualist, subjectivist theory of value was the central unifying principle of Menger's economic theory. Like Jevons and Walras, and like the German historical school, Menger was convinced that the labor theory of value of the Ricardian school was incorrect. Instead of basing value in objects or the consequences of actions, he located the source of value in individual valuations of the usefulness of goods for the purpose of fulfilling their needs.

Like other discoverers of the principle of diminishing marginal utility, Menger proposed that people rank-ordered their needs and applied successive units of goods to satisfying less and less urgent needs. The value of any part of a stock of goods was equal to the least important use to which a portion of the stock was put ([1871] 1981:122–128). As we have seen, this formulation, only later termed "diminishing marginal utility"[6] was what earned Menger the reputation of having been one of the coparticipants in the marginal revolution. In addition, the method of his presentation of the idea contributed to the view that he was an incomplete neoclassicalist.

Menger illustrated his theory with a chart that showed numerical representations of the diminishing degree of importance to a hypothetical consumer of varying quantities of ten different goods, and argued that the consumer would bring the satisfaction of one good "into equilibrium" with the satisfaction of the other goods (127). However, since he included no given income endowment, it was impossible to figure out from his table what the equilibrium consumption basket for his hypothetical consumer would be. Hence he was credited with developing only part of the neoclassical theory of consumer choice. In addition, all of Menger's subsequent discussions of allocating increasing quantities of the same good to successively less important uses was viewed as imprecise verbal elaboration on the same utility-maximizing theme.[7]

---

6 Streissler (1987:921) explains that Wieser coined the term *grenznutzen*, which Marshall later translated as "marginal utility."

7 Even Menger's English translators, Dingwall and Hoselitz, felt compelled to point out Menger's "error" in a lengthy footnote on p. 126 of the *Principles*. I argue in Vaughn (1987:440), that the scale-of-values table that Menger included in his text was meant only to be illustrative of a general principle, to illustrate why an individual would consume combinations of valued goods rather than exhausting his desire for the most important before moving on to the less important good, and that it was not meant to be sufficient to "solve" for the optimal consumption basket. Certainly, his numerical chart was not intended to substitute for his verbal analysis. Rather, his genuine articulation of the principle of marginal use is found in the verbal discussion following the tables.

This is not the only reason for regarding Menger as a primitive neoclassicalist. Although one can argue over the full definition of neoclassical economics, it seems clear that neoclassical economics is a theory of the determination of equilibrium prices under varying degrees of competition in markets. On this score as well, Menger seems to be in the neoclassical camp. His theory of exchange in particular is a barter model where individuals trade horses for cows depending on their marginal valuations of each, and price is shown to fall within standard equilibrium limits. Further, Menger explored the consequences for price determination of increasing the size of the market, showing that the range of equilibrium prices narrows with increasing numbers of traders. He not only seems to be engaged in equilibrium reasoning in these cases, he specifically describes prices as "symptoms of an economic equilibrium between the economies of individuals" (191).

The whole notion of setting the limits to economic exchange implies some equilibrium underlying human action.[8] It is true that for Menger, economic equilibria are at best partial and ephemeral: The world is characterized more by constant flux than by equilibrium states. However, there is an underlying equilibrium that can be defined and that perhaps may obtain in the real world from time to time:

The foundations for economic exchanges are constantly changing, and we therefore observe the phenomenon of a perpetual succession of exchange transactions. But even in this chain of transactions we can, by observing closely, find points of rest at particular times, for particular persons, and with particular kinds of goods. At these points of rest, no exchange of goods takes place because an economic limit to exchange had already been reached. ([1871] 1981:188)[9]

Although the above passage pretty clearly describes a notion of partial equilibrium, Menger also discusses in his later work on methodology, *Investigations into the Method of the Social Sciences with Special Reference to Economics*, "economic prices," a notion that bears some resemblance to prices in general equilibrium ([1883] 1985:71). Prices are "correct" to Menger only when everyone protects his economic interests, people have complete knowledge of their goals and means of achieving them, they understand the "economic situation" (all market opportunities are

---

[8] Menger also makes passing, if somewhat murky, reference to an equilibrium between present and future consumption with respect to goods of a higher order ([1871] 1981:159).

[9] The notion of equilibrium as "points of rest" really means only that individuals temporarily stop trading because they have reached the best deal within the context of their knowledge and opportunities. It does not imply anything in particular about the possibility of reaching a general equilibrium in the system. In fact, Menger's notion of general equilibrium, such as it is, is more in the order of a logical foil than an end point in an economic process. In this matter, Mises was faithful to Menger's notions of equilibrium (Mises, 1963:247).

known and taken into account in personal calculation), and they have the freedom to pursue their goals. In this discussion, he views economic prices as the benchmarks for measuring the deviations of real prices from those that reflect full economic awareness – an analogue to general equilibrium.

His theory of diminishing marginal valuation of goods, his barter model of trade, his exploration of price under varying market conditions culminating in a market that without much of a stretch of the imagination could be construed as perfectly competitive, and his identification of the "full economic situation" as one in which all relevant information is known and all prices equal costs, all argue for Menger as an early neoclassicist. Furthermore, there are insights in Menger's writings that anticipate some rather modern neoclassical theories such as his discussion of the effect of transactions costs on prices ([1871] 1981:189), his mention of patents and trademarks as economic goods (54), and his brief references to public goods problems.[10]

There is no doubt that one can extract many instances of neoclassical reasoning from Menger's writing. Yet to read him solely as a half-formed neoclassical economist requires a certain willingness to ignore the context in which his neoclassical-like pronouncements are offered. One must ignore his many references to problems of knowledge and ignorance, his discussions of the emergence and function of institutions, the importance of articulating processes of adjustment, and his many references to the progress of mankind. When that context is taken into account, it becomes clear that the Menger-as-neoclassical economist view only tells part of the story. It is the rest of the story that both provides Menger's claim to real originality and forms the theoretical origins of an Austrian alternative to neoclassical economics.

Menger as alternative theorist

To begin to appreciate the reasons why Menger can be viewed as providing an alternative to neoclassical economics, it is necessary first to consider the context of his writing. The professional preoccupation with the origins and development of mainstream economics led historians of economic thought earlier in the century to underestimate the deep roots Menger had in German economics and in German philosophy. Such an

---

10 In particular, Menger identifies public goods as those that, in advanced societies, are generally provided by governments, such as education and pure drinking water. Since they are provided free to all takers, they lose their "economic character" for consumers. They are intermediate between free goods whose natural supply is so abundant that it is not necessary to economize on them and scarce economic goods (103–104).

oversight is surprising not only because of the close connection between German and Austrian academics in the nineteenth century, but even more because Menger dedicated the *Principles* "with respectful esteem to Dr. Wilhelm Roscher," leader and founder of what was later to be called the older German historical school.[11]

The older German historical school, which included not only Roscher but also Knies and Hildebrand, was united both in its opposition to the British classical school and in its concept of proper economic methodology. Its members agreed that economic laws are different from the laws of physics, that human motivations are far more complex than the assumption of universal egoism admits, and that one cannot deduce laws of economics from simple principles, but must arrive at them through a process of induction based on detailed historical study of concrete economies (Alter, 1990:60). They were not against theory so much as against monocausal deductive theory of the Ricardian type. They wanted to claim the historical method as the sole method of economic analysis.

Why, then, did Menger dedicate his first major theoretical book to Wilhelm Roscher? The simple answer is that he believed he was providing an organizing principle to historical research.[12] One could not give a satisfactory historical account of economic phenomena without some theory of how human beings acted within history. Menger's theory of human action and particularly his theory of value was his answer to how human beings relate to goods and thereby bring about historical change. Menger described himself once as writing the *Principles* in a state of "morbid excitement" (Hayek, 1964:347). Such an emotional state is consistent with someone who believes he has found the answer to a long-standing, troubling problem and is eager to share his truth with his teachers.

[11] Undoubtedly, Menger himself contributed to the general perception that he was more different from the Germans than he was similar. The extreme acrimony of the *methodenstreit* led both Menger and Schmoller to dichotomize their positions to the point that it appeared to onlookers that they had little or nothing in common (Schumpeter, 1954:816).

[12] Menger's preface to his *Principles* is revealing in this regard. He criticizes those who deny universal laws of economics and argues that the so-called inductionists (presumably the Germans, although he does not name them) misunderstand the Baconian method, but he nevertheless acknowledges that his "reform" of economics is "built upon a foundation laid by previous work that was produced almost entirely by the industry of German scholars." His work, then, is to be regarded as "a friendly greeting from a collaborator in Austria, and as a faint echo of the scientific suggestions so abundantly lavished on us Austrians by Germany through the many outstanding scholars she has sent us and through her excellent publications" (49). Although one can undoubtedly detect a note of sycophancy in the homage Menger pays to the Germans, there is no doubt that he did see himself as building upon and contributing to the German research program far more than to the British classical school.

Although his German audience did not see Menger as the savior of their research program that he aspired to be, his ambition does help to explain the parts of Menger's writings that do not fit into a Menger-as-neoclassical-forerunner interpretation. Indeed, if we consider his German context, it is likely that the most inconvenient Mengerian statements from a neoclassical perspective are really the most important for a coherent interpretation of Menger. In particular, Menger's inconvenient bits about knowledge, process, plans, and the growth of institutions require close attention.

Menger's assumptions

Menger begins his treatise with a statement that is surprising in an economics text:

All things are subject to the law of cause and effect. This great principle knows no exception, and we would search in vain in the realm of experience for an example to the contrary. Human progress has no tendency to cast it in doubt, but rather the effect of confirming it and of always further widening knowledge of the scope of its validity. Its continued and growing recognition is therefore closely linked to human progress. ([1881] 1981:51)

In this statement, we get immediate hints concerning Menger's central question in the *Principles*. He is interested in explaining human progress, or more specifically, "the causes of the progress of human wealth" (71). Like the German historical school, his concern is to understand the process of historical change, but unlike his German contemporaries, he intends to ground his theory of historical processes in a causal theory that includes human action as well as physical causes.

But what are these causal relationships that lead to the progress of human wealth? This is the question that leads him to develop his general theory of human action and human valuation. It is conventional in neoclassical economics to describe the economic problem as the allocation of scarce resources among competing ends. While there is nothing to deny that statement in *The Principles*, Menger saw the economic problem facing human beings as a much wider one. Humans can only economize on what they have if they have knowledge about their wants and their circumstances, and if they have the power to affect their condition. For Menger, humans have inherent needs that can only be satisfied through knowledge and action. Hence the primary economic problem is to learn the "causal connection between things and the satisfaction of their needs" in order to make reasonable decisions about their economic well-being.

Menger takes less for granted than typical neoclassical economists. Consider for example, his enumeration of the prerequisites for a useful thing to become a good:

1. A human need.
2. Such properties as render the thing capable of being brought into a causal connection with the satisfaction of that need.
3. Human knowledge of this causal connection.
4. Command of the thing sufficient to direct it to the satisfaction of the need. (52)

We can think of properties one and four as statements of preferences and constraints, but we have no conventional category in which to place two and three. Two is an objective condition of reality, namely, that something can serve human purposes. Number three, however, homes in on the central ingredient of economic growth: knowledge, a feature that is only assumed in neoclassical economics.

Indeed, throughout the *Principles*, Menger stresses the importance of the combination of knowledge, power, and will to the pursuit of economic well-being and economic development. Economic life is built around gaining knowledge and power; knowledge of causal relationships between things and satisfactions (52), knowledge of the relationship between goods of a higher order (capital goods in our parlance) and goods of the first order (56–57), knowledge of available quantities of goods (89), knowledge of trading opportunities (170), knowledge of the "economic" situation (224), and the power to make the best use of one's knowledge. The acquisition of knowledge is an integral part of man's struggle to provide for his economic well-being.

Throughout the *Principles*, we see repeated examples of how increasing knowledge of the causal relationship between goods and their ability to satisfy wants contributes to human progress. In fact, Menger explicitly criticizes Adam Smith for too narrowly identifying the "progressive division of labor" as the source of wealth (72). Rather, Menger argues,

The quantities of consumption goods at humans' disposal are limited only by the extent of human knowledge of the causal connections between things, and by the extent of human control over these things . . . . [T]he degree of economic progress of mankind will still, in future epochs, be commensurate with the degree of progress of human knowledge. (72)[13]

[13] Menger's main point in criticizing Smith is that Smith fails to distinguish between simply dividing up a known method of production into several parts and discovering new methods of production and new ways to satisfy needs. While dividing up known methods can produce some increase in output, actual economically progressive people increase their wealth by innovation both in techniques of production and in kinds of products. Hence, "the further mankind progresses in this direction, the more varied become the kinds of goods, the more varied consequently the occupations, and the more necessary and economic also the progressive division of labor" (73). Of course, Menger's criticism of Smith is not fair. Smith does clearly note the importance of

Interestingly, Menger's zealous adherence to the idea that economic progress was caused by the growth of knowledge has opened him up to the criticism (Lachmann, 1978c:58) that he was not sufficiently subjectivist.

Menger believed that there were objective laws of nature and that goods had objective properties that made them more or less capable of fulfilling human needs. Hence, people needed to learn of the causal relationship between the properties of a good and its ability to satisfy needs. However, people could be in error about either the objective properties a good possesses or about the nature of their need for it. So, for instance, people could at a more primitive time believe that witch doctors cured disease, but with the advancement of knowledge they would come to realize that such a belief is in error. Hence, Menger included in his lexicon the category of "imaginary goods" (53).

For a pure subjectivist, this category is anathema.[14] If goods are defined by individual subjective evaluations, why would any good be more imaginary than any other? For Menger, the obvious answer was that although value at any moment in time depended upon subjective evaluations of needs, over time, people would learn to correct their mistakes.

If one is going to talk about progress, one must be able to define it. Menger could not define it in terms of national wealth since he did not think one could aggregate the wealth of individuals in a sufficiently precise way as to come up with a meaningful measure of national wealth.[15] The measure of progress had to be an individual one, yet if one held that an individual's subjective evaluations could never be incorrect

inventions of machinery to increased productivity and gives several examples of such innovations ([1776] 1981:9–10). It is true, however, that Menger stresses the multiplicity and variety of consumer products that marks economic progress more than does Smith. An emphasis on heterogeneity of products is important to the modern Austrian school.

[14] Jeremy Shearmur (1990) documents the objection to Menger's use of the construct of imaginary goods. He also argues that Menger's willingness to include an objective component to the circumstances of human choice might be a useful addition to Austrian theorizing.

[15] Regarding the concept of national wealth: "Here we have to deal not with the entire sum of economic goods available to a nation for the satisfaction of its needs, administered by government employees, and devoted by them to its purposes, but with the totality of goods at the disposal of the separate economizing individuals and associations of a society for their individual purposes. Thus we have to deal with a concept that deviates in several important respects from what we term wealth. . . . [U]nder our present social arrangements, the sum of economic goods at the disposal of the individual economizing members of society for the purpose of satisfying their special individual needs obviously does not constitute wealth in the economic sense of the term but rather a complex of wealths linked together by human intercourse and trade" (112–113). Note the similarity to Mises' and Hayek's use of the term catallaxy to represent the nexus of economic activities of individuals rather than an economy.

even in the light of his own later knowledge, how could one ever speak of "progress"? Hence, Menger took the position that people value goods according to their subjective assessments of the relationship between the good and the need it could satisfy, but that people can be mistaken in their understanding in the sense that once they acquired better information, they would recognize their mistake. Witch doctors objectively do not cure disease. Progress means that people come to realize this and, as a result, will substitute better forms of medicine:

> As a people attains higher levels of civilization, and as men penetrate more deeply into the true constitution of things and of their own nature, the number of true goods becomes constantly larger, and as can easily be understood, the number of imaginary goods becomes progressively smaller. It is not unimportant evidence of the connection between accurate knowledge and human welfare that the number of so-called imaginary goods is shown by experience to be usually greatest among peoples who are poorest in true goods. (54–55) [16]

So many of Menger's observations have to do with the way in which civilization progresses that it seems inescapable that Menger's main goal in the *Principles* was to provide a theory of economic development and not a theory of static economic allocation. In fact, once one reads the *Principles* with this purpose in mind, it is difficult to see how it could ever have been read in any other way.

Progress is a consequence of increasing human knowledge about the causal relationship between goods and the satisfaction of needs, but it also has a dimension that is only imperfectly recognized in the neoclassical research program: the dimension of time. To Menger, "the idea of causality, however, is inseparable from the idea of time. A process of change involves a beginning and a becoming, and these are only conceivable as processes in time" (67).

Human beings live in time and hence are not only plagued with limited knowledge about their needs and circumstances, they also have to make decisions in the present that will have consequences in the future. That man is ignorant and constantly must try to improve his knowledge implies that his economizing activities cannot be passive and reactive. Insofar as men recognize their ignorance and try to overcome it, they must engage in some learning process and take some actions that lead to a future different from the past. Human beings engage in intentional action to satisfy their needs through time.

Menger's concern with human action in time is especially evident in his

[16] Of course, one need not agree with Menger to understand his argument. Considering some of the examples Menger used to illustrate his concept of imaginary goods (i.e., cosmetics), a student of contemporary culture might argue that one consequence of progress may be that we invent at least as many new imaginary goods as we discard.

theory of higher-order goods (67–71). Consumption goods are goods of the first order, but goods of the first order are the product of all of the intermediate stages of production that are necessary to produce them. Hence, in order to provide for their consumption, humans must produce goods of a higher order that will only lead to consumption goods at some future time. They must invest in the production of goods of a higher order, moreover, in a context of uncertainty about the full nature of the production process and the vagaries of time (71).

The importance of time in production processes is a well-known hallmark of early Austrian capital theory,[17] leading to a distinctive if often criticized view of business cycles (Mises, 1981; Hayek, 1931, 1941). But capital theory is not the only way in which time enters into Menger's view of economics. It is also an overlooked feature of Menger's celebrated but only partly understood theory of value.

We have seen that Menger's theory of value can be viewed as a simple, although incomplete, approximation to a theory of consumer equilibrium with given information. That interpretation, however, requires that one read only the middle of his exposition and ignore the beginning and the end. Menger's statement of his theory of marginal utility,[18] his claim to neoclassical stardom, is preceded by a discussion of an individual's need to plan for an uncertain future (80–84).

In order to meet their requirements adequately, people must anticipate their needs and their resources over a planning period so that they can take steps to correct any potential shortfall in resources.[19] The plan includes the recognition that, over time, needs may change and so men must plan for a variety of contingencies.[20] Once the estimation is made,

---

[17] Early Austrian capital theory is known mostly through the writings of Bohm-Bawerk, who developed a time-preference theory of interest, linked productivity to the roundaboutness of lengthy production processes, and tried to measure the degree of roundaboutness by defining an "average period of production" ([1888] 1959).

[18] The term "diminishing marginal utility" is misleading for characterizing Menger's value theory. His theory is a description of how successive units of a good are applied to successively less important uses. It is the importance of the least important use that determines the value of any particular unit of the good. There is no appeal to utility in Jevons's sense of a psychological state, despite the fact that the Austrian school was sometimes called the "psychological school."

[19] He calls their estimated needs "requirements" (*bedarfs*), a concept for which we have no modern equivalent, although Stigler (1941:140) has argued that requirements are the quantities of goods sufficient to make marginal utility go to zero (all the economic goods men could possibly consume and not reduce their total utility). I regard this explanation, however, as an attempt to make Menger's alien idea fit the procrustean bed of neoclassical economics. Requirements are neither preferences nor objective needs. They seem to be estimates of projected consumption of commonly used goods in a household.

[20] Notice Menger's implication that needs (or the modern term, "tastes") are not assumed to be stable. People learn how to identify their needs as well as their resources. This

they must then actively seek out additional resources if they believe their currently anticipated supplies are inadequate. More than just allocating given resources among competing ends, economizing behavior requires foresight, imagination, planning, and action. And the whole concept of planning implies that it is a process in time.

Although there are indubitable references to equilibrium states in Menger's writing, they are overshadowed by his attention to active processes. Consider, also, Menger's theory of exchange and price. It can be interpreted as a laborious definition of equilibrium prices, but it is more appropriately viewed as a theory of economic processes.

The same principle that guides men in their economic activity in general, that leads them to investigate the useful things surrounding them in nature and to subject them to their command, and that causes them to be concerned about the betterment of their economic positions, the effort to satisfy their needs as completely as possible, leads them also to search most diligently for this relationship wherever they can find it, and to exploit it for the sake of better satisfying their needs. (180)

Menger's traders are not simply solving a maximization problem. They actively search out trading partners and exploit the differences in valuation between them. And, since the activity of trading requires knowledge and effort, not everyone will come to the same conclusions. Actual trades will depend on actual circumstances that will differ from individual to individual. The economist's job is to show the principles by which individuals bargain with one another once a trading partner is found, and to develop general principles for the formation of prices in more developed markets. Hence, Menger's theory of price describes the limits of economic prices and does not primarily attempt to determine equilibrium prices.[21]

The relationship between trade and economic equilibrium is further revealed in Menger's explanation of the effects of increasing competition on trade and prices. In a modification of typical neoclassical procedure, Menger begins with isolated monopoly and then shows how the range of potential prices would narrow with increases in the numbers of buyers and sellers in the market (194–225). His emphasis here is not so much on deducing equilibrium prices under different market models as it is on giving an analytic and historical account of how increasing competition leads to lower prices, greater output, and the more complete exploitation

alone puts him outside of strictly neoclassical research programs as defined by George Stigler and Gary Becker (1977).

[21] Hans Mayer, holder of Menger's chair in the 1930s, described Menger's theory as one of price formation rather than price determination (Lachmann, 1986:62; see also Moss, 1978).

of every economic opportunity. In fact, Menger's chapter on price formation is more an integral part of his analysis of the characteristics of economic progress than it is an analysis of equilibrium prices.[22]

Menger believed that progress was synonymous with increased knowledge, better and more diverse products, economic complexity, greater stability, and more complete satisfaction of human needs. This would be brought about as people's economic knowledge improved so as to make real prices more closely approximate economic prices – that is, prices that reflected widespread knowledge of the causal connection between goods and the satisfaction of needs as well as widespread knowledge about available supplies. Economics was the science devoted to explaining how such progress was possible.

Methodology

The *Principles* was intended to be the first in a four-part treatise on economics. Menger never wrote the other three volumes, nor did he ever succeed in revising the first volume to his satisfaction. Instead, his only other major work was his book on methodology, *Investigations into the Methods of the Social Sciences with Special Reference to Economics* ([1883] 1985). The story of its publication and professional reception goes a long way toward explaining both why Menger developed the reputation of being an early neoclassical economist and why his connection to the historical school was for so long overlooked.

After its publication, the *Principles* was well received in Austria and quickly came to dominate the research agenda of the circle of economists who formed the backbone of the Austrian school. This group included Menger's most famous colleagues, Friedrich von Wieser and Eugen von Bohm-Bawerk, along with colleagues less well known outside of Austria: Emil Sax, Johann von Komorzynski, Robert Zuckerkandl, and H. von Schullern-Schrattenhofe, all of whom published works in the Mengerian tradition. However, Menger's reception in Germany was not as warm as he would have liked.

While Menger thought of himself as correcting the theoretical lacunae in the program of the German historical school, the Germans, unfortunately, did not see Menger's theory in exactly that same light. Roscher reviewed Menger's book and although he gave it a mildly favorable opinion, he did not regard it as the salvation of the historical school. Perhaps puzzled by the lukewarm nature of his reception in Germany,

---

22 Streissler argues that Menger's discussion of the adjustment of prices to equilibrium is a "social process and a most laborious one to boot." Whereas "Walras's tatonnement takes a minute; Menger's tatonnement takes a century!" (1972:440).

Menger began work in 1875 on his second book, and the one for which he was most well known until the middle of this century, the *Investigations,* a book spelling out the relationship Menger saw between theory, history, and economic policy.

Menger divides economics into three related areas: the historical-statistical, which investigates the unique or "individual" aspects of economic phenomena; the theoretical, which investigates the "general" nature of economic phenomena; and the "practical sciences of national economy," roughly equivalent to economic policy. Although the historical school attends only to the unique or concrete aspects of economic phenomena, he argues that their investigations are incomplete without reference to economic theory or "exact laws." Historical data can be understood as aspects of *types* that form *typical* relationships. Economic theory is composed of exact laws of general types and typical relationships.[23]

Although Menger insisted on the "scientific" nature of the exact laws of economics, scientific, to him, as to the older historical school, did not mean identical to the laws of physics. The laws of economics were clearly not as strict as those of physics, but this was also true of many other sciences. In fact, all sciences vary in their degree of strictness, and "the number of natural sciences which absolutely comprise strict laws of nature is also small, and the value of those which only show empirical laws is nevertheless beyond question" ([1883] 1985:52). This undoubtedly was the source of the later claims by Mises and Hayek of the differences between the social and natural sciences.

The reason economic laws are not like physics is that they happen to manifest themselves in complex reality in which their consequences are altered by the noneconomic goals of observable human beings. Hence, one can never refute exact laws of economics by pointing to contrary empirical cases. Such a procedure would be analogous to testing the laws of geometry by measuring triangular shapes.[24] But if this is so, how does one find the causal laws that explain events?

In contrast to the Baconian method of natural science, what Menger calls the empirical realistic approach, the procedure that he advocates for social science is the "exact" approach (59). "It seeks to ascertain the simplest elements of everything real, elements which must be thought of as strictly typical just because they are the simplest" (60). The application

---

[23] Menger's discussion of ideal types was to influence Max Weber's methodology of sociology as well as Mises' and Lachmann's own attempts to formulate a methodology for economics. See Mises (1963:59ff.) and Lachmann (1986).
[24] Cf. Mises' claim for the apodictic and irrefutable characteristic of praxeology (1963:31–32).

of the exact approach to economics "consists in the fact that we reduce human phenomena to their most original and simplest constitutive factors. We join to the latter the measure corresponding to their nature, and finally try to investigate the laws by which more complicated human phenomena are formed from those simplest elements, thought of in their isolation" (62). To Menger, the simplest elements of economic theory are human valuations from which can be derived more complicated economic relationships. This is obviously an individualist methodology.

The example Menger uses to contrast the exact approach with the "realistic-empirical" approach that deals with empirical phenomena is worth examining since it also illustrates his use of equilibrium constructs. Menger claims that the exact method can be used to predict "economic prices," even though one rarely observes true economic prices in the real world. Although the laws that predict economic prices are true and exact, their empirical manifestations will vary because of "noneconomic" circumstances. Indeed, it would be surprising if any of the circumstances required for the establishment of "economic" prices – maximization, full knowledge of all circumstances, complete freedom of action (71) – were ever fully met in the real world. Real prices will deviate from economic prices, and the role of the realistic-empirical approach is to discover the degree of deviation, taking economic prices as the point of departure. He never explains how one might come to know the "economic" price apart from empirical prices, however, and so creates a standard of comparison that seems impossible to employ. But note the similarity between Menger's formulation and conventional economic theory that predicts directions of change of real prices on the basis of a theoretical presumption of economic prices.[25]

The theory of unintended orders

Menger spends the first book of his volume in setting out his less than fully convincing methodological position and the second book in criticizing somewhat ungenerously the limitation of the historical school. However, book three, the shortest one in the *Investigations,* contains the most important contribution of this much misunderstood volume. Here, Men-

---

[25] Although Menger insisted on the importance of exact theory to understanding economic reality, he did not believe that human beings were pure homoeconomicus. Economics provides exact laws, but only of a subset of human actions. A full understanding of social reality requires a broader science of man, as well as a full understanding of the historical context within which man acts. Economics describes man guided exclusively by self-interest in the provision of his material wants, but this is only a partial account of the full richness of human motivations. Economics pertains to a part, but not the totality of human experience (64).

ger shows how the principle of individual valuation developed in the *Principles* can provide a theory of history, a theory of organic social change. Here, more clearly than anywhere else, Menger shows how historical descriptions of the rise of social institutions are illuminated by a theory of human action.

In the tradition of the Scottish Enlightenment,[26] Menger defined the problem of exact research to be to discover "how institutions which serve the common welfare and are extremely significant for its development come into being without a *common will* directed toward establishing them" ([1883] 1985:146). His answer, developed using examples of such social institutions as money, law, language, markets, the origin of communities, and of the state itself, was that individuals following their own economic interests provide spillover benefits to others in the form of increased knowledge of potential advantages or increased ability to pursue their interests.

Menger first developed a theory of organic orders in the *Principles* in his discussion of the origin of money. Money is the unintended outcome of individuals' attempts to improve their chances to get what they want through barter. Because of the double coincidence of wants required for a successful exchange in a barter system, some people find that if they trade less marketable commodities for more marketable ones they can increase the barter opportunities open to them. It is far easier to trade a sack of wheat for something else one might want than to trade a pair of custom-made shoes, for example. Eventually, as people engage in more and more indirect trade of less marketable for more marketable commodities in order eventually to get what they want, one commodity will emerge as the most marketable of all and become institutionalized as money ([1871] 1981:257–260). This process from which money emerges is neither deliberately designed nor predictable in advance. The institution that emerges from the process was never deliberately sought after but is an unintended consequence of deliberate economic action.

Although money was Menger's most carefully worked out example of an unintended order (some might argue, his only worked out example), he alludes to others in the *Investigations*. New localities develop as individuals of different abilities and different professions settle in new areas because they believe they have a better market for their skills. States mostly come into being as families living in close proximity to each other

---

[26] Menger shared in the project of David Hume and Adam Smith as well as Adam Ferguson, who described social institutions as "the result of human action, but not the execution of any human design" (1767] 1980:187). To show how social order can arise as an unintended by-product of purposeful human action seems to be a prerequisite to any theory of history.

through a process of increasing cooperation eventually decide it is to their advantage to unite. Most such social organizations, Menger argues, were not the consequences of conscious planning, but the unconscious result of human will directed toward other, more personal ends. This is the nature of organic development in human communities.

What makes Menger's discussion of "organic" orders particularly interesting is that he not only describes them, but he also provides a brief theoretical analysis of how they can develop. He mentions in his theory of the origin of money that some individuals will be quicker than others to recognize the advantages of acquiring more marketable commodities because it helps them to come closer to their own ends. Not everyone will discover the advantages of indirect exchange at once, but they will soon learn because "there is no better means to enlighten people about their economic interests than their perceiving the economic success of those who put the right means to work for attaining them" ([1883] 1985:155). Bearing no small resemblance to evolutionary biology, Menger's theory of organic development seems to be a process of discovery and transmission of new information through imitation, motivated by the interests of economic persons. It is thus an attempt to reconcile the organic and developmental approach to economics with the exact laws of economic science. It would take until the third quarter of the twentieth century for Menger's theory of unintended orders once again to take center stage in Austrian circles.

The *methodenstreit*

Given its message, one might have expected Menger's book to have begun a dialogue between German and Austrian economists. Unfortunately, Menger's rather imperious tone apparently did not invite cordial scholarly interchange. Further, the book was not published until 1883, by which time Roscher was no longer the dominant force in German academics, having been replaced by Gustav Schmoller, who, as leader of the younger historical school, was intransigent in his opposition to a priori, universal theory. So although Roscher had been mildly disposed toward Menger's new work, Schmoller was actively hostile.

Schmoller reviewed the *Investigations* in 1883 (Schmoller, 1968) in a particularly insulting manner, causing Menger to respond with an impassioned, polemical pamphlet entitled *The Errors of Historicism* in 1884. Hayek later wrote that Menger succeeded in ruthlessly demolishing Schmoller's position (1964:355), but if so, Schmoller never acknowledged defeat. For a final crushing insult, Schmoller returned Menger's book unread and wrote a final, scathing attack on Menger in his journal.

This unsavory exchange is referred to in the literature as the *methodenstreit*, or war of methods, a war that had no clear winners at the time nor led to any mutually acknowledged resolution of opposing views. Ultimately, Menger's position was far closer to the methodological turn economics took in the twentieth century, and ironically, by the end of his career, Schmoller had conceded almost all of Menger's points defending the necessity of theory. But the professional consensus in the non-German academy was that the whole debate was a waste of time.[27]

Although one might agree that Menger's time might have been better spent developing his economic theories than arguing over method, that was not the only casualty of the war. The more profound loss was to Menger's reputation and to the understanding of his position outside Austria. The extreme hostility of the feelings between Menger and Schmoller seemed to polarize their positions in the minds of the profession, and Menger's careful attempt to carve out a place for theory in empirical research was reduced to a polemic for pure theory. So, whereas Menger began his career attempting to develop an organizing principle for historical research, he came to be viewed as the archenemy of history. Whereas he wanted to show the relationship between theory, history, and economic change, he became known as the defender of an extreme understanding of a priori theorizing, and whereas he wanted to present a theory of the individual embedded within historical circumstances, he was viewed as an exponent of extreme individualism and "lightning calculators."[28] Menger's major insights to the problems of ignorance, time, uncertainty, processes, and unintended orders were lost in the dust of battle.

---

[27] For a contrasting view that the *methodenstreit* was not a waste of time but a genuine clash of contrasting epistemological views, see Bostaph (1978). Bostaph argues that the difference between Menger and Schmoller depended on their respective views of concepts, which in turn implied different views of economic laws. Schmoller held that concepts were "labels attached to universal summarizations that are subject to alteration depending on how extensive the data is from which they are derived" (8). Hence, any attempt to describe a complex entity would be contingent upon the extent of one's observation and open to revision. The economic laws that Schmoller could derive from such concepts would be contingent or "short-run" (9). Menger, on the other hand, viewed concepts as "abstract generalizations from only a few instances that have universal applicability" (8). When one had understood the essence of a phenomenon, therefore, it would be possible to deduce exact laws of economics from those concepts that would be universally applicable.

[28] The term "lightning calculator" was the work of Thorstein Veblen, who ridiculed all attempts to develop the notion of economic man in the early twentieth century. Although Veblen's criticism might be warranted by the developing neoclassical orthodoxy of his time, Menger's theory should certainly be well out of the path of his barb (1919:73).

Menger and the fate of the "older" Austrian school

As I have argued, Menger's claim to being a founder of neoclassical economics, while genuine, reflects only part of his message in the *Principles*. His theory of value was easy to cast in a neoclassical mold, but it was embedded in a larger attempt to answer what was basically Adam Smith's question: What are the causes of the progress of the wealth of nations? He identified the source of progress as man's increasing knowledge of the causal connections between goods and human needs and showed how it was brought about by the active efforts human beings take to satisfy their requirements. Seeking after ways to satisfy human needs leads to both greater knowledge and greater command over resources.

For Menger, the concrete manifestations of economic growth were increased complexity in the economy and prices that more and more closely approximated those that would obtain within the "full economic situation," which seemed to mean conditions of perfect competition. Complexity was evident in the proliferation of products in society, in the highly developed division of labor, and in the number and variety of economic institutions that emerged to satisfy man's desire for more complete economic information and to facilitate exchange. Notions of equilibrium were clearly present in Menger's writing – two-party exchange resulted in an equilibrium of sorts, for instance – but equilibria were either ephemeral and rapidly changing to reflect persistent change in the economic conditions, or described some distant goal that was never fully to be achieved.

We have also seen that while Menger's value theory was accorded full scholarly recognition, his larger theme of growth and development through increasing knowledge was lost to his contemporaries. Those who would have most appreciated Menger's project, the German historical school, reacted so adversely to his theoretical structure that they, too, ignored the implications for economic history. But what of Menger's immediate colleagues in Austria? Were they not sensitive to the distinctiveness of Menger's message? Ironically, both Wieser and Bohm-Bawerk, Menger's closes associates and best-known colleagues, developed aspects of Menger's thought that belied his distinctiveness from neoclassical economics.

Consider,first, Friedrich Wieser. The theory of marginal utility, its relationship to exchange and to price intrigued him so much that he took it as the starting point for his own work and developed it in ways that brought it closer to the emerging neoclassical theory of marginal utility. Wieser's best-known book, *Natural Value* ([1893] 1971), developed the implications of Menger's theory of value to an extraordinary degree of detail. Not only did he restate and provide detailed exposition of the law of diminishing marginal utility and extend it to a theory of opportunity cost, he also gave a verbal description of a demand curve (41–42), showed the identity between the law of costs and the law of value (183–185), and developed the principle of imputation of factor values from the value of goods of the first order far more than had Menger (Bk III, pt. 1).

It is instructive to note that Wieser himself was one of the first to place Menger within the neoclassical camp. In his preface to *Natural Value*, he clearly identified Menger as one of the four discoverers of the principles of value, including not only Jevons and Walras but also Hermann Heinrich Gossen in his tribute. However, he regarded Menger's formulation of value to be superior to that of his "co-discoverers" because Menger's theory of value was more general and lent itself to wider application than that of the others (xxxiii).[29] In particular, Wieser criticized Walras's formulation because of his use of mathematics. Value theory, according to Wieser, was more than an "expression of the law of amounts."

The obscure conception of value is to be made clear; all its manifold forms are to be described; the service of value in economic life is to be analyzed; the connection of value with so many other economic phenomena is to be shown; in short, we have to give a philosophy of value which needs words, not numbers. (xxxiii)

Hence, in Wieser's eyes, Austrian economics, insofar as it was in any way distinct from other formulations within the marginal utility school, was more or less a theory of value in words, not numbers. In this, Wieser was simply expressing a view of Menger's contribution that was to be generally accepted for much of the next century.

Even at the time, Wieser's (and Menger's) view of mathematics must have seemed a bit old-fashioned to the ever-increasing numbers of economists who were using graphical and mathematical formulations seemingly to say in a few lines what took Wieser pages and pages to argue in words. Not surprisingly, the Austrians became known as the economists who backwardly rejected the latest scientific techniques in their refusal to endorse mathematical economics. And as long as the problem was confined to working out the implications of value theory, the critics of the Austrians had a point. For the particular problem neoclassical economics was attempting to answer at the end of the nineteenth and the beginning of the twentieth century, graphical analysis and mathematical formulation

---

29 Wieser attributes Menger's superiority here to his debt to the German school "with its patient untiring labour in formulating the general economic conceptions, and pressing forward from concrete phenomena to that height of abstraction from which the phenomena are to be logically arranged. It may be said that, in great part, the German school long ago formulated the conceptions, leaving for us only the task of filling them out by adequate observation" (xxxiv).

did seem to save time and add precision to their reasoning. The fact that the problem Menger had initially addressed was wider and more complicated than simple price theory and its implication for factor pricing was not considered, even by Wieser.

Ironically, Wieser was so successful in narrowing the focus of the Austrian school and ignoring questions of knowledge and time, of growth and active processes, that by 1932, when Lionel Robbins, reflecting the influence of the Austrian economists, wrote his classic, *The Nature and Significance of Economic Science,* he cast the Austrian message in a way that lent itself to focusing on questions of allocation rather than wealth creation.[30] His definition of economics as "the science which studies human behavior as a relationship between ends and scarce means which have alternative uses" ([1932] 1962:16) can very easily be regarded as a static equilibrium formulation despite the more general sense in which Robbins seems to have meant it.[31]

In these early days of Austrian economics, concerns with economic change manifested themselves in the theory of capital and interest as developed by Eugen von Bohm-Bawerk. Menger has been reported as saying that Bohm-Bawerk's theory of capital and interest was "one of the greatest errors ever committed" (Schumpeter, 1954:847) because of the Ricardian elements Bohm-Bawerk reintroduced into capital theory, such as a classical wages fund, and because of his attempt to define an average period of production, which essentially homogenized a complex production process. Nevertheless, Bohm-Bawerk's theory of the structure of production and his "three grounds for interest" (two of which were subjective in nature: declining marginal utility of income over the planning horizon and the declining marginal utility of goods the further in the future they become available [Hennings, 1987:256]) did maintain a focus on time and processes. Further, later theories of business cycles that were based largely on Bohm-Bawerk's theory of production also were

[30] Robbins's purpose in writing his little book was to counter the "materialist" definition of economics with one that focused on the problem of choice, and to uphold the strict value freedom of economic science in the manner that the Austrians argued. He argued that economics is a science of a particular kind of action, and hence is generalizable to all human endeavors that share the characteristics of scarcity and multiple ends. "It follows from this, therefore, that in so far as it presents this aspect (scarcity), any kind of human behavior falls within the scope of economic generalizations" (17).

It is instructive to note that in his preface to the first edition of his book, Robbins acknowledges his special debt to both Ludwig von Mises and to Philip Wicksteed in formulating his own arguments (xvi).

[31] Israel Kirzner (1973) first called attention to the limitations of Robbins's definition of economics when he contrasted "Robbinsian maximizing" behavior, which is purely reactive and calculative, to his own vision of entrepreneurial "alertness," action that perceives and brings about changes in the means–ends framework (32–37). See also chapter 7.

noted for their emphasis on the interrelation between time and production. Capital theory could not be divorced from notions of process. Nevertheless, the formalism of Bohm-Bawerk's approach dominated the substantive particulars of his theory, and hence his views, though hotly debated,[32] were nevertheless debated within a neoclassical context. Not surprisingly, the Mengerian themes of processes and heterogeneity of capital goods were less important to the scholarly community at large than the Ricardian and formalistic framework within which Bohm-Bawerk developed his ideas.

Hence, even the disciples chose to glean from Menger ideas that were more congenial to the emerging neoclassical conversation than was true of the overall thrust of Menger's work. And, Menger increasingly could not speak for himself. His potential German-speaking audience was closed to him partly because of his bitter dispute with Schmoller, who managed to keep Mengerians out of academic positions in Germany and partly because of Menger's refusal to have his *Principles* reprinted, making access to his written work difficult. As for the increasingly important English-speaking world, the Marshallian hegemony that became established by the turn of the century made it doubtful that Menger would have been much noticed even if his *Principles* had been available to interested economists.

This is not to say that the Austrian school after Menger did not remain faithful to his alternative message in some respects. Austrians never did completely lose their awareness of the importance of knowledge, time, and process, no matter how much they assimilated into the neoclassical orthodoxy. However, in order to be part of the greater scholarly community, it was necessary more and more to develop their "Austrian" ideas in neoclassical parlance. Clearly, this was true of Joseph Schumpeter, Gottfried Haberler, Fritz Machlup, and Oskar Morgenstern, for example, all later-generation Austrians who became part of the neoclassical mainstream through their development of Austrian themes.[33] Interestingly, as

---

[32] Bohm-Bawerk carried on an intense debate with J. B. Clark over the nature of capital that set the stage for a subsequent debate between Hayek and Knight on substantially the same grounds. Both Clark and Knight regarded capital as a continuous, self-perpetuating fund of value that yields a return, whereas Bohm-Bawerk and Hayek pointed to the importance of the time dimension and the composition of the capital stock and emphasized the necessity of deliberate choice to maintaining an income from capital.

[33] Haberler's work on business cycles was within the purview of process theory (1937), Machlup's work on knowledge and information theory (1962) was an Austrian theme in a neoclassical setting, and Morgenstern's game theory (Morgenstern and von Neumann, 1944) arguably can be said to be an attempt to model individual interactions in a broader context than Mengerian and Bohm-Bawerkian exchange models. Schumpeter was an even more interesting case. While retaining much of the Austrian concern with process and institutions, in particular in *The Theory of Economic Development* (1934),

we will see in chapter 4, it was also true to a lesser extent of Ludwig von Mises, the most identifiably Austrian economist of this group and the man whose name became synonymous with Austrian economics in the United States.

No wonder, then, that by the 1920s most economists, including the Austrians themselves, believed that there was no longer any discernibly different Austrian school (Mises, 1984). All of the major contributions of the Austrians were either easily absorbed into the mainstream of neoclassical thought or served as topics for family feuds. Instead of Austrian economics, then, one thought of economic ideas that happened to originate in Austria. The forgotten bits of Menger that spoke of knowledge and ignorance, time and process were either subsumed into ceteris paribus or deemed not relevant to the central core of neoclassical discussion. However, underneath this ecumenical consensus were real differences in understanding about the functioning of an economic system. These differences were shortly to explode the seeming unity of thought between Menger and the Marshallian-Walrasian branch of neoclassical economics, not through a direct confrontation over differing points of theory, but through a confrontation over the possibility of socialism.

Business Cycles (1939), and Capitalism, Socialism and Democracy (1942), he nevertheless embraced the static equilibrium economics of Walras as the epitome of economic science. One is never sure if Schumpeter actually believed in Walrasian economics, but he certainly used it to berate less "scientific" Austrians in his later life.

CHAPTER 3

Economic calculation and the rediscovery of Mengerian themes

In the 1930s the problem of how one could organize a socialist economy became a major concern among economists. Partly because of the affinity many intellectuals felt for the "Soviet experiment," and partly because of the perceived shortcomings of "unfettered capitalism" that were increasingly the subject of academic investigation,[1] working out the economics of socialism presented an exciting challenge to economic theorists. However, the theoretical inquiry eventually represented far more than an exercise in the application of economic principles to an alternative institutional arrangement. It evolved into a debate between two contrasting visions of how an economic system functioned in the first place and hence became a means for deepening theoretical understanding of private-property regimes as well as of communist regimes. And more important for our story, the debate that developed over the economics of socialism eventually demonstrated the wide gap that existed between the Mengerian vision and the neoclassical vision of economic reality.[2]

The topic of the economics of socialism was not new to Austrian economists in the 1930s; it had occupied the attention of prominent Austrians from the beginning. Indeed, Menger himself had been a liberal in the nineteenth-century sense,[3] and one of his aims in developing his

[1] Not only were business cycles and their perceived irrationality the topic of intense investigation in the early part of the twentieth century, the 1920s saw the publication of Pigou's *The Economics of Welfare* (1920), which developed the concept of externalities and market failure. In addition, Piero Sraffa was criticizing the internal consistency of the perfectly competitive model (1926) leading to Joan Robinson's work on imperfect competition (1933). Few professional economists during this time (except for Ludwig von Mises) would have argued for the obvious superiority of free markets over some kind of government planning.

[2] The "economic calculation debate," as it has come to be known, has been a topic of much interest to modern Austrians, and for good reason. As we see below, the debate really marked the divide before which it was possible to think of Austrian economics as simply a part of a general consensus on economic theory and after which no such easy assimilation was possible. On this, see Caldwell (1988), Kirzner (1988), Lavoie (1985a), Murrell (1983), and Vaughn (1980a).

[3] Although Menger never seems to have written anything directly on economic policy, there is one arena in which he showed his policies to be even more liberal than those of Adam Smith. Menger served briefly as tutor to Crown Prince Rudolf, whose notebooks, corrected by Menger, have come to light. In these notebooks (which were produced from Menger's lectures), Menger severely limits the scope for government policy and

value theory was to refute decisively the labor theory of value and its radical implications for private property and wage labor ([1871] 1981:168). Bohm-Bawerk carried on Menger's project by criticizing Marx in *The Positive Theory of Capital* ([1888] 1959). His best-remembered attack on Marx, however, was his long essay *Karl Marx and the Close of His System* ([1896] 1949), in which he showed that there was a fatal contradiction in Marx's critique of capitalism: It could not be the case both that goods would exchange at their labor values in the long run and that the returns from capital in all occupations would be equalized at the same time (28). Since Marx's theoretical proposition was at odds with fact, his system had to be incorrect (101). However, Marx's mistakes had to do with his critique of capitalism, not with his vision of a future socialist economy. Since there was little hint in Marx as to the nature of the socialist alternative he was proposing, Bohm-Bawerk's refutation of Marx's economics was basically a critique of a critique.

Bohm-Bawerk's efforts notwithstanding, intellectual interest in Marx continued to increase in turn-of-the century Vienna. Marxist discussion flourished in the university and even in Bohm-Bawerk's famous seminar there were a number of students who were to become noted Marxist thinkers.[4] Later, the disastrous conclusion of World War I widened the audience for Marxist ideas among war-weary and disillusioned young Austrians, while the success of the Bolshevik revolution in Russia lent contemporary urgency to the discussion of the nature of a socialist economy.

One young Austrian who was not convinced of the promise of socialism was Ludwig von Mises. A brilliant student of Bohm-Bawerk's and a participant in his seminar, Mises early in his career made a name for himself as an up-and-coming force in monetary theory with his publication of *The Theory of Money and Credit* ([1912] 1980). This work carried on Menger's ideas by applying Menger's theory of value to monetary theory. Mises was concerned to counter the quantity theory of money with an account of the value of money that relied on the subjective valuations of

expresses a confidence in the ability of the market to serve most of people's needs in society (Streissler, 1990:110).

[4] The most prominent among them was Nikolai Bukharin, whose first book, *Economic theory of the Leisure Class* (1919) was a detailed critique of Bohm-Bawerk and the Austrian school in general. Mises, however, mentions in particular two other Marxists, Otto Bauer and Otto Neurath, who participated along with him in Bohm-Bawerk's seminar. Mises had great respect for Bauer's intelligence, although not for his character, while he had nothing but contempt for Neurath (Mises, 1978:39–40). Not surprisingly, Neurath and Bauer were the two Marxists who, along with Karl Kautsky, were the targets of Mises' scathing criticism of socialist plans to eliminate capitalism (Mises, [1920] 1935).

individual economic actors. In particular, he wanted to explain the value of money as an instance of Menger's theory of marginal utility.

The problem that Mises addressed was this: In order for an individual to assess the marginal utility of a money unit to him, he must know its objective purchasing power. But the objective purchasing power depends upon the money prices of goods and services available in the marketplace on any given day. How can an individual dispose of money according to its marginal utility before market prices are established in the day's trade? But how can market prices be established until money trades actually take place (130)? This was known as the circularity problem.

Mises found the solution in an extension of Menger's theory of the origin of money. At any moment in time, an individual determines the marginal utility of money to him with reference to the objective exchange value of money that existed in the immediate past. On this basis, he will determine his demand for money to hold and will enter the market. Although subsequent market activity will change the objective value of money, this new value will provide the basis for the next day's assessment. Similarly, yesterday's assessment will depend on the exchange value of money on the day prior to that, and that day's, on the day before that. At some point in this historical regress one reaches the point where money emerges from barter, and the value of money to an individual then depends not on its previous purchasing power as money, since that does not exist, but on its value as a commodity (130–131). In this way, Mises not only accounted for this historical emergence of money from commodity barter as had Menger, but he tied the ability of individuals to assess the marginal utility of the money unit to this historical process. Money was by nature a product of a historical continuity, and not the product of agreement or government fiat. As we shall see, the continuity of evolved institutions became an important element in modern Austrian theory.

In addition to a theory of the value of money, Mises' book contained a pure time-preference theory of interest, and an extensive analysis of contemporary fractional reserve banking theory, banking institutions, and banking policy both before and after World War I.[5] At the end of the book (388–404), Mises combined his theory of interest and his understanding of banking practice to point to a theory of economic crises. Following on Wicksell, he identified the gap between the natural rate of interest and the money rate as the consequence of credit expansion. Insofar as the money rate was below the natural rate, he argued, producers would invest in

---

[5] Hayek was later to remark that Mises was most probably the only man who really understood the causes of the postwar Austrian inflation. He also agrees with Mises' own assessment that if the Austrian authorities had listened to Mises, the worst effects of the inflation could have been averted (1992:8).

more roundabout production processes than were warranted by the preferences of individuals. When the credit expansion came to an end, whether because of the limits of a gold standard, conventional banking practice, or because interest rates could no longer be driven lower, a "counter movement" would set in leading to a crisis. Hayek's later work on the "Austrian" theory of the business cycle was largely an elaboration and further enhancement of Mises' theoretical suggestions in *The Theory of Money and Credit*. It is noteworthy that both Mises and the early Hayek framed the problem of business crises as a process of markets attempting to adjust to a disequilibrium situation caused by fractional reserve banking.

In addition to showing a talent for monetary theory, Mises also gained a name as a formidable opponent of socialism. Early in his studies, Mises underwent an intellectual conversion from a lukewarm socialist to a passionate advocate of classical liberalism ([1962] 1978:16, 20). Consequently, almost from the beginning of his career, he was out of step with the political views of his contemporaries, whom he regarded as naive and unthinking. While such later famous Marxists as his classmates Otto Bauer and Otto Neurath were advocating some sort of utopian reforms that would do away with the institutions of capitalism such as private property, money, and markets for capital valuation in order to replace them with the ideal society in which social value would dictate economic decisions, Mises' studies served more and more to convince him of the widespread benefits of liberalism.[6] Shortly after his return from active duty during World War I, Mises wrote an article to challenge some of the more utopian views of his Marxist compatriots. This article was to touch off the debate that, by the middle of the twentieth century, would change the nature of Austrian economics completely.

The impossibility of socialist calculation

Mises had been Wieser's student as well as Bohm-Bawerk's, and as such he had learned from Wieser that socialism could not avoid the problem of rational valuation of alternatives. Already in *Natural Value* ([1893] 1971), Wieser had indirectly addressed the socialist critiques of capitalism by investigating the nature of value apart from the particulars of property ownership and distribution. He defined natural value as "value as it would

6 Mises recounts how his researches into housing and into changes in the law regarding domestic servants convinced him that "all real improvements in the conditions of the working classes were the result of capitalism; and that social laws frequently brought about the very opposite of what the legislation was intended to achieve" (1978:20). It was his further study of economics that clinched the case against interventionism for him.

arise in a communist state" (60) undistorted by differences in income. He argued that even where incomes were equal and property was owned by the state, scarcity would still be the condition of human life and hence, "the elementary laws of valuation . . . would be entirely and unlimitedly effective for the whole community" (60). Clearly, contra Marx, labor would not be the only valuable input into the production of goods. Land and capital would also be valuable and hence would require rational economic decisions to be made about their disposition in society.

The "natural value" of resources would have to be calculated in some way to determine their relative value. Since no one person could make such complicated evaluations of the contributions of all factors of production to utility, some means of calculating value is necessary for society: no one person could possibly know enough to make such decisions unaided by some form of numerical calculation (211). Although some might hope that government statistics could solve the problem, government statistics could never calculate individual marginal valuations, which were exactly the information necessary to make rational use of resources. Wieser concludes with the observation that "in so far as prices represent natural value, an enormous and arduous mental labour of calculating the exchange value of things is saved" (213). Socialism can only function if it finds some way to calculate value.[7]

In 1920, Mises published an article entitled "Economic Calculation in the Socialist Commonwealth" ([1920] 1935). In an effort to combat some of the more utopian claims of contemporary Marxists, Mises developed two major points. First, he reasserted and elaborated upon Wieser's earlier argument: The substitution of state ownership for private property does not eliminate want, scarcity, or the problem of rational calculation.[8] Mises went further than Wieser, however. He asserted that the only way to make rational calculations of value was with the aid of market prices. Market prices are the result of people trading their property in ways that improve their satisfaction. Without private property, there can be no

---

[7] In *Social Economics* ([1927] 1967), Wieser argues that because of the division of labor, economic activities "will be executed far more effectively by thousands and millions of human beings, seeing with thousands and millions of eyes, exerting as many wills; they will be balanced, one against the other, far more accurately than if all these actions, like some complex mechanism, had to be guided and directed by some superior control. A central prompter of this sort could never be informed of countless possibilities, to be met with in every individual case, as regards the utmost utility to be derived from given circumstances or the best steps to be taken for future advancement and progress" (1971:396–397).

[8] The same argument had also been made by N. G. Pierson in 1902 ("The Problem of Value in the Socialist Community") and by Enrico Barone in 1908 ("The Ministry of Production in the Collectivist State"). Both papers were reprinted along with Mises' 1920 article in Hayek (1935:41–85, 245–290) and served as the opening salvo to Hayek's participation in the calculation debate.

market prices to reflect the consensus of individual valuations (111). Without market prices, there can be no rational economic calculation.[9] Hence, he concluded, if socialism meant rational calculation without the aid of private property or free market exchange, socialism was impossible. Even if socialists allowed ownership of consumer goods that could be priced in markets, this still would not solve the calculation problem because rational use of resources could only be based on prices established in resource markets. Without private resource markets (which of course would be impossible without private resource ownership) there would be no way for any central authority to decide whether in making a resource decision, it was sacrificing a less valued opportunity for a more highly valued one, or using a valued resource in the production of a less valued product.

Mises' second point was that centralized, state enterprise cannot substitute for private enterprise in the production of wealth. State-appointed managers of enterprises are fundamentally bureaucrats with different incentives and different ambitions from private owners. Bureaucrats will not treat state property the same way they would treat their own, nor will they make the same kind of entrepreneurial decisions that private owners would make. The bureaucrat who is required to follow orders is fundamentally different from the manager, promoter, and man of affairs who risks his own capital and reputation in his business ventures (119).

Mises' article reads like a condensed version of a larger argument. He states his points emphatically and with little discussion. His central argument comes through loud and clear: Socialism requires some means of calculating relative values if it aspires to rationality in resource use. However, several of his supporting arguments cry out for elaboration, an elaboration that was forthcoming two years later in his monumental treatise, *Socialism* ([1922] 1981). *Socialism* is an impressive tour de force that covers far more ground than one expects from the pen of an economist. Tucked in the pages of this volume is a wide-ranging analysis of the philosophical and empirical differences between liberalism and socialism, a theory of social change and social evolution, a critique of Marxism, an analysis of the various forms of socialism proposed by various groups, and an examination of the ethics and morals of socialism. Of course, there is also a detailed analysis of the economics of a socialist community that is fuller, but not substantially different from the position

---

[9] "As soon as one gives up the conception of a freely established monetary price for goods of a higher order, rational production becomes completely impossible. Every step of the way that takes us away from private ownership of the means of production and from the use of money also takes us away from rational economics" (104).

Mises took in his 1920 article ([1922] 1981:part II).[10] Although most of this section is an extension of arguments he already made in shorter form, the treatment of the problem of economic calculation in *Socialism* is notable for a change in emphasis in his account of the difference between socialist and liberal economists.

Socialists, he argues, assume that the economy is basically static and undergoes little change in parameters (213). As he pointed out before, in such a state, it would be in principle possible for economic prices to be calculated either from the memory of the earlier nonsocialist state, or from prices derived in the nonsocialist world. The real world, however, was characterized by constant change.[11] The sources of change were external in nature; population, capital goods, techniques of production, the organization of labour, and changes in demand. He points out that such changes will change economic valuations, but without market prices to serve as guideposts, neither the magnitude nor the directions of change can be known. Although this argument is familiar, the conclusion Mises draws from it reflects a new emphasis. He observes that "in any economic system which is in process of change all economic activity is based upon an uncertain future. It is therefore bound up with risk. It is essentially speculation" (181).

Here, then, our attention is drawn to the importance of time in the analysis of economic systems. Economic life is characterized by change. Change implies an uncertain and unpredictable future, which means that speculation cannot be avoided by changing the institutions of society. "Economic activity is necessarily speculative because it is based upon an uncertain future" (182). All that one can accomplish is to change the form in which speculation is handled. Unless socialism can develop institutions that permit it to adjust to constant change in a responsible way, it will remain an impractical solution to the economic problem. It was this issue of the dynamics of an economic system that was to lead to so

[10] As an example of the extreme breadth of Mises' treatment of his subject, it is interesting to note that Mises had a discussion of "socialism and the sexual problem," in which he credited capitalism with substituting the idea of marriage as a contract between equal partners for the older idea of marriage in which women were considered the property of men. The older idea reflected the age of violence in which all that mattered was the brute force men could inflict on women. Capitalism ushered in an age of contract in which women gained status as property owners and hence could demand and assert rights as full human beings (76–83). It is doubtful that many feminists credit Mises as one of their theorists, but he clearly ranks with, say, John Stuart Mill as a champion of female equality.

[11] "The idea of a stationary state is an aid to theoretical speculation. In the world of reality there is no stationary state, for the conditions under which economic activity takes place are subject to perpetual alterations which it is beyond human capacity to limit" (173).

much misunderstanding between the Austrians and the advocates of socialist planning in the next decade.

Mises also elaborated on his argument about the differences in incentives facing private managers and socialist managers, tying it to the issue of speculation and change. In a system of private property, private owners realize that they will be the ones to gain or lose by their speculation, and hence they have strong incentives to speculate responsibly. To the extent they succeed, they make profits. To the extent that they fail, ownership of resources will pass out of their hands and into the hands of those who have proven themselves better at the game.[12] In either case, society benefits from the efforts of individuals to predict the future correctly and to take appropriate action. In socialist institutions, on the other hand, one observes the "crippling of initiative and a sense of responsibility" (183).

Interestingly, the failures of socialist bureaucracy are not necessarily due to malfeasance so much as to basic features of human nature. Socialists too often ignore a fundamental principle of human action: "Men have their own thoughts and their own wills" (183), a principle that Adam Smith had already adduced in *The Theory of Moral Sentiments*.[13] Men will pursue their own interests and act on their own judgment. Private enterprise sets up incentives for individuals to identify their own interests with those of the firm. Bureaucracy, with its committee structure and painstaking rules, pits the interests of the individual worker against organizational goals.[14]

We all know the appearance of the apparatus of socialist administration: a countless multitude of office holders, each zealously bent on preserving his position and preventing anybody from intruding on his sphere of activity – yet at

---

[12] Note this early sketch of a selection process that tends to direct resource use to productive ends. Mises later develops this idea into a theory of entrepreneurship in markets (1963: 289 ff.).

[13] "The man of system . . . is often so enamored with the supposed beauty of his own ideal plan of government, that he cannot suffer the smallest deviation from any part of it. . . . [H]e seems to imagine that he can arrange the different members of a great society with as much ease as the hand arranges the different pieces upon a chess-board; he does not consider that the pieces upon the chess-board have no other principle of motion besides that which the hand impresses upon them; but that, in the great chess-board of human society, every single piece has a principle of motion of its own, altogether different from that which the legislature might choose to impress upon it" ([1759] 1982:233–234). Cf. Mises' statement that "men have their own thoughts and their own wills. . . . [I]t is not to be supposed that they would suddenly, of their own free will, make themselves for all time the passive tools of *anyone* out of their midst – even though he were the wisest and best of them all" ([1759] 1982:183).

[14] It is interesting to note that Mises built his argument about the disincentives of socialism around the assumption that individuals would pursue their own interests in government agencies as well as in private enterprise, the insight that was later reintroduced by James Buchanan and Gordon Tullock in their pathbreaking work on public choice, *The Calculus of Consent* (1962).

the same time anxiously endeavouring to throw all responsibility of action on to somebody else. (183)

Furthermore, in socialist firms, there will be no incentive to innovation. Bureaucrats "content themselves with imitating what goes on in similar privately-owned undertakings. But where all concerns are socialized there will be hardly any talk of reforms and improvements" (184).[15]

Mises' 1920 article and his book-length critique of socialism had little effect on the progress of events in his native Austria, but it did have an effect on the scholarly community. In fact, Mises' clear and unequivocal assertion of the impossibility of economic calculation in socialism changed the course of the debate within a decade of its publication. However, for the next stage of the debate, it was not Mises playing the lead center stage, but his younger colleague and informal student, Friedrich von Hayek.

Hayek and capital theory

Hayek's role in the debate over socialism came about largely as a side issue in his intellectual life that eventually grew to all-consuming proportions. His first professional work was in business cycle research and capital theory, but because of the prominence he achieved in this field, he became a strong voice in the exploration of socialist economics. His expertise in capital theory led him to be in the right place at the right time to allow his arguments to be heard, if not particularly well understood.

Soon after completing his formal studies,[16] Hayek joined the Institute for Trade Cycle Research, an organization begun by Ludwig von Mises in

[15] Mises anticipates the criticism that private corporations are subject to the same bureaucratic inefficiencies as public firms and hence socialism will not change the basic behavior of firm managers. He asserts (without much in the way of evidence) that "success has always been attained only by those companies whose directors have predominant personal interest in the prosperity of the company" (184). Although his statement may not be immediately convincing, it could be restated to suggest that the degree of success of a firm is related to the degree to which managers are rewarded financially for their achievement. However, later, in *Human Action*, Mises argues that it is foolhardy to reward managerial success with a share of profits since, in the absence of any penalty for loss, this will only encourage risky behavior. Instead, he relies on capital markets and their implicit evaluation of managerial performance to discipline managers to behave in the interests of stockholders (1963:306–307).

[16] Hayek's interest in business cycles theory was inspired by a trip he took to the United States early in his career. Armed with letters of introduction he obtained from Joseph Schumpeter, Hayek toured the major academic centers in the United States during the 1923–1924 academic year. During this time, he met with most of the well-known economists of the day. That was an era when Wesley Clair Mitchell and institutional economics were in the ascendancy. Although Hayek was fascinated by the problem of the interrelationship of capital and monetary theory, the lack of theoretical foundations to support the statistical analysis produced by the American institutionalists, in his own

his capacity as economic and legal adviser to the Austrian Chamber of Commerce. Hayek's position with the institute allowed him to undertake a study of business cycles from the perspective of Austrian capital theory, combining Bohm-Bawerk's theory of the structure of production with monetary and interest theories drawn from Mises and Wicksell. Hayek carried on his research at the institute for seven years, rising to the position of director and becoming a recognized authority in the field of business cycle research. His work attracted attention beyond the borders of Austria: A set of essays that Hayek published in 1928 led Lionel Robbins, then very much attracted to the Austrian point of view, to invite Hayek to give a series of lectures at the London School of Economics during the 1930–1931 academic year on the topic of capital theory.

Hayek's published papers so far had been concerned with fleshing out the Mises–Wicksell theory of money and the trade cycle with a more complete theory of capital.[17] For his London lectures, however, he essentially wrote a new book, which he later published under the title *Prices and Production* (1931). His aim in these essays was to integrate monetary theory with a Bohm-Bawerkian notion of the structure of production to explain a "typical nineteenth century business cycle" (O'Driscoll, 1977:66).

After his arrival in London, there was at first no small enthusiasm for Hayek's ideas. Hicks, in telling the "Hayek story" (1967), explains the fascination many had with his unusual and difficult view of capital and production. As Hicks later reported, in the early thirties, Hayek was the principal rival to John Maynard Keynes in trying to explain economic crises. Hayek's ideas were hotly debated as most prominent economists at the London School of Economics tried to master Hayek's alien system. However, after the publication of Keynes's *General Theory of Employment, Interest and Money* ([1936] 1964), Hayek's ideas lost ground until eventually it was generally conceded that Keynes had the more promising view of capitalist processes. Nevertheless, Hayek continued to refine his theory of the business cycle for well over a decade, often in response to heated debate from his English colleagues.

As had Mises and Wicksell, Hayek viewed business cycles as the conse-quence of distortions of the information content of the price signals that inform the decisions of entrepreneurs and investors. When economic expansion is financed by bank credit that is not backed up by voluntary

words, "sent me rather back to Wicksell and Mises and made me attempt to build on the foundations they had laid" (1992:19).
[17] His early essays, published in German in 1928, were translated in 1933 as *Monetary Theory and the Trade Cycle* ([1933] 1966).

savings, Wicksell had explained, interest rates will fall below the "natural rate" and entrepreneurs will think that consumers are demanding more long-term investment projects and fewer short-term consumer goods. For Hayek, the lower interest rate will induce investors to substitute lengthier, more capital-intensive production processes for shorter more labor-intensive ones, thereby reducing the flow of consumer goods. However, since there is no new saving to offset increased investment, the new bank credit will cause factor prices to be bid up. The resultant increase in factor incomes eventually leads to increasing prices of consumer goods as consumers reassert their undiminished demand for first-order goods in relation to higher-order goods. This disequilibrium between consumer and producer expectations brought about by inappropriate price signals results in a crisis triggered by a mechanism Hayek later referred to as the Ricardo effect.[18]

As the prices of consumer goods are bid up, the profitability of short-term projects in relation to long term-projects will increase. The consequence will be abandonment of unprofitable capital projects that signal a recession. The boom could be kept going for a while by ever expanding bank credit, but eventually, the Ricardo effect would assert itself and lead to a bust. Hayek's ultimate message was that cycles were caused by credit expansion – Mises' original insight from *The Theory of Money and Credit* – and that the only cure for a boom was a bust that would permit correct relative prices to reassert themselves (Moss and Vaughn, 1986:55ff.).

Such a conclusion must have been particularly unpalatable during the throes of the Great Depression, and must be at least part of the reason that Hayek lost out to Keynes in the debate over macroeconomic theory.[19] There are undoubtedly many other reasons, some theoretical and some sociological, why the profession decided that it was Keynes and not Hayek who "was right" about macroeconomics and economic crises, but here we need only note that Keynes, at least as he was interpreted by his followers,[20] shifted the central macroeconomic questions from problems of growth and time-consuming processes to static models that equilibrated flows of income and expenditure at a moment in time. His problem was

---

[18] Hayek discussed the Ricardo effect mechanism in three places ([1939] 1975:3–71, 1948:220–254, 1978a:165–178). See also O'Driscoll (1977:92–135) and Moss and Vaughn (1986).

[19] Hayek continued to work on the problem of economic fluctuations throughout the 1930s and into the 1940s. In addition to numerous journal articles, his most important works on the subject are *Profits, Interest and Investment* ([1939] 1975) and *The Pure Theory of Capital* (1941).

[20] We will see later that the more subjectivist and "disequilibrium" aspect of Keynes's thought was to influence Austrian economics in a positive manner in the 1970s and 1980s largely through the intermediation of G. L. S. Shackle and Ludwig Lachmann (chapter 6).

simply different from that with which Hayek concerned himself and was clearly more amenable to the static equilibrium framework so familiar to neoclassical economics. In addition, where Keynes paid little attention to the characteristics of the capital stock and its relationship to economics growth, Hayek's background assumption was one of economic growth through increasing complexity of a heterogeneous and interrelated capital stock, a background assumption that fit uncomfortably, if at all, within a static equilibrium bed.

Furthermore, fundamental to Hayek's explanation of business cycles were problems with subjective perceptions of actors, their level of knowledge, and the expectations that they formed from the signals they received from the price system. The reason the crisis occurs is that producers are fooled about relative scarcities from incorrect factor prices, and their expectations about future profits are misled by inappropriate credit availability. All this led Hayek to develop a theory of genuine disequilibrium processes that resulted not in over- or underinvestment, but in the wrong kind of investment projects that inadequately meet consumer demand; investment that results in costly errors that have consequences for the future shape of capitalist processes. Even the correction of errors would not return the system to the previously achieved equilibrium (Hayek, 1978a:172–173).

Hayek's analysis of business cycles, then, relied on Mengerian concerns with time, knowledge, and processes. At the same time, Hayek attempted to theorize about a problem that arose fundamentally because of issues of subjectivity, knowledge, and time in an equilibrium framework that was familiar to his English colleagues. The result was a theoretical structure that was vaguely, but imperfectly, neoclassical. Hicks later was to claim that Hayek was not doing "English economics" (1967:204); we might rather say Hayek was doing Austrian economics within an "English" context. It was a mismatch from the start.

The economic calculation debate

The themes of perception, expectations, information, and disequilibrium processes were also to figure prominently in Hayek's writings on socialism during the 1930s and 1940s. And, where Keynes was Hayek's major rival for capturing the profession's view of capital theory and trade cycles, ironically, his most formidable rival over the economics of socialism was none other than Leon Walras – or Walras as interpreted by his followers in the 1930s. Unlike the Marxist advocates of socialist economy in the early decades of the twentieth century who had been Mises' primary antagonists, the most forceful spokesmen for socialist economics during the 1930s were neoclassical economists who were doing no more than applying conventional economic theory to an alternative institutional setting (Vaughn, 1980a).

The most well-respected theorist of the economics of socialism and the one who was credited with refuting both Mises and Hayek on the subject, Oscar Lange, took as his starting point Walrasian general equilibrium theory (Lange and Taylor 1938:70ff.). Perhaps it was the very sharpness with which Lange applied conventional economic models to the institutional setting of an ideal socialism that permitted a more clearly defined Austrian view of economic processes to emerge during the course of the debate.

Not surprisingly, it was Ludwig von Mises' 1920 article that induced the neoclassical socialists to try to work out the economics of socialism. While Mises' emphatic, unqualified pronouncements invited a certain amount of academic resistance, a number of conventional English-speaking economists starting almost a decade later found his challenge irresistible.

One of the first attempts to answer Mises involved various ways of solving the pricing problem in central planning by estimating demand and supply equations from empirical data in order to compute economic prices (Dickinson, 1933). Although most economists accepted the basic premise of such solutions to the pricing problem, these proposals were quickly abandoned as practical schemes for actually running a socialist economy in the face of the overwhelming problems of data collection and processing in a precomputer era. Indeed, it was the "practical difficulty" of statistical estimation that Oscar Lange addressed with his version of "market socialism."

Lange accepted Mises' point that in order for a socialist economy to make rational decisions about resources, one needed a means of calculating relative values.[21] Lange, therefore, attempted to answer Mises' challenge by finding an alternative means to arrive at economic prices that relied neither on extensive data collection and model building nor on

[21] In fact, with obviously more than a touch of sarcasm, Lange opened his article with a "tribute" to Mises: "Socialists have certainly good reason to be grateful to Professor Mises, the great advocatus diaboli of their cause. For it was his powerful challenge that forced the socialists to recognize the importance of an adequate system of economic accounting to guide the allocation of resources in a socialist economy. . . . Both as an expression of recognition for the great service rendered by him and as a memento of the prime importance of sound economic accounting, a statue of Professor Mises ought to occupy an honorable place in the great hall of the Ministry of Socialization or of the Central Planning Board of the socialist state" (Lange and Taylor, 1938:57–58). It is a fitting irony that busts of Mises do now reside in "places of honor" (although not at the central planning boards since they no longer exist) in most of the formerly socialist countries of Eastern Europe and in Russia, given by friends of Mises in the United States to recognize the fulfillment of his prophecies regarding the impossibility of socialism.

real markets, with all their perceived imperfections. Lange's answer was to derive shadow prices from market information in much the same way that Lange believed it was accomplished in real markets and to use this information to make resource allocations in centrally controlled firms.

His scheme followed Mises' original argument by allowing for private property and a real market in consumer goods and in labor, but having all producer goods, "the means of production," collectively owned (Lange and Taylor, 1938:73). Prices for capital goods would be decreed by a central planning board (a CPB) and all production would take place in state-owned firms. The managers of all state-owned firms would be instructed to behave as perfect competitors and maximize profits on the basis of prices dictated by the CPB.

The crux of Lange's plan, and the feature that won him the most praise from his colleagues, was his plan for arriving at economic prices. Prices, he argued, were simply the terms on which alternatives were offered (60). These terms did not need to be established in free markets based on private ownership, but could be arrived at even in a centrally planned economy.

He imagined that actual pricing in real markets took place according to a Walrasian tatonnement, with the market proxy for the auctioneer arriving at the market clearing price by trial and error (81–82). Hence, Lange argued, the CPB could substitute for the market by acting as an auctioneer and adjusting prices according to trial and error as well. All they would need to do would be to increase prices in response to shortages and decrease prices in response to surpluses. Information about shortages and surpluses would be obtained from the managers of state-owned firms, who would be given two rules to follow: Minimize average cost (to arrive at optimum input combinations), and equate marginal cost to the state-declared price (to fix the correct scale of output).[22]

Lange believed his scheme duplicated all the important features of the market, and more important, he believed that the information that the CPB would gather about surpluses and shortages was all the information necessary to achieve economic prices. He had no reason to believe his brand of market socialism would be any less efficient than ideal capitalism. Furthermore, he believed that because the central planners would have much wider knowledge of the total economic system than would any

[22] Abba Lerner, who had a deeper understanding of cost than did Lange, argued that Lange had essentially overdetermined his system. Since the point of socialist production was to maximize the value of production, that would be sufficiently accomplished by instructing managers to simply equate marginal cost to price. Issues of plant size would be derivative from this formulation (1937:251).

individual entrepreneur, the trial-and-error system he envisioned would work even better than its analogue under capitalism (89). Hence, Lange was able to enlist neoclassical general equilibrium theory, including its revelation of the flaws of free markets, in the service of socialism.

What strikes one today in reading Lange's articles is the simplistic naivete of his system. All economic decisions were to be based on "parametric" prices and given technical knowledge. Production was the unproblematic solution to a simple constrained maximization problem. Socialist managers would do as they were told and could be disciplined by periodic audits of their books. Products could be defined for planning purposes and the trial-and-error process would be uncomplicated enough to maintain prices at equilibrium. To Friedrich Hayek, a man who had spent the past thirteen years trying to understand the intricacies of capital theory and business cycles, this simplicity of approach seemed totally at odds with reality. The world was far more complex than anything dreamed of in the socialists' philosophies.

Hayek first became embroiled in the discussion about the economic feasibility of socialism the year before Lange's article appeared in print. In 1935, Hayek published a volume, *Collectivist Economic Planning*, that brought together essays by Dutch economist N. G. Pierson, German economist Frank Halm, Enrico Barone, and Mises' original calculation article. By far the most important contribution to this volume, however, was made by Hayek himself. Of his two essays, the first was a summary of the early stages of the debate over socialism, while his second article, the concluding one in the book, was his own critique of some of the more recent (post-Mises) proposals for socialist economy.

Hayek's approach in this article was largely to raise questions about the feasibility of socialist prescriptions for new institutional arrangements. He contributed few positive arguments about the nature of economics but rather confined his efforts to raising objections to socialist proposals. Most of his objections, moreover, were of a very specific nature indicating his general belief that the socialists simply had not paid enough attention to the details of the market in constructing their grandiose schemes. It was as if they believed that the economists' model of perfect competition was an accurate description of reality and not a bare bones abstraction to answer some limited questions.

Some of Hayek's specific objections revolved around the following issues: What does it really mean to run a socialist firm? That is, how can socialist managers produce efficiently within the constraints of a socialist system? The socialists seem to think that once resource prices were given, production was a simple matter of finding optimal input combinations of resources and plugging them into some automatic recipe for output.

Hayek argued that in fact production depended less on objective recipes than on subjective judgments. For instance, some of the most difficult production decisions involve the amount and rate at which capital goods are used, and such decisions depend upon expectations of future product and input prices (209). Future prices, however, are simply judgments about future states of the world that have no objective status. Upon what basis are firm managers to make such judgments?

Hayek also asked what it means to refer to "given" technical knowledge? Given to whom? In a market economy, technical knowledge is the product of competition among actors each of whom possesses a limited amount of knowledge about the production process. In a planned economy, without real competition, how will this limited, dispersed knowledge be shared? Furthermore, in what does technical knowledge consist? Techniques of production should not be thought of as some sort of fixed recipe; rather, in many cases it is really more a "technique of thought," a knowledge of how to find new solutions to problems (210). How can central planning duplicate the market's ability to mobilize this kind of knowledge?

Like Mises before him, Hayek raised troubling questions about the potential behavior of managers in socialist firms. Socialists argued that managers would be directed to minimize cost, but how would managers know what minimum cost was? Costs are not objective magnitudes that can be read off accounting sheets; they are subjective estimations about the value of opportunities forgone. Since these values are only expected returns, their magnitude depends upon the estimates of the firm managers. Without a market against which to test expectations, the manager's estimates could not help but be arbitrary (226–229).

The whole question of how one monitors and rewards socialist managers, Hayek believed, is also problematic. In a system of private property, profit and loss serves to discipline the behavior of managers and direct resources to those who can use them most efficiently. In socialist firms where managers have neither property- nor market-determined profit and loss to guide them, resource allocation would be difficult at best. How, for instance, could the planning board decide to whom to allocate new capital resources? On the basis of promises of future returns? Are these not empty promises when managers have no property to serve as collateral for their loans? And how will managers' behavior be affected by the knowledge that their own wealth is not at stake when they take risks for their firms? As Mises had pointed out, the whole question of risk taking cannot be avoided in a changing world. Would socialist managers not tend to be more cautious than private managers, since they will have to justify their behavior ex post to their superiors without the example of other competing firms to separate the consequences of bad judgment from conditions outside their control? And without genuine, after-the-fact profit and loss to guide them, on what basis would the central planning board assess the appropriateness of the risky choices managers made in the past (233–237)?

The dominant characteristic of all these criticisms is much greater attention to the details of individual economic decision making than the socialists had displayed in their schemes. In their uncritical acceptance of the aggregate nature of economic abstractions, Hayek argued, they neglected the process by which the market brings about the situation they were trying to duplicate:

The essential thing about the present economic system is that it does react to some extent to all those small changes and differences which would have to be deliberately disregarded under the system we are discussing if the calculations were to be manageable. In this way rational decisions would be impossible in all these questions of detail, which in the aggregate decide the success of productive effort. (212–213)

Two years after the publication of Lange's system in book form, Hayek continued his critique of socialism (Hayek, 1948:181–208). In this later article, he reiterated most of his earlier criticism concerning the socialists' neglect of the details of the market process. He once again asked uncomfortable questions, such as how will the socialist scheme define a product when most products are differentiated from each other in some way? For how long are prices to be fixed? How will managers behave where they have no property at stake? What does it mean to minimize costs when costs are not objective entities but subjective estimate about possible future states of the world? This time, however, he was clearer on the nature of one of the basic differences between his assumptions and those of the socialists.

As Hayek (and Mises before him) had previously argued, the socialists suffered from "an excessive preoccupation with problems of the pure theory of stationary equilibrium" (188). If there was little change in the real world, he argued, the problem of planning would be much less troubling. One could approach an equilibrium through a process of trial and error if the data never changed. In the real world, however, "constant change is the rule." Which method, then, is more likely to give quick adjustments to change – planning or markets? The difference between a system of planned prices and a system of markets, he argued,

seems to be about the same as that between an attacking army in which every unit and every man could move only by special command and by the exact distance ordered by headquarters and an army in which every unit and every man can take advantage of every opportunity offered to them. (187)

When one considers how a system of planning would actually work, it is difficult to see how anyone could imagine that it would even come close to a system in which "the required changes are brought about by the spontaneous actions of the persons immediately concerned" (187).

Knowledge and process

Although Hayek's articles directly related to the socialist calculation debate were mostly of a critical nature, the issues he raised in these articles became the basis for further exploration of the nature of the market process. The essays to which his continuing exploration gave rise can be considered both answers to the socialists and attempts to advance economic understanding of market processes. In each of these articles, he emphasized the same themes that informed his critiques of socialism: the ubiquitousness of change in economic life; the importance of detailed, local knowledge; and the function of the market process in bringing about order. Hayek, by virtue of the sheer logic of the argument, had begun to discover the very Mengerian themes that were lost in the homogenizing blend of neoclassical economics.

The first issue raised by the calculation debate that he tackled directly was the whole question of what we mean by equilibrium and how it relates to the real world. Obviously troubled by the socialist use of static equilibrium theory to design their economic system, Hayek tried to develop a meaning of equilibrium that is consistent with a world of change and action. In "Economics and Knowledge" (1948:33–56), his stated aim is to separate those propositions of formal economic theory that are simply part of the logic we apply to understanding situations, the "pure logic of choice" (35), from those supplementary empirical hypotheses that are "in principle capable of verification."[23] When that task is accomplished, he argued, it will become obvious that the definition of equilibrium is part of the logic of choice, while the empirical element in economic theory, the part about adaptation to change, "consists of propositions about the acquisition of knowledge" (33).

Hayek begins by redefining equilibrium for an individual not as an optimum consumption basket, a static end-state notion, but as a plan of action that is not disrupted by new knowledge. Immediately, he calls attention to the fact that since a plan takes place in time, "the passage of

---

[23] Despite this "verificationist" criterion for accepting a scientific proposition, Hayek remained very much an Austrian in methodology. In an essay written during this period, "The Facts of the Social Sciences," Hayek emphasized that what constitutes data depends upon the theory with which you organize interpretation, and he asserted the importance of intuitive understanding of the actions of others in formulating social theories (1948:58–67).

time is essential to give the concept of equilibrium any meaning (37). This, of course, is directly contrary to the static notions of equilibrium common to neoclassical economics of that time. From here, he proceeds to argue that while equilibrium for a single individual is a relatively straightforward concept, the concept becomes somewhat less precise when applied to the interaction of many individuals.

If equilibrium among individuals is to have any meaning, Hayek mused, it must represent "some sort of balance between the actions of different individuals" (37). But since individuals all have different plans, and since the actions of one individual form the external environment of another, what sort of balance can we be talking about? His answer is to define equilibrium of the competitive system as a situation in which individual plans are consistent with one another such that the actions of one do not disrupt the plans of another. It may be the case that even if plans are consistent or coordinated, individual expectations with respect to external events may prove wrong and equilibrium may be disrupted, but as long as the disruption is not brought about by mistaken expectations about the behavior of others, the system can be said to be in equilibrium (41–43).

The advantages of such a notion of equilibrium, Hayek believes, are clear. First, it is a conception that is compatible with "a progressive society" in which prices need not always be market clearing in the conventional sense, but may still be consistent with plan compatibility and economic growth. Second, it allows us to focus on the central empirical question of economic analysis, which is to what extent is there a tendency toward equilibrium in the system?[24] What are the conditions under which such a tendency exists, and what is the nature of the process by which it is brought about? It is here that we finally get to questions of the relationship of knowledge to equilibrium and it is here that we finally get to the crux of Hayek's complaint against both socialism and current economic theory.

Socialism, just like its progenitor, neoclassical economics, has misspecified the economic problem: It assumes perfect knowledge in markets when the question that one really wants to answer is how does anyone come to know what it is we assume in the first place? As Menger had argued seventy years earlier, within a modern economy there is a "division of knowledge" from which we all somehow manage to profit. The

---

[24] As we will see later (chapter 7), this claim of Hayek's was controversial. Israel Kirzner, for example, argues that the tendency toward equilibrium is not an empirical proposition at all but an implication of human action, that man has a propensity to discover opportunities. Hence, a tendency toward equilibrium is inherent in the nature of the market process (1979:29–31).

problem we need to solve is "how the spontaneous interaction of a number of people, each possessing only bits of knowledge, brings about a state of affairs in which prices correspond to costs, etc., and which could be brought about by deliberate direction only by somebody who possessed the combined knowledge of all those individuals" (51). This is the nature of the economic problem that Hayek believed the socialists had not even identified, let alone solved.

Notice that Hayek really has two propositions here. The first is that the division of knowledge is the rationale for the market, the "spontaneous interaction of a number of people." The second is that an optimum position occurs when the spontaneous interaction leads to a situation that could be brought about by an omniscient dictator, apparently Hayek's restatement of the invisible hand doctrine. Any society will be characterized by some division of knowledge, but the various bits of knowledge possessed by individuals can be used in a variety of ways. Hayek wants to leave room to argue that under some institutional conditions (i.e., socialism) this division of knowledge will be used inefficiently in relation to other institutional conditions (markets). Without some notion of an optimum pattern of interaction among individuals (or at least a notion of better or worse), it would be difficult to see how he could argue that markets work better than socialism.

Hayek in this article does not go very far along the way of articulating those subsidiary empirical propositions about how knowledge is acquired and used that he claimed were necessary to understand the market order. Instead, he ends by making a few suggestions about how particularized knowledge might be linked in a market economy to form a "sort of optimum."[25] However, nine years later he was to come back to the problem of those subsidiary empirical propositions in his essay "The Use of Knowledge in Society" (1948:77–91).

In this essay, Hayek explores the nature of the knowledge that is important to the market process and the way in which the market mobilizes and economizes on its use. He once again focuses on the true nature of the economic problem that he sees as being wider than what is conventionally accepted. "The economic problem of society . . . is how to secure the best use of resources known to any of the members of society,

[25] He describes how one might achieve the optimum result (that could be achieved by an omniscient dictator) as long as people with specialized knowledge are linked together by overlapping trades. That is, people at the margin know what is necessary for them to get the best deal in their particular circumstances and are connected to the wider set of potential traders by others whose links extend outward (53–54). This is a rather wordy version of the argument that not everyone has to know everything in order for the perfectly competitive result to obtain as long as there are marginal traders who bring about adjustments to equilibrium.

for ends whose relative importance only these individuals know. Or . . . it is a problem of the utilization of knowledge which is not given to anyone in its totality" (77–78).

The recent bias for planning, he argues, seems to be partly a consequence of a misunderstanding of the nature of the knowledge that is relevant for economic activity. Despite the prevailing prejudice in favor of "scientific" knowledge, Hayek emphasizes that the knowledge that really makes the market process work is not scientific so much as "the knowledge of the particular circumstances of time and place" (80) – once again, the details of everyday life. Everybody, he points out, has some specialized knowledge of events and facts personally relevant to him. In this sense, everyone has some particular knowledge advantage over others from which he can profit. And in the course of his profiting from it, others are able to benefit from it as well. This is the kind of knowledge that markets utilize most effectively, yet it is exactly particularized knowledge that is washed out in the aggregative statistical data used by planners (83).

The problem facing society is how to encourage people to use their particularized knowledge in a way that results in their benefiting others. Here Hayek once again emphasizes the implications of constant change for economic activity:

If we can agree that the economic problem of society is mainly one of rapid adaptation to changes in the particular circumstances of time and place, it would seem to follow that the ultimate decisions must be left to the people who are familiar with these circumstances, who know directly of the relevant changes and of the resources immediately available to meet them. (83–84)

If we do this, it is not necessary that everyone know everything in order for the result to be successful. In a price system, it is clear that people really have to know very little about changes in the circumstances of production and of distribution in order for them to make the correct changes in the use of resources. If the price goes up, this is a signal to use less. If the price goes down, it is rational to use more. In this way, the price system economizes on knowledge while making it possible for people to benefit from the division of knowledge that is unavoidable in human life.

The marvel is that in a case like that of a scarcity of one raw material, without an order being issued, without more than perhaps a handful of people knowing the cause, tens of thousands of people whose identity could not be ascertained by months of investigation, are made to use the material or its products more sparingly; that is, they move in the right direction. (87)[26]

---

[26] Kirzner argues (1984) convincingly that Hayek's vivid description of the knowledge conveyed by prices led to an overemphasis on the information content of equilibrium prices. Concentration on equilibrium prices obscured the more important insight implied by Hayek that in actuality it is *disequilibrium* prices that are important for informing people of the need for change and bringing about efficiency in the market process (201).

In a foreshadowing of his later work on social evolution, Hayek quotes Alfred North Whitehead, who said that "civilization advances by extending the number of important operations which we can perform without thinking about them" (88). By this criterion, central planning is a step backward rather than an improvement on the price system.

There are two more important Hayek articles that must be mentioned here. Although they were published several decades apart, they seem to form two parts to the same argument. Their titles lend credence to such an assessment: "The Meaning of Competition" (1948:92–106) and "Competition as a Discovery Procedure" (1978a:179–190). In the first of these articles, Hayek examines the relationship between the perfectly competitive model and real-world competitive practices. In the second, his last on the general subject of the economics of the price system, Hayek combines the insights of his essays on knowledge with his understanding of the competitive market process.

The target audience of "The Meaning of Competition" was less market socialism than the economics of imperfect competition. Once again, Hayek's overall message is that the perfectly competitive model is misleading about the real nature of competitive processes. Because it is static in nature and it assumes homogeneous products and perfect knowledge, the model manages to eliminate all those activities from consideration that constitute real competition. In perfect competition, there is no explanation for advertising, for product differentiation, or for price competition, yet these are all the very ways in which real businessmen try to compete for consumer purchases (1948:96). Even more egregious, perfect competition explicitly excludes "personal relationships" among market participants from the model. Yet in actual life, our limited knowledge makes reliance on personal relationships and their proxy, brand names and good will, imperative. This, however, in no way reduces the intensity of competition; it simply describes how it is undertaken. To call this kind of competition "imperfect" (as had Joan Robinson) is certainly misleading. Given the limitation of knowledge in the real world, such competition is as "perfect" as possible. In fact, such "imperfect" practices are the very reason that the "market would still bring about a set of prices at which each commodity sold just cheap enough to outbid its potential close substitute" (99). Hayek regarded that as no mean accomplishment.

Hayek's important point here, both for central planning and for regulation, is that one must be careful not to make the wrong kind of comparison. The comparison should not be between the fictitious model of perfect competition that may be a reasonable abstraction for markets for standardized goods like those sold in agricultural markets but that is too abstract to explain much about other markets; the comparison should be between real markets in which there is free competition and the situation that would exist if there were no competition at all (100). Here, Hayek cut to the heart of the problem with the economics of socialism. One cannot criticize the market according to criteria that ignore the basic problems the market is designed to solve – heterogeneity and lack of omniscience. One must judge the market by comparing it to realistic alternatives.[27]

In this article, Hayek touched lightly on an issue that was to be the subject of his last article on the theory of markets. All economic activity is always future oriented; "It is always a voyage into the unknown" (102) in which the consequence is the discovery of new ways of doing things and new products, the idea behind the title, "Competition as a Discovery Procedure" (1978a:179–190).

In this last essay, finally, the distinctive Hayekian (and not surprisingly, Mengerian) message becomes clear. Markets are about knowledge and change. The knowledge important for market decisions is specialized, detailed, particularized according to time and place. It is also sometimes tacit and unreportable.[28] The information that is generally assumed in economic models is really the product of a market process in which competition is rivalry among partly ignorant suppliers who, through a genuine process of trial and error, seek to earn profits by learning about and providing information to partly ignorant consumers. Since even the best plans of the market-socialists assumed the existence of knowledge that was yet to be discovered and provided no satisfactory means to duplicate the market process in generating that knowledge, market socialism must be presumed to be unsatisfactory. Because they misunderstood the nature of a market economy, the neoclassical socialists had not even begun to appreciate the central problem of socialist economy. They addressed the problem of calculating value without understanding how the market accomplished the task.

These articles clearly point to a different understanding of the nature of the competitive process than was current during the time Hayek was writing. They were eventually to form the core of modern Austrian

---

[27] Ironically, Hayek's opponents made a similar charge against him. He was accused of comparing real socialism with an idealized market (Bergson, 1948).

[28] The implications of tacit knowledge for market organization is an important theme in modern Austrian economics that can be traced back to Hayek's work on competition. Yet, in "Competition as a Discovery Procedure," Hayek just barely alludes to the role of tacit knowledge in market processes,"the . . . combinations of knowledge and skills, which the market enables them (market participants) to use, will not merely, or even in the first instance, be such knowledge of facts as they could list and communicate if some authority asked them to do so" (1978a:182). By the time he publishes the first volume of *Law, Legislation and Liberty*, however, he fully integrates tacit knowledge into his analysis (1973).

understanding of the nature of markets and to provide the link between Menger and the modern Austrians. Yet, at the time they were published, although Hayek's writings were widely read and respected, they were by no means fully understood. It was not so much that his colleagues thought he was wrong in anything he said. They just did not see how what he said mattered, either for the calculation debate or for economic theory in general.

The prevailing attitude toward Hayek's objections to socialism can be effectively captured by consulting Schumpeter's *Capitalism, Socialism and Democracy* ([1942] 1962). Despite his early ties to the Austrian school, on the specific matter of the theory of socialist calculation, Schumpeter sided entirely with the socialists. He argued that there was "nothing wrong with the pure logic of socialism" (172) and dismissed Mises' arguments against socialist calculation with the sweeping claim that "consumers in evaluating ('demanding') consumers' goods *ipso facto* also evaluate the means of production which enter into the production of those goods" (175). He further asserted that socialism "in any normal situation would command information sufficient to enable it to come at first throw fairly close to the correct quantities of output in the major lines of production, and the rest would be a matter of adjustments by informed trial and error" (185). Indeed, in socialist economies, far from operating at a disadvantage, planners and managers would probably do better than under capitalism because they would have more information at their fingertips (194). Schumpeter simply missed entirely Hayek's arguments about timing and knowledge because he presumed economic equilibria could be achieved and persist for long periods of time. He regarded all Hayek's objections as practical impediments, which, although they might seriously interfere with the actual performance of socialist economies, did not touch the logic of the theory.

In sum, Hayek's larger exploration of the problem of knowledge and processes in economic order seemed to fall on deaf ears. Consequently, he became increasingly frustrated with the gulf that existed between him and his neoclassical colleagues. When Hicks suggested that Hayek's capital theory was misunderstood because he was "not doing English economics," he could just as well have been referring to Hayek's role in the economic calculation debate. It is no wonder, then, that by the end of the 1940s, Hayek ceased writing primarily for an audience of economists. He was simply not in the same conversation as everybody else. He had to wait twenty more years for his message to be heard.

CHAPTER 4

Ludwig von Mises: Austrian economics in America

Although it was Friedrich Hayek who brought Austrian economic ideas to England, it was his older colleague and mentor, Ludwig von Mises who is most identified with Austrian economics in America. This is not to say that Mises was the first Austrian economist to emigrate to the United States. Indeed, Mises was the last who can be said to have been pushed out of his native country by the advance of Hitler's armies during the interwar period. Preceding Mises had been such eminent figures as Joseph Schumpeter, Gottfried Haberler, Fritz Machlup, and Oscar Morgenstern, all of whom obtained good academic appointments in major American universities and assimilated themselves nicely into the indigenous academic scene. Mises, on the other hand, arrived in the United States in 1940, never acquired a tenured academic appointment, never fully assimilated into the contemporary academic milieu, and ended up becoming the controversial symbol of Austrian economics in America. It also turned out, undoubtedly because of his professional isolation from the mainstream academic community, that Mises' ideas became the focal point for the Austrian revival of the 1970s.

As we have already noted, Mises was one of the younger generation of Austrian economists who studied under Bohm-Bawerk and Wieser at the University of Vienna in the opening years of the twentieth century. Mises received his law degree in 1906, and after a brief stint as a law clerk, he accepted a position at the Vienna Chamber of Commerce in 1909 (Mises, 1978:71). He continued in his capacity as primary economic and legal adviser to the chamber throughout his life in Vienna, where he was recognized as a major figure in economic policy formation during these years.

Although Mises' formal employment was with the chamber, he also taught regularly at the University of Vienna as a Privatdozant. There was some expectation among Mises' colleagues that he would at some point be offered a chair at Vienna, but despite Mises' generally recognized eminence, when a chair became available, it went instead to Hans Mayer, another of Wieser's students whose level of accomplishment never came close to that of Mises. Mises himself attributed his lack of academic appointment to his outspoken liberal ideas, but others have noted that

Mises also suffered from two other handicaps in interwar Vienna: He was a Jew and he was "difficult to the point that many people thought him 'personally obnoxious' " (Craver 1986:5). Although this last characterization is a matter of opinion, the first two were indisputable barriers to advancement in academic circles in the Vienna of his day.

Mises may have been an outsider to formal academics, but he was nevertheless a major player in the production of economic ideas throughout the Viennese stage of his life. In addition to the course he generally taught at the university, for fourteen years (1920–1934), Mises conducted a private seminar in his office at the chamber. This seminar was not only the main vehicle for Mises' teaching, it also seemed to have been the heart of his intellectual life in Vienna.[1] Once every two weeks from October to June, younger scholars and intellectuals would meet to discuss questions of economics, sociology, and philosophy with Mises. The quality of the seminar can be gauged by the regular participants, including economists Friedrich Hayek, Oskar Morgenstern, Gottfried Haberler, Fritz Machlup, Paul N. Rosenstein-Rodan, and philosophers Felix Kaufman and Alfred Schutz.[2] Participants were later to write glowingly of the intellectual rigor combined with an atmosphere of genial toleration that characterized the Mises seminar. Hayek remembers:

These were not instructional meetings, but discussions presided over by an older friend whose views were by no means shared by all members. . . . [T]he discussions . . . frequently dealt with the problems of the methods of the social sciences, but rarely with special problems of economic theory (except those of the subjective theory of value). Questions of economic policy, however, were discussed often, and always from the angle of the influence of different social philosophies upon it. (Hayek, 1992:29–30)

Apparently, this seminar provided the training ground for serious Austrian economists of the twenties and early thirties.[3]

The seminar ended in 1934 when Mises accepted a position as professor of international relations at the Institut Universitaire des Haute

---

[1] Mises also reports that he was instrumental in forming the Economic Society in Austria in 1908, and although it was formally presided over by Hans Mayer, Mises remained an active member until his departure from Vienna in 1934. The society lasted as a viable entity for only four more years, at which time Mayer, acting on Nazi orders, dismissed all non-Aryans from membership. After this craven action, Mayer's name became anathema in Austrian circles and his contributions virtually ignored (Mises, 1978:98–99; see also Craver 1986).

[2] Interestingly, of the twenty-six people Mises mentions as regular participants in his seminar, six were women (1978:100). Apparently, Mises practiced what he preached about equality between the sexes in *Socialism* (1981:89).

[3] Fritz Machlup also remembered Mises, the teacher, fondly. He reports that he only began to become an active economist when he joined Mises' seminar at the University of Vienna. He wrote his dissertation under Mises and joined the privat-seminar in 1924 (Machlup, 1980:9).

Etudes Internationales in Geneva, Switzerland. Mises found the conditions at Geneva both congenial and satisfying, and he might have spent the rest of his productive life there if France, right across the border from Geneva, had not fallen to the Nazis in 1940. The precariousness of the situation was not lost on him, and he was finally convinced to follow so many other German and Austrian intellectuals into exile from their native land to the safer shores of the United States.[4]

Although many Austrian economists had preceded him to the United States and quickly established themselves in their new home, Mises found the going somewhat rougher. In the first few years in the United States, Mises was kept busy establishing new intellectual contacts. He traveled frequently, giving lectures at universities such as Princeton, Columbia, New York University, Harvard, and the Fletcher School, and to business groups; he wrote articles for the *New York Times*;[5] he formed a long-term association with the National Association of Manufacturers; he became a member of the staff of the Foundation for Economic Education; and for several years, he was a paid associate of the National Bureau for Economic Research. From 1945 to 1949, Mises was on the regular faculty at New York University, although not in a tenured position. From 1949, when his official contract was not renewed, until four years before his death at age 92 in 1973, he continued to teach at New York University supported by the Volker Fund, which underwrote Mises' weekly seminar.

Mises also continued to write prolifically during all his years in the United States, publishing books and articles at a steady pace. Yet, despite all of his speaking engagements, his teaching, and his writing, he was never more than a peripheral figure in American academic circles. In Austria, he did not hold a formal academic chair, yet his prominence as economist and legal adviser to the powerful Chamber of Commerce coupled with his part-time teaching at the university, his scholarly publications, and his famous private seminar guaranteed his role as a major player in Austrian economic circles for over thirty years (Craver 1986:14). In the United States, his experience was very different.

There are a number of reasons why Mises never gained the stature in the United States that he had in Austria – or even that other Austrian economists who preceded him to this country achieved. The reason most often supplied by some Mises supporters is that his unflinching opposition to socialism and interventionism at a time when academics believed

---

[4] For an exciting account of Mises' harrowing trip through France as he and his wife worked their way to America, see Margit von Mises, *My Years with Ludwig von Mises* (1984: 51–56).

[5] Mises' long-time friend and admirer Henry Hazlitt wrote for the *New York Times* and helped to get Mises' articles published.

that socialism was not only technically possible but also likely to be an improvement on capitalism barred his entry into academic circles. Mises and Hayek, we should remember, were judged to have lost the calculation debate.

There is no doubt that Mises' politics played a major role in his lack of academic success in the United States,[6] yet other factors entered in as well. One must have been his age.[7] Mises was almost sixty when he emigrated to America, and starting over to build a career in a new land in the seventh decade of life is never easy. Perhaps a better reason, however, was the nature and style of Mises' publications during the American stage of his life.

There is no question that despite the creativity of his mind and the breadth of insight he brought to economics, the tone of his writing was imperious and his context was unfamiliar to American academic audiences. He wrote with a certainty in the correctness of his argument that brooked no opposition. He was convinced that the economics profession was straying further and further from good science, and the longer he wrote, the less tolerant he seemed to become of what he viewed as foolish opposition. Worse, from the perspective of a contemporary American audience, he was often fighting battles that had long since ceased to interest professional economists or that they had never heard of in the first place. Many pages of his text are devoted, for example, to refuting the German historical school, naive Marxists, and thirties-style behaviorists. In his writing, he resolutely carved out his own field of play and defined his own opponents, but the cost was that others simply refused to play his game.

---

[6] It was not that Mises was entirely overlooked by the academic world in America. While still in Geneva, Mises received an offer of a visiting appointment at the University of California (Margit von Mises, 1984:49). Since visiting appointments were often a first step for European refugees to secure permanent academic appointments, the position in California might have been the entree that Mises needed to get a foothold in American academics. He refused to accept the position, however, preferring instead to live in New York, which he considered the intellectual center of America. Furthermore, he reported to Hayek that he could have a position at the New School for Social Research, but that he did not want to take it (letter dated October 27, 1940, Hayek correspondence at the Hoover Institution, Box 38, file 24; I am grateful to Peter Boettke for locating this reference and the following one during his research at the Hoover Institution in 1992–1993). It should not be forgotten as well that he did hold a regular appointment, although not a chair, at NYU from ages sixty-four to sixty-eight. Although politics may well have played a role in terminating Mises' appointment, age sixty-eight is not too far off the usual retirement age for academics to consider the failure of NYU to renew his appointment as solely a political move.

[7] In a letter to Hayek of December 22, 1940, Mises himself blames his age for some of his difficulties in integrating himself into a new academic culture, but reassures Hayek that he will have it easier because he is younger.

Mises' refusal to join in the contemporary economic conversation was partly cause and partly effect of another aspect of his American life. Largely because he was known as a staunch advocate of free markets at a time when the enthusiasm for them had reached a nadir in American intellectual life, Mises quickly attracted a following among the "old right." He became a spokesman for an economic point of view that was largely absent in professional economic circles of the time and hence was a rallying point for free market groups who were looking for intellectual leadership. Mises' long-term association with the Foundation for Economic Education is one example of his new constituency. It is no surprise, further, that his seminar at New York University was underwritten by the Volker Fund, another free market foundation.[8]

Mises conducted his New York University seminar for approximately two decades, yet it had surprisingly little impact on the economics profession.[9] Unlike Vienna, where all the most important economists to pass through Austria at least visited Mises' seminar, New York, with a few notable exceptions, brought him no students who were to become major players in the economics profession.[10] And whereas in Vienna, Mises had served as a discussion leader in his seminar, in New York, he was more the professor instructing the faithful students who treated him with corre-

---

[8] The Volker Fund also provided Hayek's salary at the Committee on Social Thought at the University of Chicago during his stay there from 1950 to 1962. Apparently, the publication of *The Road to Serfdom* (1944), which explicated his views on the similarity of the totalitarian natures of Nazism and Communism, and his belief that interventionism was leading inexorably toward totalitarianism in the so far free countries made him too controversial to employ on regular appointment, even in the economics department of the University of Chicago.

[9] It is instructive to note the contributors to a Mises Festschrift edited by Mary Sennholz in 1956. By this time, he had been a resident of the United States for sixteen years and had been actively teaching for most of those years, yet out of the nineteen contributors, only three – Murray Rothbard, Louis Spadaro, and William Peterson – were American economists who had studied with Mises. The others were either former colleagues and friends from his earlier life in Vienna (i.e., Rueff, Roepke, Machlup, Lachmann, Hutt, Hayek) or people associated more with his libertarianism than his economics (Hazlitt, Harper, Read, Greaves). Certainly, no contemporary American economists who were not "disciples" (a word bandied about a great deal in Mary Sennholz's introduction) of Mises were represented in this volume.

[10] The obvious exception, of course, was Israel Kirzner, who achieved the rank of professor at New York University and who has taken the most prominent role in the Austrian revival. Murray Rothbard, on the faculty first at Brooklyn Polytechnic Institute and now at the University of Nevada, Las Vegas, was also a regular participant in the Mises seminar and for a time was considered the foremost spokesperson for Austrian economics in America. However, Rothbard's work has never achieved the mainstream academic respectability that Kirzner's work receives. Several other Mises seminar attendees went on to academic careers as well: William Peterson, George Reisman, Hans Sennholz, and Louis Spadaro are a few names that come to mind. But although these names are well known within Austrian circles, they are less well known within the mainstream of the economics profession.

sponding reverence.[11] Consequently, he rarely received any overt criticism. The esteem with which he was held tended to stifle academic debate and intensify his isolation from his academic peers. Symptomatic of the isolation of Mises' work from mainstream economic thought was that, for the first time, something called "Austrian economics" was self-consciously identified by Mises' followers.

During most of the years of the NYU seminar, Austrian economics seemed to stand for opposition to Keynesian economics and interventionist policy coupled with a steadfast belief in the superiority of free markets for economic prosperity and individual freedom. These were the issues that increasingly occupied Mises' thought during the interwar period in Austria and Switzerland, and these were the issues that were central to Mises' life in America. They were also the issues that brought students to study with him at New York University. Not surprisingly, Mises' New York University seminar became more a focal point for conservative and libertarian thought during the 1950s and 1960s than a training ground for contemporary economists.[12]

Mises, the scholar, of course supported his anti-Keynesian and classical liberal views with his carefully developed economic theory and methodology, delivering erudite lectures on the wide range of subjects that he had at his command. Further, as a utilitarian he never argued the case for the market on ethical grounds, but only on pragmatic ones. He believed in value-free science, but he was convinced that scientific analysis showed that free markets were the only possible way in which human beings could live in peace and prosperity. As he argued in *Human Action*, "The choice is

---

[11] Richard Cornuelle, a member of Mises' seminar in the 1940s, describes his experience as follows: "When I joined Mises's seminar, it was meeting twice a week in the late evening in a low-ceilinged cellar room, as befitted an underground movement, in the shadow of Trinity Church in lower Manhattan. We were usually about a dozen. Mises arrived last, always on the stroke of the appointed hour, impeccably dressed. He took a single page of notes in German from a small envelope, grasped the edge of the table with his palms flat on the top and his thumbs under, and spoke without interruption for an hour and a half, in a kind of accented chant as if he were reciting scripture from memory. Then there were questions, which he usually answered by repeating, almost word for word, the part of his recitation the question suggested. His method seemed entirely appropriate. We sensed we were in the presence of a towering and uncommonly disciplined intelligence, martyred and misunderstood. We knew Mises had paid dearly for his beliefs. . . . We would, except for the practical difficulties, have carved our notes in stone" (1992:2).

[12] At one point, Ayn Rand, the novelist-philosopher, decided that Mises' economics was consistent with her philosophy of Objectivism and advised all of her followers to read his works. This connection seemed to provide an entry way into Austrian economics for a significant number of people associated with libertarian ideas. Even when, after a time, Rand decided that the subjective theory of value was subversive of objective reality and withdrew her support, this link between Objectivism and Austrian economics was not completely severed.

between capitalism and chaos. . . . Socialism is not an alternative to capitalism; it is an alternative to any system under which men can live as human beings. To stress this point is the task of economics as it is the task of biology and chemistry to teach that potassium cyanide is not a nutriment but a deadly poison" (1963:680).

However, during Mises' American life, he was surrounded by people who agreed with his political views and accepted his economic pronouncements almost without question. As a consequence, he never entered contemporary American debate, he rarely received a hard argument that made him clarify or restate his propositions in more moderate form, and he became increasingly more rather than less isolated from his academic peers as the years went on.

One might argue that this isolation was not necessarily a bad thing, that perhaps at the margin Mises' unqualified support for free market policies during those decades of interventionist ideology was a more important contribution to American intellectual life than his contributions to economics. Others would undoubtedly vehemently disagree. Whatever one's judgment on that matter, the fact is that Mises' economics was barely heard during the decades of the 1950s and 1960s. And his magnum opus, *Human Action*, a best seller by the standards of academic publication, probably sold more copies to businessmen and conservative intellectuals than it did to academics.

Human action

In the German phase of Mises' career, he was most known for three areas of research. His publication at a young age of *The Theory of Money and Credit* established him as an expert on monetary theory and banking institutions. He continued to write articles on money and banking theory throughout his career. Second, his article "Economic Calculation in the Socialist Commonwealth" followed by his comprehensive book on *Socialism* led him in two directions. His critique of socialism led him to investigate further the economics of market systems, and it also led him to a deeper analysis of the political philosophy of liberalism. The second concern was evidenced in his 1927 book, *Liberalismus*, a book that defends free markets and liberalism on utilitarian grounds.[13] Finally, Mises' Mengerian heritage manifested itself most directly in the methodological studies he produced during the 1920s and 1930s.[14] To his American

---

[13] This book was translated as *Liberalism in the Classical Tradition* ([1927] 1985).
[14] See in particular, *Epistemological Problems of Economics* (1981), the English translation of *Grundprobleme der Nationalokonomie*, originally published in 1933. For an overview of the development of Mises' ideas during the 1920s and 1930s, see the collection of Mises'

audience, however, it was more the first two areas of expertise rather than the third for which Mises was known. That was to change after the publication of *Human Action*.

Human Action (1963), published in the United States in 1949, was both a summary and an expansion of Mises' life work.[15] A treatise in the grand manner, *Human Action* is a difficult book to categorize. Beginning with a philosophical exploration of economic epistemology and method; moving on to an analysis of markets and market pricing, the theory of money, interest and capital; and ending with a treatment of socialism, capitalism, and interventionism as economic policy and political theory – it seems to have in its pages a little bit of everything. Most people confronting it for the first time are not quite sure what to make of it. It contains much material that is familiar to economists in general, but it is phrased in unfamiliar ways. There is, as one reviewer put it, much that is "sound, interesting and valuable" (Wright, 1950: 229) in it, but it is also full of overstatement and free market polemic. The tone is one of stating what is true of economics in general, yet it takes a line far different from conventional understanding on many issues.[16]

Mises' overt aim for *Human Action* was to write a comprehensive treatise on economics (vii). Notice, he did not plan to write a comprehensive treatise on *Austrian* economics. In fact, despite his later identification as

essays edited by Richard Ebeling under the title of *Money, Method and the Market Process* (1990).

[15] *Human Action* was a completely rewritten and expanded English language version of his *Nationalökonomie, Theorie des Handelns und Wirtschaftens* published in Geneva in 1940. This was not an auspicious year to publish a German-language analysis and defense of free markets and liberal politics, and hence his book was largely unread and unavailable to his potential audience.

[16] I have criticized Mises' tone several times in these pages. In fairness, it should be pointed out that he did not have a monopoly on imperious style. His critics were prone to answer his statements in kind, and even, on occasion, to do him one better. Although *Human Action* received several thoughtful reviews by economists who, while not agreeing with him on many points, nevertheless saw the grandeur of his construction (see Schuller, 1950), Mises' political "opposition" cannot be credited with such generosity.

Seymour Harris, in a review in the *Saturday Review of Literature* entitled "Capitalist Manifesto" (1949), espousing a doctrine of arriving at scientific truth by counting heads, argued that "this book could just as well have been written in 1900 as in 1950, for the author has little use for twentieth-century economics. . . . Von Mises remains static in his thinking, quarantining himself against every advance in economics since 1900: mathematical economics, the new theory of monopolistic competition, Keynesianism, new planning theory. . . . Mises is wrong to assume that the tens of thousands of economists in the twentieth century, relatively and absolutely well trained, could not have added something to the foundations built by economists of earlier centuries numbered in the hundreds" (31). He then goes on to list several of Mises' more provocative statements without any attempt at argument, simply calling them "errors and misrepresentations."

John Kenneth Galbraith, in his review in the *New York Times* (1949), castigated Yale University Press for even publishing a book with such overt free market sentiments.

the leader of the Austrian school in America, Mises himself never believed there was an Austrian economics distinct from other economics. In part this was a semantic distinction. Given his belief in the a priori certainty of economic theory, anything that did not agree with his rendition of economics would simply have been wrong, not an alternative school of thought. In part, however, Mises believed there was a core of economic truth that was widely known and needed to be pulled together in treatise form. Economic theory needed to be systemized, purged of its errors, and placed within the proper methodological and philosophical context. *Human Action* was intended to accomplish just the tidying up that economic science required. Regardless of what Mises thought he was doing, it is also possible to read *Human Action* as essentially a subversive but incomplete project.

Mises set out to establish the philosophical and existential foundations of a science of human action. However, contained within the basic axioms of his system are Mengerian elements of time and knowledge that challenge the basic paradigm not only of neoclassical economics, but of Mises' own account of economic order. Despite the length and breadth of his masterpiece, I would argue that Mises did not finally achieve what he set out to achieve: that is, to reformulate a generally accepted economic theory that both is deduced from the praxeological categories he identifies (including the category of time) and that supports his contention that the free market leads to the harmony of rightly understood interests. My interpretation of Mises leads me to conclude that he tried too much to blend some fundamental Mengerian insights with the apparatus of neoclassical price theory to the detriment of both. The project was flawed, but it was at once so learned and complex that it would take decades to unravel its central contradiction. In fact, Mises' edifice inherited a basic incompatibility between the Mengerian and the neoclassical approach that is still a source of controversy among modern Austrian economists.

Praxeology: the science of human action

Mises saw economics as merely a subset of a larger scientific discipline he called "praxeology," the science of human action ([1949] 1963:3). Praxeology was for Mises the theory appropriate to all social science, an approach that would provide a unified social science with a firm theoretical foundation. Subsidiary to praxeology were catallactics, the science of all market phenomena (233), and economics, the study of "the determination of money prices of goods and services exchanged on the market" (234).

Praxeology is an axiomatic system that has as its ultimate given that human beings act; they use means to pursue ends. All of human life can be seen as a manifestation of this fundamental axiom, and from this axiom all of economic theory can be deduced. Action consists in choosing one alternative over another, of exchanging a less desirable state for one that we expect to be more desirable. This is the meaning of the term "action." From the fundamental action axiom, subsidiary praxeological categories can be deduced to provide the core of economic theory.

By beginning with an axiomatic, deductive approach to economic theory, Mises was doing nothing particularly different from accepted microeconomic theory, with its assumptions of preference functions and resource constraints. What made Mises' approach distinctive, and also suspect to the overwhelming majority of the economics profession, was his claim that the axioms of praxeology were a priori true and were not subject to refutation by empirical test. In an age of allegiance to empirical verifiability, or later, to conceptually refutable hypotheses, a claim for a priori truth and "apodictic certainty" would surely have seemed bizarre to his contemporaries.

In making his claim, Mises was following up on Menger's methodological work by making a sharp distinction between economic theory and history. All "data," Mises pointed out, are historical data. One cannot even define data without some theoretical structure to distinguish between relevant and irrelevant events. And even good data require interpretation according to some theoretical structure. However, not just any theoretical structure will suffice: it is the role of praxeology to provide the correct theoretical structure based on true statements about human action in order to interpret historical data correctly.[17]

According to Mises, there is no choice of starting place to develop an axiomatic theory of human action. We know the fundamental action axioms through appeal to our reason because reason and action are two different aspects of the same thing.[18] Adopting a broadly Kantian ap-

[17] Mises' methodology became known as extreme a priorism, which meant that the construction of economic theory is totally insulated from particular historical events. Theory is prior to history, but it serves as our tool for interpreting history. There is no sense, in Mises, of any interpretive interaction between theory and history, as if theory could be deduced in pristine form from the mind of a totally ahistorical, isolated individual. Although fiercely defended by some of Mises' followers (Rothbard, 1957), some later Austrians were to criticize this aspect of Mises methodology as paying insufficient attention to the limitations of the human mind (Lavoie, 1986b).

[18] "The real thing which is the subject matter of praxeology, human action, stems from the same source as human reasoning. Action and reason are congeneric and homogeneous; they may even be called two different aspects of the same thing. That reason has the power to make clear through pure ratiocination the essential features of action is a consequence of the fact that action is an offshoot of reason. The theorems attained by correct praxeological reasoning are not only perfectly certain and incontestable, like

proach to epistemology, he argued that the human mind is structured in such a way that the only way we can understand action is as the use of means to pursue ends. When we attempt to explain an action, what we mean by explanation is the identification of the means and the ends perceived by the actor. Any other starting point would not be recognized as *human* (as opposed to animal or vegetable) action. The behaviorist project is not only incoherent, it fails to take into account a source of knowledge we as human beings have about other human beings – our knowledge of action. Once we recognize the fundamental nature of the action axiom, however, we can develop a set of propositions that allow us to make sense of otherwise chaotic reality. The way we do this is to interpret events as the consequences of the actions of purposeful human beings.[19]

Although at one level, Mises' exhaustive discussion of the action axiom (that people use means to pursue ends) might seem little more than a more general exposition of familiar neoclassical assumptions about preferences, as Mises proceeds in his argument, he introduces ideas and clarifications that challenge conventional theory. One such clarification concerns the individual's "scale of values," a notion that is sometimes interpreted as a verbal description of an individual's preference function.

Menger, as we may remember, described individuals as having a scale of values of goods arrayed from most important to least important for their purposes and included a numerical chart for illustration. Perhaps concerned about the potential for misinterpretation of such a chart, Mises emphasizes that the notion of a "scale of values" is simply an organizing principle for interpreting action. These scales "have no independent existence apart from the actual behavior of individuals. . . . [They] are nothing but an instrument for the interpretation of a man's acting" (95). All we really know is that at the moment of choice, an individual prefers the thing chosen to what he gives up. Later, Mises draws the further implication that since these scales of values do not really exist, it makes no sense to think of them as stable over time. This both distinguishes his theory from the usual neoclassical theory of consumer choice and has important implications for his own theory of market processes.[20]

the correct mathematical theorems. They refer, moreover with the full rigidity of their apodictic certainty and incontestability to the reality of action as it appears in life and history. Praxeology conveys exact and precise knowledge of real things" (39).
[19] We should also point out that by stressing the primacy of the means–ends relationship, Mises was not arguing that man necessarily pursues any particular kind of end. He was not arguing, for example, for homoeconomicus – man who reduces all choices to cost calculations or pursues material benefits exclusively. Instead, he saw the means–ends relationship as a purely formal means of understanding the actions of individuals.
[20] Mises' statement that the scales of value "have no independent existence apart from the actual behavior of individuals" might be taken to be a formulation of revealed prefer-

Mises continues his discussion of the "praxeological categories" of human action further by introducing conditions of action that rarely find their way into foundational discussions of microeconomic theory. Action, Mises continues, implies change, and change implies the notion of temporal sequence or time. "Human reason is even incapable of conceiving the ideas of timeless existence and of timeless action" (99).

Some of the most provocative and promising statements in *Human Action* can be found in Mises' very short chapter on time. Building on the work of Henri Bergson, Mises discusses the relationship between action and time. It is action that makes man aware of the passage of time (100). Although from a philosophical perspective, time is an ineluctable flow in which the present is only an ideal, never-existing boundary,[21] humans actually experience the present as having duration. Mises calls this the "real present . . . the continuation of the conditions and opportunities given for acting" (101). Every action has some set of conditions that make the action coherent. Those conditions define the real present for acting human beings. The catch is that the "present" has different meanings for different people and for different projects undertaken by the same person. Time, therefore, is subjectively experienced by individuals.[22]

This discussion of real time might have led immediately to a discussion of the implications of the experienced "real present" for the pursuit of plans and projects and for the compatibility of plans over time, a problem so much on Hayek's mind not too long before the publication of *Human Action*. Or, he might have examined the implication of time for human learning and change in the use of knowledge, a theme so important to

ence. As Rothbard (1956) points out, however, revealed preference theory presumes that the underlying utility function is stable across observations, whereas Mises makes no such stability assumption. To Mises, the scale of values is simply an analytic device that changes sometimes with great frequency. Rothbard calls Mises' utility theory ".lemonstrated preference" to differentiate it from revealed preference.

[21] Cf. Shackle's many discussions of time in which he argued that the present has no duration and all that is experienced is the past through memory and the future through imagination ([1958] 1967, [1961] 1969). Both Shackle and Mises were grappling essentially with the same problems associated with time – its ineluctable passage, the unknowability of the future, and the subjective experience of time that characterized the human condition. As we will see in chapter 6, it was Ludwig Lachmann (1976a) who identified the link between Mises and Shackle and introduced Shackle to the postrevival Austrians.

[22] To put this highly abstract discussion in some more concrete terms, consider that conventional economic theory already contains some of this notion of "real present" in its concept of long run and short run. These are analytic devices that refer to the persistence of constraints on specific plans and actions and are generally recognized to be different for different firms. Although Mises didn't make this particular application, he did much later on in his book talk more about the implications of subjectively experienced time in connection with capital and interest theory. One cannot help but be a bit dissatisfied, however, that Mises did not write more explicitly about the implications of subjective time for economic theory.

Menger and later investigated by Lachmann. Instead, Mises passes over such considerations and addresses implications of the praxeological category of time that were of more immediate interest to him. The notion of real time, for example, is the source of one of Mises' strongest complaints against the "mathematical or logical systems of thought," an attitude for which he became noted and most often criticized.

Criticism of the use of mathematics in economic analysis is a hallmark of Austrianism from Menger to the present but is considered wholly anachronistic by most economists. Mises nevertheless offered profound questions about the applicability of mathematics to economics that remain largely unanswered. These questions all center around problems caused by time and the uncertainty surrounding human action.

Within a logical or mathematical system, Mises argued, notions of time, or "anteriority and consequence," have no meaning. There is no implication of time or causality. Praxeology, on the other hand, is inseparable from time and causality, from actions and consequences, and from the "irreversibility of events." In this setting, the language of mathematical functions is merely metaphor, and not very apt metaphor for actual time-consuming processes (99).[23]

Mises also points out that the fact that man exists in time – he is born, grows old, and dies – implies that time itself is scarce and must be economized. Hence, rational action necessarily has a time dimension, and the economic problem cannot solely be thought of in a static allocational sense, a point he will elaborate later on in his theory of capital. Action through time, however, has another fundamental implication, pervasive uncertainty.

Recognizing pervasive uncertainty, according to Mises, must make us skeptical of any claims by determinist theorists of human beings.[24] Really, there are only two ways of looking at human choices. If, on the one hand, all action is determined by laws of the universe outside of man, then there would be no uncertainty, but there would be no reason for man to act

[23] O'Driscoll and Rizzo discuss in greater detail the incompatibility of mathematical symbolism and the passage of real time in their book (1985:54–56). Mathematics can only capture "Newtonian" conceptions of time, which represent change as a "series of states, each of which is homogeneous . . . and consequently does not (itself) change" (Henri Bergson, quoted in O'Driscoll and Rizzo, 1985:55). "A Newtonian system is merely a stringing together of static states and cannot endogenously generate change" (55).

[24] In an article titled "Comments about the Mathematical Treatment of Economic Problems" ([1953] 1977), Mises emphasized again the incompatibility of undetermined, uncertain human action and mathematical equations. He reiterated that praxeology is not like natural science, statistics can offer no proof of economic theory, at best it is a tool for historical research, economics has no units of measurement, and one loses rather than gains knowledge by translating natural language into mathematical formulae.

either. If the future is determined and man has no free will, we can only observe the unconscious motions of automata, not the actions of human beings, but then the "we" who are doing the observing are also simply responding to stimuli and cannot possibly be said to have created a theory of human action. If, on the other hand, action is freely chosen in the sense that there are no uniquely predictable antecedents to any action, then man can never know the future unfolding of events, and the future is by definition uncertain. A deterministic social science of human action is a contradiction. This is an issue raised by Mises that was to so intrigue George Shackle in his later work ([1958] 1967) and was to call into question the whole nature of social science.

Mises' recognition of the importance of time and uncertainty to human action led him to present an interesting critique of statistical modeling in social science. In a world of uncertainty, all action is based on the anticipation of probable outcomes and not on knowledge of the future. In order to act, human beings have to form assessments of possible future outcomes of their actions, but the assessments that pertain to human action are not probability estimates in the conventional sense of instances of a class of events, but what Mises calls "case probability."

Mises points out that human actions are unique events, not members of a class of repeatable trials like tossing a coin. Case probability refers to situations in which we understand some of the causal factors that will lead to some future event, but not all of them. It is a probability based on limited knowledge of causal relations, not on the outcome of one instance of a class of events. Hence, discussions of the very high probability of the stock market declining after an oil shock, for example, are simply statements about one's belief system and the models one is applying to human behavior. To place probability numbers on such events is again to make metaphorical statements about the strength of our beliefs. This discussion provided the basis for the later Austrian skepticism toward econometric modeling in empirical economics.[25]

Mises makes two further comments about the praxeological category of time that must be noted. First, not surprisingly, he points out that in a world of time, without certainty, all action is speculation, an observation that will play an important role in his theory of entrepreneurship. The

[25] It should be noted that Mises himself apparently had no objection in principle to statistical analysis. As the founder of the Austrian Institute for Business Cycle Research, he was deeply immersed in techniques for empirical economic research. Mises' objection to quantitative analysis was rather that a means of organizing and analyzing data was misrepresented as economic theory. "Statistics is a method for the presentation of historical facts concerning prices and other relevant data of human action. It is not economics and cannot produce economic theorems and theories" (1963:351).

second comment is surprising in that it seems to undercut all he has said about the relationship between time and uncertainty until this point.

Mises claims that despite the uncertainty that individuals face in all of their actions in the real world, praxeology still "makes it possible to predict with apodictic certainty the outcome of various modes of action" (117). This is, on the face of it, an amazing statement. If individual actions are undetermined, if all action is speculative, and if the future can never be known with certainty, how can he possibly speak of certainty with regard to economic theory? Once again, he really is saying something not so very different from conventional ideas. He simply means that theoretical causal relationships, what Hayek called qualitative predictions, can be made with certainty. What cannot be predicted is the quantitative level of predicted outcomes.[26] Economics theory can predict that an increase in the price of apples will reduce the quantity of apples purchased, but not by how much.[27] Estimates of "how much" are left to the methods of "understanding," where "understanding" refers to some sort of empirical techniques that Mises never discusses. His failure to discuss in *Human Action* any appropriate methods of doing "history" or empirical economics was a serious lack that made Austrian economics after Mises seem completely isolated from any contact with reality. While Mises' argument, suitably translated, is equally applicable to standard economic theory, his one-sided presentation was at the very least a serious tactical error that left the impression that Austrians were not interested in empirical work.

Mises ends his methodological section by stating three propositions that he claims follow from the action axiom: the law of diminishing marginal utility, the law of returns, and human labor as a means. These are instructive since they reflect the whole gamut of achievements and problems with Mises' text. First, we see an insightful discussion of diminishing marginal utility along Mengerian lines that shows up the limitations of simple constrained maximization problems applied to consumers. Here, Mises emphasizes that the concept of utility is a fiction, that all we can know is that at the moment of decision one thing is preferred to another, that the value attached to a good is the use to which it is put, and that people fulfill more urgent uses before less urgent ones; hence, marginal utility diminishes.

[26] Not surprisingly, Mises' views are echoed by Machlup when he argues that because of the limitations of ceteris paribus, economics is not very good at positive prediction even of a qualitative kind, although he thinks the value of economics for negative prediction, ruling out highly unlikely events, is substantial. He has no patience at all, however, for forecasting, an activity that he calls "foolish" (1980:9–10).

[27] Interestingly, Mises does not explicitly state the ceteris paribus caveat here, although his claims about theoretical certainty are incomprehensible without it. We must assume he took it for granted.

The second two laws, however, read like clumsy presentations of standard neoclassical economics. The law of returns is particularly obscure, although not obviously different from more conventional formulations,[28] and the law of labor as a means makes the assumption that labor is always a means and never an end somewhat arbitrarily. And if Mises claims that the praxeological categories are deducible from the action axiom, neither the law of returns nor the assertion of labor as a means fits the bill. The first is a physical law and the second is either an assumption about preferences or a definition of labor.

Here we come to a common complaint about Mises' project. He wants to establish the apodictic status of praxeological laws and compares them to the laws of geometry. He then wants to use these laws to interpret complex reality or historical data. If he could establish that praxeology follows inexorably from the action axiom and if he could convince us that there is no other possible starting point for understanding human action, then we would have to grant the certainty of praxeological laws and their ability to give us knowledge of real things. The application of theory to the interpretation of historical data would still be more a matter of art and judgment than unquestionable truth, but the theory in any case would be beyond dispute. However, Mises does not deduce all of praxeology from the action axiom. He slips in subsidiary statements that can only be viewed as hypotheses and not certain truth.

This, of course, need not be devastating to his project. Economists generally consider the law of returns a physical law of nature, and the claim that labor is a means and not an end is a broadly accepted generalization about human attitudes. Indeed, Mises even notes the exceptions when he discusses the "creative genius" who works for the sake of his creations (139).[29] However, rather than claim that his system is a priori true because it is based on certain and true axioms derived from

---

28 Consider, for example, Mises' introduction to the law of returns: "Quantitative definiteness in the effects brought about by an economic good means with regard to the goods of the first order (consumer goods): a quantity a of cause brings about – either once and for all or piecemeal over a definite period of time – a quantity α of effect. With regard to the goods of the higher orders (producers' goods) it means: a quantity b of cause brings about a quantity β of effect, provided the complementary cause c contributes the quantity γ of effect; only the concerted effects β and γ bring about the quantity p of the good of the first order D" (127). It only gets worse from there. Although when translated into more commonly understood form, Mises is more or less saying that outputs depend upon the quantity and variety of inputs, the effort of translation simply does not seem worth the return.

29 Mises wards off the claim that the creative genius derives satisfaction from work itself, however. He argues within the spirit of nineteenth-century Romanticism, "Neither does the genius derive immediate gratification from his creative activities. Creating for him is agony and torment, a ceaseless excruciating struggle against internal and external obstacles; it consumes and crushes him" (139). Such activities cannot be construed as normal labor.

reason alone, Mises would have found more sympathetic listeners had he made the lesser claim that praxeology begins from widely shared and empirically obvious propositions about human beings and the world they inhabit that may not have the certainty of geometry, but are nevertheless overwhelmingly convincing.[30]

While methodology is one of the main areas for which Mises is known, his methodology can only partly be viewed as a continuation of Menger's program. His insistence that theory is prior to experience of particular events, that one can only interpret events with respect to a theoretical structure is a direct restatement of Menger's position during the *methodenstreit*. The attempt to provide a complete axiomatic, deductive theory that required no interaction with real-world events to speak to its legitimacy is Mises' attempt to improve on Menger. Unfortunately, this extreme methodological position served to obscure Mises' contributions to economics rather than to highlight them.

The theory of the market process

Austrian economics in the last quarter of the twentieth century claims to be a theory of the market process as opposed to a study of equilibrium conditions. To a large degree this is a consequence of adopting Mises' understanding of market activity. In the spirit of Adam Smith as well as of Carl Menger, Mises emphasized that in advanced economies characterized by the division of labor and exchange, the market is a primary means by which human beings can profit from cooperation with one another. He described the gains from trade in terms of the "Ricardian law of association," which he took to explain how "collaboration of the more talented, more able, and more industrious with the less talented, less able, and less industrious results in benefits for both" (159). In fact, he based his primary argument for the general benefits of markets on this law. However, Mises further emphasized far more than his intellectual predecessors, an important prerequisite for market exchange – the institution of money. Markets are only possible because of the use of money. The only way humans can plan for their future actions and assess the consequences of their actions is through the use of monetary calculation.

The importance of monetary calculation in market economies is a persistent although largely unappreciated theme in Mises' writing, begin-

---

[30] Rothbard argued in several places (1957, 1973) that it was not necessary to claim a priori status for the action axiom. Instead, Rothbard argued that it could be regarded as a statement of broad, general empirical nature that was so pervasive that, given our understanding and experience of the world, it would be impossible to imagine its contradiction. In Rothbard (1973) he specifically links Mises' praxeological approach to a tradition that is at least as old as J. B. Say and Cairnes.

ning with his first major work, *The Theory of Money and Credit,* and continuing throughout his career. For example, when he wrote his 1920 article on "economic calculation in the socialist commonwealth," his central claim was that complex economies required prices to measure relative wants and scarcities, and that only money prices arrived at in markets would do. Lange, we remember, accepted the first proposition, that prices were required for economic calculation, but denied the second, that only market prices would do the job. In doing so, he revealed that he hadn't really grasped Mises' argument – as neither did the rest of the profession that accepted Lange's "refutation" of Mises. When Mises asserted that only money prices could be used for calculation, he was saying simply that there could be no complex real economy without money and markets because one could not arrive at meaningful prices without money.

Unfortunately, Mises did not provide detailed reasons for his claim. However, one can construct an argument that is consistent with Mises and probably captures his meaning. As Mises points out, the economist's theoretical approach of solving the system for barter prices and then defining one commodity as a numeraire is fundamentally flawed. The patently obvious fact that no complex set of equilibrium barter prices could ever in reality be established without the aid of money was one reason.[31] The other was that the very act of trade was necessary to form preferences. As Mises insisted in the early pages of *Human Action,* fully articulated preferences do not exist apart from the act of exchange; in a complex economy, the only way to form preferences over an array of goods is with the help of monetary calculation to provide a system of accounting. The idea that humans could fully understand and rank-order all possible goods over which they could form preferences was, for Mises, fantastic. There were no fully formed preference function and therefore no "ipso facto" imputation of values to prices. Preferences could only be learned through confrontation with alternatives, and this could only take place with any degree of complexity in a money economy.

According to Mises, the market process is one of continual change, brought about by changing value judgments as people learn of their alternatives through real possibilities. Shifts in external constraints are

---

[31] Loasby (1982) links Mises' insistence on the importance of a money economy to Marshall's view that it would be unlikely for a sequence of barters to lead to a true general equilibrium. Loasby argues that "this argument leads to the paradox that microeconomic equilibrium cannot safely be analyzed in real terms (as is the standard practice) except in a monetary economy." He then goes on to argue that since monetary processes are not necessarily stable, the whole equilibrium analysis requires some modification (114).

not the primary motivator in this view of the market process.[32] One of the most important differences between the Austrian and the neoclassical view of the world is that people's preferences are not fixed. They are constantly reevaluating both means and ends and hence altering their market activities, leading to adjustments in prices that in turn affect the market behavior of others. Within this roiling mass of change, human beings save, invest, acquire capital goods, produce output, and hope to earn a living from their correct anticipation of future wants. This can only be accomplished with the aid of monetary calculation.

To Mises, monetary calculation was at base a method of thinking about possible alternative courses of behavior (229). In a changing world, the only way to attempt to anticipate the outcome of some business plan is to anticipate future prices, and the only way to assess whether or not the plan has been successful is to calculate monetary profit and loss. Money makes it possible to maintain capital accounts, which enable businessmen to judge the profitability of various ventures, and it permits the conversion of assets to better reflect individual needs and plans. Hence, he argues, Goethe was right to call double-entry bookkeeping "one of the finest inventions of the human mind" (quoted on 230).

As necessary as money is to complex exchange, Mises does not argue that monetary calculation is perfectly efficient in the neoclassical sense. Mises was always suspicious of neoclassical definitions of efficiency as the achievement of general equilibrium. Prices and costs are far too subjective to be taken as exact measures of either costs or benefits, let alone some abstractly defined notion of general welfare. For instance, business accounts may seem exact, but the numbers are often estimates of future conditions that may or may not come about.

What monetary calculation gives one is a means of weighing real alternatives and possible future consequences against one another, not exact measures of utility or cost. But, as inexact as money calculation may be according to an external abstract standard, "economic calculation is as efficient as it can be" (214). It measures alternatives open to individuals; it gives no clues about social accounting. It only works in a system of private property and free markets, because money prices are the outcome of innumerable adjustments individuals make to changing circumstances.

Here Mises makes another one of his provocative statements that cries out for further elaboration. He is clearly countering the entire social

[32] "The market is not a place, a thing, or a collective entity. The market is a process, actuated by the interplay of the actions of the various individuals cooperating under the division of labor. The forces determining the – continually changing – state of the market are the value judgments of these individuals and their actions. . . . The market process is the adjustment of the individual actions of the various members of market society to the requirements of mutual cooperation" (1963:257–258).

welfare literature, but he makes no attempt to explain why money prices, in addition to presenting individuals with a means of calculating the importance and consequences of alternatives, does not also give us a measure of social resource cost. Since no concept of social cost appears in his system, it is as if he feels no need to acknowledge any other interpretation of prices regardless of how deeply entrenched it may be in conventional theory. One could perhaps expand his argument by pointing out that conventional social welfare theory requires all prices to be in equilibrium for prices to bring marginal social cost and marginal social benefits to equality (Vaughn, 1980b). Since Mises posits not equilibrium, but continual change, the concepts of social welfare theory simply do not apply. Mises, however, does not even go this far to argue his case. Had he done so, however, he would have had to address an even more fundamental problem: What specifically is the function of prices outside of equilibrium?

Equilibrium constructs

Mises' whole treatment of equilibrium constructs and their relationship to market phenomena is surprisingly unsatisfying. He posits not one, but three notions of equilibrium that he claims underlie his analysis. The first, the "plain state of rest," is a temporary state in which all currently desired transactions have been made and, for the moment, no one wants to trade. His example of such a state is the close of the trading day in the stock market. When the market closes, all desired transactions have taken place and a set of market prices has been established. However, once the doors open in the morning, new trades will take place and new prices will be established. One might compare this temporary "state of rest" to Marshall's market period.[33]

The second equilibrium notion Mises employs is the "final state of rest," the state toward which the market tends if there is no change in the data. This apparently is Mises' analogue to general equilibrium. Whereas the plain state of rest is a phenomenon that is routinely found in markets, the final state of rest is an "imaginary construction" in that it can never be

---

[33] Unfortunately, Mises' example is poorly chosen. The only reason trading stops in the stock exchange is because of the convention of closing for the night. If the exchange were open all night long, trading would be continuous. In no sense, then, is a "plain state of rest" achieved for an array of tradable stocks, although the trading in specific stocks may cease for periods of time during which there are no bids or asks. One could, then, perhaps say that the market for that particular stock had cleared for a time. Note, however, that Mises does not define the plain state of rest as one in which prices clear the market, but as a cessation of trade. Presumably, they mean the same thing to him, although one wonders why he was not more explicit about the role of price here.

achieved in reality, although it is a necessary analytic tool for understanding the direction of price changes.[34]

Finally, Mises posits yet a third equilibrium notion, the "evenly rotating economy," or the "ERE." This, too, is an imaginary construction of what the market would be like if there were no changes in the data. In this construction, however, people continue to be born, to live, and to die, and capital is accumulated at a rate just sufficient to maintain current patterns of consumption and investment. It is a condition in which the same products are consumed and produced over and over again, and all prices equal the prices established in the final state of rest (246–247). Mises sees the purpose of this construct differently from the purpose of the final state of rest. For Mises, the evenly rotating economy is necessary "in order to analyze the problems of change in the data and of unevenly and irregularly varying movement" (247). To do this we compare the real world to the fictitious state in which neither change nor irregular (uncoordinated) movements occur.

Whereas the first two notions have their analogues in contemporary economics, the ERE seems to be unique to Mises.[35] Instead of describing a direction toward which current forces can be said to be tending, it provides a foil against which to understand aspects of reality. Specifically, by constructing the ERE, a construct without change, it is possible to grasp what economic activities are related to change. The most important

---

[34] It should be emphasized that Mises regarded the "method of imaginary constructs" as the only appropriate method for praxeological reasoning. An imaginary construct is "a conceptual image of a sequence of events logically evolved from the elements of action employed in its formation. It is a product of deduction, ultimately derived from the fundamental category of action, the act of preferring and setting aside" (236). Since it is a hypothetical model of sequences of action based on the logical implications of action, it can never be judged by its conformity to reality. Its purpose is to highlight some feature of action that might be obscured in complex reality and its usefulness depends upon the truth of its assumptions. Two examples of imaginary constructs that Mises employs are the evenly rotating economy and the pure, unhampered market economy, neither of which can exist in reality, but both of which help us to understand essential features of real markets.

[35] Cowen and Fink (1985) follow Rothbard (1962b) in confounding the final state of rest with the ERE. They are not the same thing nor do they serve the same purposes. The final state of rest is the direction in which the current market is moving before it gets disturbed. Although Mises does not specifically say so, it is reasonable to assume that this is a construct useful in qualitative prediction. He posits no such tendency in the ERE. This very different construct is purely used as a foil to show what the world would be like without change. It is an ideal type that points up the importance of prices and entrepreneurship to a changing world. Fink and Cowen are correct, however, to criticize Mises' contention that the ERE can be used for comparative static analysis as if the process of change has no impact on the outcome. This seems a violation of the central problematique of economic process analysis. Mises himself seemed to confuse his two distinct notions of equilibrium, and Fink and Cowen are correct to argue that "the ERE either can be an initial state for an economy that is about to experience change, or it can be a foil, but it cannot be both" (868).

payoff to Mises' construction of the ERE is the identification of the one function that is missing in a world of no change: the function of entrepreneurship.

The entrepreneur

In Mises' system, the entrepreneur is a direct implication of the fact of time in human action. The passage of time implies both uncertainty and the unavoidability of entrepreneurship.[36] The entrepreneur is "acting man exclusively seen from the aspect of the uncertainty inherent in every action. In using this term one must never forget that every action is embedded in the flux of time and therefore involves a speculation" (254). All action has entrepreneurial aspects, then, since there can be no action that is not uncertain to some degree. This is especially the case in all activities that involve provision for the future. Hence, all capitalists, all people who take action in the present that will only have consequences in the future, are acting entrepreneurially (253). Hence, "entrepreneur means acting man in regard to the changes occurring in the data of the market" (254).

It appears that, given Mises' definition of action, there can never be anything other than entrepreneurial action, an implication that would call into question Israel Kirzner's later attempt to reconcile Austrian entrepreneurship with neoclassical economics by distinguishing between maximizing behavior and pure entrepreneurship (see chapter 7).

In a broad sense, it is also true that everyone who successfully deals with uncertainty earns profits, "the gain derived from action" (289). Although all action is at base entrepreneurial, Mises also argued that in the market, "The specific entrepreneurial function consists in determining the employment of the factors of production" (291).

Mises had a specific name for those entrepreneurs who specialize in employing factors of production: "promoters and men of affairs." These are people who are "especially eager to profit from adjusting production to the expected changes in conditions, those who have more initiative, more venturesomeness and a quicker eye than the crowd, the pushing and promoting pioneers of economic improvement" (254). Promoters are pacemakers in the market, the leaders who point the way for their less imaginative competitors. They are "the driving force of the market, the element tending toward unceasing innovation and improvement" (255).

The specific way in which promoters earn profit is by anticipating successfully the demands of consumers (293). In fact, in the market

---

[36] Entrepreneurship is "acting man in regard to the changes occurring in the data of the market" (254).

process that Mises describes, consumers are the true "sovereigns" whose choices determine the success or failure of market ventures.[37] Promoters and entrepreneurs compete with each other to best satisfy consumer wants because it is only through such action that profits can be made.

The principle mode of entrepreneurial action in the marketplace is what Mises calls "catallactic competition" (274). Unlike the competition one finds in sporting events, where there are winners and losers, catallactic competition is a form of social cooperation. Although it is true that producers compete with each other for the consumer's dollar, in principle it is possible for anyone to make profits by satisfying some previously unsatisfied want. Catallactic competition "is emulation between people who want to surpass one another" in attracting the attention of consumers. Unlike war, the success of one does not mean the defeat of the other. Those who lose out simply find another place in the market nexus of social cooperation in which to pursue their aims. Catallactic competition, then, is "the opportunity to serve the consumers in a better or cheaper way without being restrained by privileges granted to those whose vested interest the innovation hurts" (276).

By vested interest, Mises means those who would pass laws hampering certain competitive activities. If left unhampered, he argued, competition would be pervasive and beneficial to consumers. Even so-called monopoly would not be a problem. Monopoly means exclusive control over the supply of a definite commodity. In this sense, Mises argued in the same vein as had Joan Robinson ([1933] 1965), that virtually every product that is in any way distinct from others is a monopoly. Unlike Joan Robinson, however, Mises did not see this as a failing of the market process. Even where there are monopolies, this does not imply the absence of catallactic competition. Every good competes with every other good, thereby placing limits on monopoly power to raise prices.

Mises' short discussion of monopoly is worth noting because it reveals a common problem with his micro analytics. His general statement about catallactic competition points toward later notions of effective competition and away from purely price-cost differentials as measures of monopo-

---

[37] Mises' invocation of consumer sovereignty seems to imply that the entrepreneur's sole role is to satisfy consumer wants and has no persuasive element involved. Yet, Mises has already argued that there are no stable preference functions, and humans only decide what they want at the moment of choice. In such a world, it would seem that entrepreneurs are also in the business of presenting consumers with alternatives they had not already considered and of persuading them to buy their product rather than someone else's. Consumers still may be "sovereign" in the sense of having the final word on what they consume, but the process seems far more interactive than either conventional economics or Mises' economics consciously implies.

ly. However, he also seems to want to minimize criticism of monopoly by arguing that monopolists may not always charge monopoly prices. Hence, he argues that monopoly of supply does not necessarily affect price unless "the demand curve for the monopoly good concerned is shaped in a particular way" (278). He then goes on to argue in essence that monopolists will only restrict supply and charge a monopoly price if the elasticity of demand is less than one. Obviously, here either Mises means different things by the words he uses from conventional economics, or his argument is particularly weak. It is a matter of simple analytics that no producer facing a downward-sloping demand curve will charge a price in the inelastic region of the demand curve. It is also the case that profit maximization occurs where marginal revenue equals marginal cost, implying that monopoly prices must always be higher than perfectly competitive prices.[38] If Mises had explicitly rejected the applicability of the convention of comparing "a world of monopolies" to perfect competition here, or if he had given any reason at all why normal demand analytics were incorrect, his argument could have had more force. Instead, he makes a simple assertion as if it were incontrovertible fact and leaves it to the reader to sort out the details.

Time and the theory of capital

While entrepreneurship is one important implication of the time dimension in human action, a more familiar implication of time is the analysis of capital and interest. In his theory of capital, Mises picks up directly on Menger's view of capital and is more true to it than any of Menger's successors except for Ludwig Lachmann.

One important feature of Menger's writing was that the theory of capital was not treated separately from the theory of value or markets. Capital was simply "goods of a higher order" that derived their value from the consumer goods they helped produce. The inherently time-consuming nature of all production processes that was implicit in Menger was made explicit in Bohm-Bawerk's theory of capital and became a cornerstone of Austrian theory. It became incorporated in a sense into the Mises–Hayek theory of the trade cycle, in which the fact that production is a sequential process of time-consuming steps makes it especially vulner-

[38] Mises may simply have been confusing revenue maximization that takes place at a demand elasticity of unity with profit maximization that must occur at a price in the elastic portion of the demand curve. Or he might have simply been suggesting that monopolists can only raise price above the competitive price if the demand curve is less than infinitely elastic, but one would expect Mises to regard this as the normal rather than an exceptional case.

able to the faulty information generated by an expansionary banking system.

In *Human Action,* Mises reiterates his theory of the trade cycle, but more important, he elaborates upon the meaning of capital in a way that links it directly to the entrepreneurial market process. Here he clearly harks back to Menger's initial structure of thought.

Mises is well known for his pure time-preference theory of interest,[39] but this is not the aspect of the relationship between capital and time that is most interesting for our purposes. Mises' more important analysis is his explication of the relationship between capital goods and the functioning of the entrepreneurial market process. The market is an entrepreneurial process of catallactic competition that results in serving consumer demand. But serving consumer demand leads to the production of capital goods, Menger's goods of a higher order, the specificity of which conditions future entrepreneurial action.

Whereas competing theories such as those of Fisher or Knight or Hicks reduce capital to a fund of value or to a homogeneous commodity, to Mises, as to Menger, capital is always embodied in a set of heterogeneous goods in process.[40] These goods are defined as capital goods not because of any physical characteristics but because of the plans that their owners have for their use (514–515). Further, capital goods are the consequence of previous plans made by entrepreneurs to engage in potentially profitable ventures; they are "intermediary steps on the way toward a definite goal" (502). Mises recognizes that not all goals are met and that entrepreneurs often make mistakes or find that their perfectly reasonable plans are thwarted by unexpected events. In a well functioning market, however, capital goods that were created for one purpose can often be converted to other purposes.[41] Their convertibility is possible because

---

[39] The theory that the interest rate reflects the discount people apply to future consumption compared to present consumption. According to this theory, the market rate of interest is not the price that equilibrates the supply and demand for loanable funds or capital, nor is it the return to capital. The supply and demand for capital will accommodate to people's time preference (524ff.). See also Kirzner (1976).

[40] Mises does also refer to capital in the sense of capital accounting – the money value of assets minus liabilities. He argues, however, that "capital accounting serves one purpose only. It is designed to make us know how our arrangement of production and consumption acts upon our power to satisfy future wants. The question it answers is whether a certain course of conduct increases or decreases the productivity of our future exertion" (514). Needless to say, there is no meaning to notions such as aggregate capital value.

[41] Actually, Mises distinguishes among four levels of convertibility. Some capital goods are useless for purposes other than the one they were created for; some are adaptable to other purposes, although they would not be the most efficient capital goods had one been starting from scratch; some are adaptable and are the most efficient means; and

they can be bought and sold, but the inevitable inference to draw is that at any moment in time, the future path of production is conditioned by the array of capital goods that already exists. A catallaxy cannot deviate too much from the course of action chosen by its forbearers. Because material wealth is always embodied in concrete capital goods that are not perfectly substitutable for one another, action is directed to specific paths. "The choice of ends and of the means for the attainment of those ends is influenced by the past. Capital goods are a conservative element" (506). As a conservative element, capital goods both limit the range of options for future action and provide a stabilizing element in the economic environment.

Mises also discussed the role of the investor in directing the path of the market process. One characteristic of the investor is his freedom to alter the nature of his investments by buying and selling shares of ownership in companies. Profit and loss is a consequence of specific decisions to use factors of production in definite projects, but the stock exchange determines on whom the profits or losses will fall (517). All investment is in some degree speculative. Speculation cannot undo past mistakes, but it can prevent additional investments being made in enterprises that speculators regard as mistakes. Further, speculation also expands the use of resources in successful ventures. In other words, the actions of speculators on the stock market serve to contain previous entrepreneurial errors and to support the expansion of successes by bidding prices up and down to reflect speculator's anticipations of the value of capital goods in various enterprises.

Mises never discusses the possibility of systematic speculative error except in the context of his trade cycle theory, in which speculators-investors are misled by improper monetary signals emanating from a fractional reserve banking system. Yet if the future cannot be predicted, or, as Shackle would say, if the future is created out of the actions of the past, why is it not at least conceivably possible for speculative activity to be on net incorrect at least some of the time? Certainly, we have the empirical evidence of speculative bubbles that are endogenous to markets as an example of market instability. One would think that the extent and potential limiting factors that affect such endogenous instabilities would be of great importance for fully understanding market orders, yet it is an issue surprisingly missing in the Austrian literature. Hence, although we can appreciate the force of Mises' argument as far as it goes, it seems that a

some are completely transferable (502). The convertibility of capital was a factor that also fascinated Ludwig Lachmann in his own work in capital theory, which drew much inspiration from Mises (see, e.g., Lachmann, 1977:197–213).

crucial part of the case for the effective functioning of a market economy is missing.

Market coordination

Clearly, in Mises' view, the market process is generated and coordinated by entrepreneurs, promoters, and speculators who can only earn profits by responding to consumer wants. But how does Mises visualize the problem of market coordination? What is his overarching picture of the emergent patterns of order in the catallaxy he so vividly describes in his writing? In answering this question, one is obviously drawn to considering the equilibrium constructs he introduces early in his analysis. However, it is not at all clear that Mises' market process is really related in any important way to the equilibrium constructs he describes.

Consider the construct of the final state of rest. Mises argues that the final state of rest describes the direction toward which the market is tending at any point in time. But Mises also assumes that consumers are constantly reevaluating their ends and that the data are constantly changing. How then is the construct of a final state of rest in any way useful? Even if the market were at any moment in time aiming in a theoretically describable direction, if the target is constantly shifting around, how can one distinguish the actual pattern of movement from random motion? Mises claims that the direction of market activity is a matter of praxeological certainty, that ceteris paribus, economic theory can always predict the outcome of action. However, praxeological certainty seems singularly irrelevant in a world too volatile to be able to perceive or predict actual patterns of change.

Mises obviously did not think that the market was so volatile as to preclude the perception of order. In fact, he describes market conditions that give direction and cohesion to market processes. Entrepreneurs can only hope to earn profits by satisfying consumer demand. However, enterprise is a process of trial and error. Successes lead to profits as well as increased command over resources while errors are contained by losses that lead to less command over resources. The whole process is directed by a stock market that makes it possible to convert the concrete by-products of losses, capital goods, to other profitable uses. In that way, consumers get to choose from an array of consumption goods thrown up by competition, and resources are continually being shifted to more profitable uses.

This verbal description of an entrepreneurial market process is notable in two respects: notions of some predictable end state are irrelevant to describing it, and prices do not play a particularly central role in explaining the market. These two respects are not unrelated. Microeconomic theory is basically a theory of the establishment of equilibrium prices and the cessation of trade or of change of any kind. Mises' economics is predicated on continual change. In such a setting, the level of prices themselves are not nearly so important as the process by which prices are formed and the flexibility with which they can change to reflect new circumstances. Mises, then, very much like Menger, was more interested in a theory of exchange and all its concomitant aspects than he was in drawing precise analytics of price determination.

Mises' attitude toward prices and equilibrium helps to explain his disdain of conventional notions of efficiency. He repeatedly argues that prices do not measure anything, and certainly not social benefits and social costs. Conventional efficiency requires the attainment of general equilibrium, a patent impossibility. The efficiency of the market, however, is not dependent upon the attainment of equilibrium prices, but rather on freedom of contract. It is freedom of contract that permits the attainment of the "harmony of rightly understood [or long-run] interests" (673).

Mises argued, like Adam Smith, that the division of labor and exchange is responsible for increasing wealth. The higher productivity of the division of labor further removes the natural conflict of interests among humans; catallactic competition in which everyone shares in the winnings, Mises argued, substitutes for biological competitions, in which some win and others lose. Hence, everyone has an interest in preserving the level of the division of labor that characterizes modern societies. He also argued that since everyone is a consumer, it is in everyone's interest that the consumer be sovereign. The capitalist market process is the only social arrangement in which profit has to be earned by serving consumer interests. Capitalism, thus, is the only social arrangement compatible with increasing and widespread wealth.

Once again he reiterates his earliest critique: Socialism could not duplicate the level of production and consumption possible under capitalism because there could be no economic calculation under socialism. Further, Mises argues that any encroachment on the free market – interventionism – would lead inexorably to unintended misallocations and discoordinations that would engender the necessity for more controls and regulations as correctives. The final result would be an inadvertent socialism that no one intended in the first place. Hence, there were only two choices, "capitalism or chaos" (680). The market is efficient simply because there is no alternative organization of society that could come close to matching it for the production and widespread distribution of wealth.

But, again, what about sources of discoordination and disorder in markets? Mises really had very little to say about such problems, and in fact one concludes that he thought disorder was a relatively minor problem. As we have noted, the only obvious sources of instability or disorder in his system were the consequences of bad banking institutions and destabilizing intervention on the part of government. Trade cycles were brought about by misguided credit policies. Unemployment was a consequence of minimum wage rates. Inflation was an increase in the quantity of money brought about by government policy. Externalities were the consequence of imperfectly specified property rights. He never considered possible sources of disorder internal to the market; disorder was an exogenous phenomenon brought about by government regulation.

In this attitude, we should recall, Mises is really not very different from many neoclassical economic theorists (although perhaps more consistent and more outspoken than others who shared his basic evaluation of the market). The resemblance of his policy conclusions to those of the Chicago school, for example, have often been noted. Indeed, to outsiders, it has often been difficult to see much difference between the Austrian and Chicago schools simply because of the similarity in policy conclusions. Obviously, however, there is a huge gulf in foundational assumptions that are often overlooked because of the political similarities.

Although Mises' a priorism and his insistence on the importance of the truth of one's assumptions contrasts markedly with Friedman's argument for the irrelevance of assumptions (Friedman, 1966:15), that is probably the least important of the differences between the two schools. Regardless of their epistemological differences, both Mises and Friedman subscribe to a basic notion of individualism and rational choice as the fundamental starting point of economic analysis. Indeed, it has been argued that Menger's and, by implication, Mises' understanding of rational action bears a striking resemblance to Stigler–Becker's household production function in that they see people as using goods to satisfy more basic wants (O'Driscoll and Rizzo, 1985:45–47).

A much more important difference is in their respective assumptions about the nature and stability of preferences and the attainment of equilibrium. As Reder (1982) has explained, fundamental to the Chicago school are the beliefs in stable preferences and "tight prior equilibrium," the assumption that all observations are equilibrium states. Nothing could be further from Mises' analysis. To Mises, preferences are always being reevaluated, and could hardly even be said to exist apart from acts of choice. Equilibrium, further, is a purely fictitious state. However, where the Chicago school's laissez-faire conclusions follow directly from assumptions about choice, equilibrium, and economic order (and more recently, rational expectations), it is not so clear that the same is true of Mises' similar conclusions.

If all action is speculation, if people are constantly reevaluating their preferences, if entrepreneurs make losses as well as profits, can we be so certain that markets are fundamentally orderly? Perhaps our world is one in which individual rationality leads to overall waste and error. Certainly, that is the conclusion of those who stress third-party effects in economic exchange. Even more to the point, in a world of constant change, how can people's plans come to be realized? Why are speculators likely to be more right about entrepreneurial prospects than the entrepreneurs themselves? And how is successful rational action distinguishable from pure luck? What are the regularities in economic life that can be counted on to lend stability and predictability to an otherwise bewildering world?

These are questions that naturally occur once it is admitted that time passes, and that all human action is suffused with uncertainty and partial ignorance. Hayek essentially had argued during the calculation debate that markets give us a better chance of taking advantage of decentralized knowledge than do bureaucracies, but he said little about the problem of expectations and time. Mises proposed to take account of time and uncertainty, but he too said little about the problem of expectation formation in an uncertain world. He did assert a trial-and-error process of production by which people presumably learned from their errors, but his casual assertions cry out for more discussion about the fundamental orderliness and beneficial nature of the process he was describing. His only argument, albeit a very powerful one, about the "efficiency" of the market process was a relative one: In the production of goods and services valued by consumers, markets were more efficient than socialist bureaucracies. However, to make the claims that he did – that the only choice we face is between markets and chaos, and that everyone gains through catallactic competition – would have required a more searching examination of the institutions that surround and nurture a market process. Despite all of the volumes that Mises wrote, this was a question he did not directly address.

CHAPTER 5

The Austrian revival

Ludwig von Mises' *Human Action* came to define Austrian economics in the 1950s and 1960s. Although Mises continued to write and publish, largely in the areas of methodology and public policy, *Human Action* was the ultimate authority on all things Austrian during this time. Similarly, Mises' New York University seminar was the major outpost of "Austrian economics" in the United States.[1] To be sure, other Austrian emigres to the United States were actively involved in academic pursuits. Fritz Machlup was teaching first at Johns Hopkins University and then at Princeton, Oskar Morgenstern at Princeton, Gottfried Haberler at Harvard, and Paul Rosenstein-Rodan, after 1954, at the Massachusetts Institute of Technology. However, despite the fact that they were working on issues that could be considered "Austrian," as the term later came to be used, none of these economists thought of himself as an "Austrian" economist except by nationality. Even Friedrich Hayek who had moved to the United States in 1950 was not directly involved with Mises and his brand of Austrian economics. Hayek, as a member of the Committee on Social Thought at the University of Chicago was working on questions of political philosophy and psychology rather than on economic theory. Although eventually Hayek's writings on these issues were to have a significant impact on American-Austrian economics, during this period, he was by and large separated from Mises and his following. Hence, Mises was isolated not only from the American economists of the time, but also, to a lesser extent, from his Austrian compatriots.[2]

[1] Economics from an Austrian perspective, as well as being taught by Mises at New York University, was taught by Hans Sennholz at Grove City College. Sennholz had been a student at Mises' NYU seminar and Mises' good friend as well.

[2] It should be emphasized that the isolation was from American academic life and not from intellectual interaction in general. Mises kept in touch with most of the Austrian emigres through correspondence or social contact. In addition, as an active member of the Mont Pelerin Society from its beginning, Mises was involved with free market, liberal economists for most of the rest of his life. The Mont Pelerin Society, originally founded by Hayek in 1947 and dedicated to keeping alive the intellectual heritage of classical liberalism, provided a network of association for academics, policy makers, and businessmen who otherwise found themselves out of step with mainstream intellectual opinion. Among the founding members of the society were, besides Hayek and Mises, other Austrians or Austrian sympathizers such as Henry Hazlitt, Walter Eucken, Lionel Robbins, T. J. B. Hoff, and Fritz Machlup. In addition, the Chicago School was well

Compounding the effects of the isolation, as we have seen, Mises' New York University seminar served less as a locus for active scholarly debate about economic theory than as a forum for Mises to impart his wisdom to a respectful audience. Few engaged Mises in serious challenges to his economics.[3] Instead, they refined critiques of interventionist policies and of the Keynesian economics that seemed to give rise to them.[4] It is likely that few in the economics profession would ever have paid much attention either to Ludwig von Mises or his seminar had it not been for two students who were academically talented and who were determined to bring Austrian insights into the public arena: Murray Rothbard and Israel Kirzner.

Murray Rothbard and the explication of *Human Action*

Rothbard began attending Mises' seminar almost from the beginning in the late 1940s while he was still a graduate student at Columbia University. Already by then an advocate of free markets, he was introduced to Mises by the Foundation for Economic Education. Despite Rothbard's official status as a student of Joseph Dorfman at Columbia, it was Mises' economics and politics that formed the most significant influence on his economic ideas. Rothbard's dissertation and eventual book on the panic of 1819 (1962a), a descriptive account of the various attitudes and policies proposed to deal with this early business crisis, reveals as much of Mises' influence as of Dorfman's.

Mises' influence on Rothbard was central to Rothbard's two most important works in economics: *America's Great Depression* (1963) and *Man,*

represented by Frank Knight, Aaron Director, Milton Friedman, and George Stigler, who was not yet at Chicago but who came to represent that institution so completely.

[3] In fact, serious challenges to Mises' views would have been considered disruptive to seminar participants. Margit von Mises, Ludwig's widow, relates an incident in which two young economics students attended the seminar and attempted to engage Mises in debate over some issues of conventional economics. Other participants tried to have them ejected from the seminar for interfering with their ability to learn from the master. Mises himself made them welcome, however, a fact that Mrs. von Mises interprets as exceptional courtesy and generosity on his part (Margit von Mises, 1984:137).

[4] One concrete manifestation of the critical stance Mises and his followers took toward the Keynesian orthodoxy was Henry Hazlitt's 1959 book, *The Failure of the New Economics*. Hazlett was a good friend of Mises' from the time Mises first emigrated to the United States until his death. Best known as a journalist who wrote extensively for the *New York Times* and *Newsweek*, among a host of other publications, Hazlett also authored a remarkably clear little book entitled *Economics in One Lesson* ([1946] 1979) that communicates the notion of scarcity and trade-offs in straightforward, nontechnical language. *The Failure of the New Economics* is a chapter-by-chapter refutation of the assumptions and claims of Keynes's *General Theory* written in a breezy style that exudes an utter disdain for Keynes's many "fallacies." Hazlett's analysis reflects accurately the major points of Mises' view of Keynesian economics.

Economy and State (1962b). In *America's Great Depression*, Rothbard attempted to apply Mises' theory of the business cycle to the years leading up to and immediately following the crash of 1929. Predictably, Rothbard attributed the 1929 crash to monetary expansion during the 1920s, and the depth and length of the following depression to Hoover's misguided interventionist policies. Rothbard argued that in the years immediately following the 1929 stock market crash, Hoover tried to prevent bankruptcies and unemployment through setting industrial policies, and tried to shore up falling wages and prices through expansionary credit policies. Such interventionist policies interfered with the market's ability to correct the errors in the structure of production brought about by the preceding credit expansion, thereby turning a routine crisis into a prolonged and painful depression.

Rothbard's account of the depression was published in the same year as Friedman and Schwartz's *A Monetary History of the United States, 1857–1960*. This is significant since the two books came to essentially opposite conclusions as to the causes of the great depression. Rothbard argued that the Federal Reserve Board had followed an expansionary credit policy throughout the 1920s that led to an inflationary boom, a necessary prerequisite to an Austrian explanation of a business cycle, whereas Friedman and Schwartz found the 1920s to be a time of stable and/or falling prices. The difference in these two historical accounts of the 1920s was partly semantic: Rothbard used Mises' definition of inflation as an increase in the quantity of money rather than as increasing price levels, the definition used by Friedman and Schwartz (and virtually the entire economics profession). In addition, however, he defined the money supply in an unusual way by including not only currency, demand deposits, and time deposits, but also shares held in savings and loans, shares and credit deposits in credit unions and, most controversial, cash surrender value of life insurance claims (1963:83–85). The organizing principle was to include all money substitutes that were redeemable at par, but his definition seemed eccentric to the rest of the profession and hence gained no converts for the Austrian theory of the business cycle other than those already predisposed to agree with it.[5]

While *America's Great Depression* was an application of a particular Austrian doctrine to some historical episode, *Man, Economy and State* (1962b) had a much broader ambition. Rothbard's stated purpose in writing *Man, Economy and State* was to present a treatise on Austrian economics that would make Mises' work more accessible to the general

---

[5] One reviewer, Eugene Smolensky (1964) concluded that Rothbard's book contains "no new numbers or concepts . . . and its appearance neither decreases nor increases the need for further research (into the causes of the great depression) (284). On the other hand, Percy Greaves (1963) gave it a glowing review in the *Freeman*.

public. He wanted to "isolate the economics, fill in the interstices, and spell out the detailed implications . . . of the Misesian structure." Like Mises, he planned to deduce "the entire corpus of economics from a few simple and apodictically true axioms" (xi). Unlike Mises, he stuck so close to his goal that he expunged much of what was unique in Mises' original work.

Although Rothbard absolved Mises from any responsibility for his product and considered the possibility that Mises might disagree strongly with some of Rothbard's exposition, in fact, he remained remarkably faithful both to the details of Mises' economics and to his tone of argumentation. He systematized Mises' development of theoretical propositions from the action axiom ("that men employ means to achieve ends") and clarified the subsidiary nature of two further necessary postulates to the axiomatic system: that "there is a variety of human and natural resources and that leisure is a consumers' good" (xi). His treatment of subjective wants, the means–ends framework, scarcity, economizing behavior, the theory of capital, the structure of production, entrepreneurship, competition, time preference, and monetary theory are all exceptionally clear renditions of Mises' ideas. And where Mises tended to jump around in his topics and engage in long digressions on all manner of political, historical, and philosophical phenomena, Rothbard stuck inexorably to the logic of the exposition. Indeed, even the flow of the analysis, although certainly nowhere close to, say, a Samuelson-like textbook division between macro- and microeconomics with the familiar sequence of topics in each, was still more recognizably a development of familiar economic topics than had been the case in *Human Action*. Even the chapter headings ("Direct Exchange," "Indirect Exchange," "Prices and Consumption," "Production," "The Rate of Interest and Its Determination," "General Pricing of Factors," "Entrepreneurship," "Monopoly and Competition," etc.) were more familiar than Mises' ("The Epistemological Problems of the Sciences of Human Action," Economics and the Revolt against Reason," "Time," "Uncertainty," "Action within the World," "The Role of Ideas," etc.). What Rothbard added to Mises was both a more accessible language and a greater analytic precision that he believed should have led to a greater appreciation for Mises' largely misunderstood contribution. This, however, was not to be.

One reason, perhaps, was that although Rothbard was indeed more analytically precise than Mises had been, his brand of economics was still considered anachronistic by the profession. Rothbard made some concession to contemporary formal techniques by illustrating his arguments with charts and graphs, but he stalwartly refused to fall prey to the siren call of mathematics in his presentation. Like Menger and Mises, he also believed that mathematics was a poor language for expressing analyses of human action.[6]

Another reason for the relative neglect suffered by *Man, Economy and State* was the eccentricity of some of Rothbard's attempts to systematize Mises. Although he strove to improve the clarity of Mises' arguments, there were occasions on which his "clarifications" seemed more like rescue attempts than expositions of Mises' doctrines. For example, we noted in chapter 4 that Mises argued that monopolists could "only" raise their prices above the competitive level if the demand curve they faced was inelastic, a statement that is either a mistake or a misuse of the concept of elasticity. Rather than presuming that Mises was incorrect in his analysis of monopoly, however, Rothbard shows a case in which Mises' analytics make sense. Rothbard began by assuming a fixed supply of some commodity and then showed how a monopolist would only raise price in this situation if the competitive price fell in the inelastic region of the demand curve. Although his analysis was technically correct, it was hardly a broadly applicable example nor one to convince economists that monopolies would not generally charge monopoly prices (594).[7]

Despite the inclusion of particular Austrian doctrines on value, time preference, production, cost (including Rothbard's ingenious explanation of why cost plays no determining role in price formation [292]), and entrepreneurship, and despite many statements about the pervasiveness of change in economic life, far more than *Human Action*, *Man, Economy and State* must have seemed to a typical reader to be more or less familiar economics presented almost exclusively in words with a few controversial definitions, and some strange discontinuous graphs. That Rothbard's, and by implication Mises', economics might represent an economics that was sufficiently different from neoclassical economic theory to warrant a different appellation would have been unlikely to cross any conventional economist's mind. Austrian economics was simply old-fashioned, sometimes correct, often incorrect, and always slightly eccentric, but largely familiar economics. Rothbard himself, and probably most of the partici-

---

[6] One reviewer (Will, 1962) compared the style of *Man, Economy and State* to early twentieth-century treatises like those of Wicksteed, Fetter, and Taussig. This was intended as a criticism as the reviewer concluded that the book was not worth buying except as a curiosity, although it strikes me that he placed Rothbard in very good company, indeed.

[7] Rothbard ultimately rejected the standard definition of monopoly that is cast in terms of ability to charge a monopoly price. He argued that in light of the ubiquitous competitive process, the only clear meaning of monopoly was "a grant of special privilege by the State, reserving a certain area of production to one particular individual or group. Entry into the field is prohibited to others, and this prohibition is enforced by the gendarmes of the State" (591).

pants in Mises' seminar, would have disputed such a characterization, but their protests would seem hollow to the mainstream of the profession.

What accounts for the familiarity of *Man, Economy and State*, despite its many particular differences from mainstream economics? The familiarity is undoubtedly the consequence of Rothbard's underlying assumption about the organizing principle for understanding market interaction, his concept of equilibrium. Although Mises had, to be sure, developed several concepts of equilibrium in *Human Action*, as we have seen, little of what is important about that great book – his discussions of time, uncertainty, probability, methodology, entrepreneurship, and capital – depends upon or even refers to equilibrium constructs. Rothbard, however, moved equilibrium notions directly into the forefront of his reconstruction of Mises.

Rothbard presumed that in individual markets, the law of one price dominated, and that market clearing happened rapidly and smoothly (124). Just as in conventional neoclassical economics, general equilibrium, the evenly rotating economy (ERE), was the direction in which the economy was headed.[8] The pervasiveness of change made it unlikely that an economy would ever achieve the ERE, but nevertheless, like a dog chasing a mechanical rabbit, it at least could explain the direction of change (274). Although Rothbard warned against taking equilibrium too seriously given the world of constant change in which we live (277), it was nevertheless his underlying assumption that markets adjust quickly to new equilibrium positions. Indeed, his justification for the basic efficiency of markets was that "entrepreneurs will be very quick to leave the losing industry" (466) when mistakes are made.[9]

Rothbard invoked notions of constant change in his writings, locating the source of that change in the same quarter that Mises had identified – the tastes and preferences of consumers. Knowledge is not perfect and demand curves are not given (641). Consumers change their minds. But why should we assume that the convergence toward equilibrium occurs faster than the changes in the preferences of consumers? And if this is not

---

[8] Here, Rothbard is not completely true to Mises' analysis. Rothbard combines the final state of rest with the ERE, two concepts that Mises treated as distinct. Although it is true that Mises' discussion of the two constructs is somewhat murky, he certainly did not think of the ERE as the direction in which the economy was headed. Presumably, Mises realized that the use of the ERE as a foil for examining a world of uncertainty and change precluded its use as an end point for a market process (Mises, 1963:246–247).

[9] It is interesting to note that there is virtually no genuine history nor real-world examples to illustrate theoretical propositions in *Man, Economy and State*. Where Mises' writings had been full of examples of real historical episodes that inspired his thinking, Rothbard's treatise studiously avoids any references to empirical practices and institutions. Indeed, even his discussions of prices avoided naming actual currencies. His prices were stated in terms of ounces of gold.

the case, how could we ever differentiate in practice a zigzagging market process from chaos?

Such questions were not addressed by Rothbard, just as they had not been addressed by Mises, largely because the implications both he and Mises drew from time and uncertainty did not include problems of differential knowledge and causes and consequences of errors in the market process. Quick, unproblematic learning was assumed, as was a relatively stable environment. Interestingly, for Rothbard, time was only examined in conjunction with the structure of production and time preference, and knowledge problems were not identified at all. Growth, for example, was explained largely as a result of increasing capital formation, with innovation getting very short shrift, indeed (470ff.). Entrepreneurs existed within the pages of *Man, Economy and State*, but they were capitalist entrepreneurs who had to decide where to invest their resources and who quickly corrected their errors. They were speculators, as Mises had described, but the uncertainties they faced were not emphasized.

Rothbard's version of Austrian economics was in principle not very different from neoclassical economics. In fact, Rothbard's treatise is fully comprehensible within neoclassical economics despite his methodological and analytic challenges: He argues consistently within the context of equilibrium theorizing despite his strictures to be concerned with processes. Processes, to Rothbard, are always tending quickly toward a describable equilibrium.

Although his economics might not be much different from the neoclassical orthodoxy, what was clearly and unquestionably distinctive about his writing was the pervasive and unequivocal free market message he delivered. Markets are the product of free exchange between two parties in which both gain from the transaction. Any order that results from such free exchanges is welfare enhancing whereas any interference reduces welfare. He criticized even Mises' use of the notion of consumer sovereignty for its possible implication that the producer did not have the right to do with his property what he wished.[10] Markets were based on "individual sovereignty," not consumer sovereignty, except in the most formal sense (560). Property itself was a completely unproblematic institution. Property rights were derivable from a Lockean process of mixing one's labor with unowned resources, which then led to a property right over those resources in perpetuity. None of even John Locke's

[10] Perhaps because he could not bring himself to directly criticize his mentor, Rothbard actually aimed his fire at William Hutt, who had originated the term "consumer sovereignty" (1963:561–566).

caveats and qualifications entered into Rothbard's schema. And virtually all policy could be related to the question of property rights.

Externalities problems, for example, were simply failures to enforce property rights (156), as if they were all clearly and unambiguously defined and as if there were no problems of transactions costs in doing so. Monopoly was virtually undefinable except as a grant of special privilege from the government, and where people were thought to have monopolies, no harm to consumers could be inferred because the ability of the monopolist to raise price by restricting output only could be profitable if the demand curve was inelastic, and if it were, well, the demand curve was after all the result of voluntary choices (564). Cartels also caused no harm to participants in the market because cartel members were merely doing what they chose with their property. If a coffee cartel chose to burn coffee rather than sell it at low prices, this was not waste. The waste was created by producing too much coffee in the first place (567). Finally, all government regulation of economic activity was analyzed under the heading of "The Economics of Violent Intervention in the Market" (765ff.).

Man, Economy and State turned out to be less interesting as economics than it was as political ideology.[11] It provided a vision of how free trade among autonomous individuals promoted economic abundance for all together with an ethical belief in moral autonomy of individuals that elevated free choice to a first principle of social desirability. It was a very radical defense of free association that brooked no compromise or admitted no ambiguity. It was exactly the right mix to have available in the mid-sixties when revolution was the dominant intellectual stance. By combining both an intense dissatisfaction with contemporary economic formalism with radical, surprising, and yet simply stated political ideology, Rothbard was able to capture the spirit of the sixties, if not the dominant message.

Further, it was precisely those qualities of rebellion against orthodoxy and loyalty to a cause that were most responsible for Rothbard's immense influence in launching an Austrian "movement" in the early 1970s. Partly because of his economics, but more because of his libertarian politics, Rothbard became a beacon to a host of young undergraduate and graduate students during those rebellious times. The students attracted to

[11] I use the term "ideology" here in the broad sense of providing an organizing framework for understanding the world, not in the sense of a set of conclusions that must be maintained regardless of the evidence. Ideology in the broad sense is a necessary prerequisite to empirical observation and provides an evaluative context for these observations. Most political ideologies are of this nature and are derivative of a larger set of theoretical propositions about how the world works coupled with an ethical system to permit judgments about the world as observed.

Rothbard generally had either read Mises, were captivated by his mix of science and politics and wanted to learn more, or had discovered some aspect of libertarianism (often through Ayn Rand and her Objectivist movement) and identified Austrian economics with libertarian politics.[12] It is arguable that Rothbard's major contribution to the Austrian revival was not so much his abilities as a technical thinker (which were formidable) as his even greater ability to energize and encourage bright young students who shared the sixties' spirit but not the ruling political presuppositions of the decade.

It would be difficult to overemphasize Rothbard's importance to the emergence of an Austrian voice in the late 1960s and early 1970s. Although his main focus was clearly on political ideology, for Rothbard, Austrian economics was the essential scientific background to support his libertarian philosophical positions. Rothbard left no one in doubt that for him, the most important aspect of Mises' message was his unflinching support for free markets, private property, and the sanctity of contract, yet it was essential to understand the economics. Hence, insofar as one was attracted to Rothbard's politics, one would become acquainted with Austrian economics. And Rothbard attracted many people to his brand of libertarian philosophy. He represented to many a radical critique of existing conventional economics and politics while at the same time presenting an individualist political alternative to the hegemony of the left. It is not surprising, then, that one of the greatest honors Rothbard could imagine was the label he later received as "Mr. Libertarian." It is also not surprising that eventually, talking to professional economists became less important to Rothbard than arguing for his political vision.[13]

---

12 The Rothbard's living room in their apartment on the upper West Side in Manhattan was probably one of the few genuine "salons" in the United States. For a number of years, their home was open almost nonstop to Austrians and libertarians who wished to drop by to discuss economics or political philosophy. Murray Rothbard's willingness to treat young budding intellectuals as equals and his wife Joey's unfailing good humor in opening her home to all comers was of inestimable importance in developing a viable libertarian intellectual force during that time.

13 Indeed, Rothbard's writing increasingly turned away from economics to questions of politics and history. He eventually published what was intended to be a third volume of *Man, Economy and State, Power and Market* (1970), a book dedicated to examining what others might call public policy or public choice but what Rothbard referred to as "violent intervention in the market." It was his most complete statement of libertarian philosophy up to that time, a defense of libertarian anarchy that included the definition and analysis of the consequences for human action of various types of intervention. It was a political economy treatise that did not recognize either public goods or negative externalities that could not be remedied by property rights enforcement. His subsequent major works have been in American history rather than economics.

Israel Kirzner and the attempt at academic dialogue

Mises' other student from his New York University seminar, Israel Kirzner, was quite a different story. Kirzner studied with Mises, wrote his dissertation under him, and, against overwhelming odds, attempted to carry on Mises' work in the context of the mainstream academic community. Rather than taking the grand treatise route that Rothbard tried, Kirzner instead focused his attention on specific Austrian themes that seemed most congenial to opening up a dialogue with mainstream economists. His first book, *The Economic Point of View* ([1960] 1976), was essentially an essay on the history of the basic assumption of rationality and valuation in economic analysis that argued for Mises' system of praxeology as the logical culmination of the tradition. His second book, *Market Theory and the Price System* (1963), was a price theory text that tried to integrate some of Mises' concepts and language, including explanations of economic processes into conventional theory. There followed in 1966, *An Essay on Capital*, an undervalued update on Austrian capital theory. Although most of these books found an audience, it was not until 1973, with the publication of *Competition and Entrepreneurship*, that Kirzner managed to make a real impact on the profession and helped to launch the Austrian revival in the process.

Competition and Entrepreneurship was an especially important book in the history of the modern Austrian school. Conceived as a kind of outreach to neoclassical economics, it was one of the first American attempts to contribute to (rather than argue against) conventional economics from an Austrian perspective. In the theory of entrepreneurship, Kirzner found a widely acknowledged chink in the neoclassical armor that he argued could be filled by a good dose of Austrian economics. Neoclassical economics had a theory of equilibrium prices, but it had no accepted theory of how these prices were attained. Kirzner set out to show that an Austrian theory of markets as entrepreneurial processes could fill this gap and provide deeper understanding of markets as well. Although we will examine Kirzner's theory of entrepreneurship in some detail in chapter 7, a cursory overview is in order here.

In *Competition and Entrepreneurship*, Kirzner develops a theory of an entrepreneur whose role is to equilibrate market prices. He presumes that at any moment in time, there are a wealth of undiscovered opportunities that are being overlooked. The entrepreneur, by virtue of the quality of "alertness," a quality of seeing what others miss, notices opportunities and exploits them to earn profit. As such, he is the motivating force for change in markets. Where Mises had emphasized uncertainty as the raison d'être of entrepreneurship and speculation as the activity of entrepreneurs, Kirzner downplays uncertainty and turns the entrepreneur into a riskless arbitrager.

Kirzner's theory of entrepreneurship leads him to criticize certain features of microeconomic theory. Following Hayek, Kirzner identifies competition with rivalry in the market. Competition occurs when entrepreneurs engage in such practices as price cutting, product differentiation, and product innovation. Once the market settles down to the standard description of a perfectly competitive equilibrium, competition ceases. This implies, however, that competition can be fully compatible with the existence of downward-sloping demand curves for particular products whose existence is the result of entrepreneurial alertness. In addition, profits may be the consequence of some temporary advantage entrepreneurs are enjoying and not a symptom of persistent monopoly power. Hence, Kirzner argues, the conventional theory of monopoly as market power or discretion over prices is not helpful in distinguishing the short-term consequences of entrepreneurship and the existence of disequilibrium from long-run persistent monopoly power (101ff.). A better classification system would be to define monopoly in terms of barriers to entry, which to Kirzner meant monopoly ownership of some crucial resource necessary to the production of a product. In that way, profits that are subject to being eroded by competition could not be construed as evidence of monopoly whereas those that were protected by right could be so construed.[14]

Since Kirzner argued that competition was characterized by all manner of attempts to seek out profit opportunities, he also defended advertising (151) and selling costs (141ff.) as manifestations of competitive and not monopolistic activity and critiqued the theory of monopolistic competition for its substitution of an inferior equilibrium analysis for a still-flawed but more useful one (113). Finally, following Hayek, he took all of welfare economics to task for presuming a level of knowledge that was not available to government planners (212ff.).

In one respect, Kirzner's book was surprisingly successful in gaining a respectful hearing for Austrian ideas in the mainstream of the profession. Kirzner developed an impeccable reputation for careful criticism and judicious Austrianism that led to his being more or less the Austrian spokesman to the profession at large. His language was familiar, he took on known opponents, and he carefully circumscribed his arguments so as not to make unsupported and sweeping generalizations, a practice in which an outsider can never afford to indulge.

[14] Note the similarity to Baumol's later work on contestable markets (Baumol, Panzar, and Willig, 1982).

Interestingly, despite the self-conscious "Austrian" character of Kirzner's work, and despite his many critiques of neoclassical practice, like Rothbard, he did not propose a radical theoretical challenge to conventional economics. And unlike Rothbard, Kirzner was self-conscious in trying to bring about a rapproachment between Austrian economics and neoclassical orthodoxy. Kirzner was deliberately trying to fill a gap in microeconomic theory that had important implications for the theory of competition and monopoly. He did not see his work as an alternative to conventional theory so much as an important supplement to it. Nevertheless, the publication of *Competition and Entrepreneurship* was an important factor in bringing about a revival of interest in the Austrian tradition.

The Austrian revival

If one had to set a specific date for the Austrian revival in America,[15] 1974 is the year that would most likely come to mind. This is not to say that rumblings of a renewed interest in Austrian economics were not being heard for several years before 1974.

In 1969, for example, James Buchanan published *Cost and Choice* in which he defied conventional opinion by claiming that the Austrians really had won the calculation debate because they understood the subjective nature of cost whereas the market socialists did not. Although Buchanan pointed out that his subjectivism, a by-product of his work on public debt,[16] was more influenced by the London School of Economics than by the Austrian tradition, he nevertheless credited Hayek with providing a methodological basis from which the London School of Economics tradition could flourish (1968:23). His serious treatment in

---

[15] I believe the term "Austrian Revival" was first used by Vivian Walsh at a meeting of the Atlantic Economic Association in 1977 during a session on Carl Menger. He was referring to the increasing interest in Menger and his followers by the economics profession in general, and not to the growing body of work in the field by those who were sympathetic to the Austrian tradition.

[16] Buchanan's 1958 book *Public Principles of Public Debt* argued, contrary to received doctrine of the moment, that the burden of the debt could in fact be passed on to future generations. His argument rested on his insistence that "burden" should be interpreted as utility loss, a subjectivist notion of debt, in contrast to the practice of considering debt burden as wealth or resource losses. This led him to explore the subjective nature of cost further and to examine its implications for other government policies. In this way, Buchanan both bolstered claims for the legitimacy of Austrian subjectivism and temporarily traveled down the same road with many of the new Austrians.

Cost and Choice not only of Hayek but also of Mises did much to enhance the legitimacy of Austrian economics in general.[17]

In 1972, George Shackle, a former student of Hayek's in London and long an admirer of Lord Keynes, followed up on some issues of time and expectations that he regarded as the essence of Keynes's message in his book *Epistemics and Economics*. This book, which broke new ground in subjectivist theory, treated the Austrians with respect and provided a set of problems for further Austrian research.

In 1973, the same year in which *Competition and Entrepreneurship* was published, Sir John Hicks, having recently found some interesting bits in Menger concerning time, edited one book on Menger, *Carl Menger and the Austrian School of Economics,* and wrote another with an Austrian theme, *Capital and Time: A Neo-Austrian Theory.* In the second book, he incorporated Bohm-Bawerkian and Hayekian notions of goods in process and roundaboutness into a theory of capital adjustment from one equilibrium position to another: hence its name "neo-Austrian."

The publication of all these books and articles not only raised important questions of economic theory but also made Austrian themes and ideas respectable again. When, in October of 1974, Friedrich Hayek won the Nobel prize in economics (shared, ironically, with Gunnar Myrdal, who because he also worked on issues of knowledge but from a "leftist" position, "balanced" the award politically), the time surely seemed ripe for a revival of Austrian economics.

As important as these academic events were to the revival of Austrian ideas, the catalyst for the revival came from another source outside the formal boundaries of the academy. In 1974, the Institute for Humane Studies sponsored a week-long conference on Austrian economics in South Royalton, Vermont. This conference brought together a varied group of about fifty economists and current graduate students whose unifying characteristic was that they had expressed some interest in the work of Mises or Hayek. The main speakers included, not surprisingly, Murray Rothbard and Israel Kirzner. More surprising was the inclusion of Ludwig Lachmann, a newcomer to most of the conference participants, and the only one among the lecturers who had not been part of the Mises circle in America.

The papers presented at South Royalton ranged from the history of the Austrian school, its method, and particular characteristics to policy and the ethical implications of Austrian economics. The conference essays were edited and published under the title *The Foundations of Modern*

---

[17] Several years later, Buchanan edited, along with Thirlby, *LSE Essays on Cost* (1973), which showed the important link between Hayek, Ronald Coase, and Jack Wiseman in the theory of subjective cost.

Austrian Economics (1976) by Edwin Dolan, who also organized and ran the conference. Dolan wrote an introductory essay to put the rest of the essays into perspective. His introduction, entitled "Austrian Economics as Extraordinary Science," is worth examining in some detail because it captures nicely the predominant assumption of that conference: that Austrians could be considered an example of an alternative Kuhnian paradigm.

Dolan began by arguing that modern Austrians give external evidence of doing "extraordinary science."

They produce relatively more books and contribute fewer articles to established journals. They do not write textbooks; their students learn directly from the masters. They are very much concerned with methodological and philosophical fundamentals. And what makes the label "extraordinary" most applicable to their work is that they share a conviction that orthodox economics is at the point of breakdown, that it is unable to provide a coherent and intelligible analysis of the present-day economic world. (4) [18]

He then contrasted this view of the Austrian paradigm with the view of Milton Friedman who, paying a friendly visit to the South Royalton conference, ruffled many feathers by pronouncing that "there is no such thing as Austrian economics – only good economics, and bad economics." Although Friedman did not specify into which category he placed Austrian economic writings, leading participants to indulge in a great deal of indignant speculation, Friedman probably did mean to state the view that any really important contribution that Austrians might make to economics could be (or perhaps had already been) incorporated into the mainstream.

In arguing against the Friedmanesque view of Austrian economics, Dolan summarized the then-current understanding of what made Austrian economics different from the mainstream: the Austrian understanding of human action, of macroeconomics, and the methodology of verbal deduction.

All of Austrian economics, Dolan explained, is the "working out of the logical implications of the fact that human beings do engage in purposeful action." He then went on to make the rather dubious claim that the Austrian notion of human action was different from "positivist" views of action in that it was composed of two claims, that human action has consequences and that without human action, the consequence would not occur. Positivism, on the other hand, he argued, deals only with

[18] Interestingly, when Dolan wrote of "the Austrians" who were actually doing this "extraordinary science," he could only have been referring to a handful of people even within the assembled group. Besides Rothbard, Kirzner, and Lachmann, there were few other Austrians at that time writing anything at all.

observable events and would deny the second half of the Austrian claim. Dolan's analysis here is mystifying and seems to be a case of perceiving a difference between Austrian and neoclassical economics, but not being quite sure what it was. This was a problem shared by many others in the years immediately following South Royalton.

Second, Dolan argued, Austrians criticize the use of macroeconomic aggregates in economics because they do not have a foundation in purposive action. Individual human beings are the sole source of action. The purpose of economics is twofold: to "make the world intelligible in terms of human action," and to explain "how conscious, purposeful human action can generate unintended consequences through social interaction." The postulating of causal relationships among macroeconomic aggregates, the procedure Austrians attributed to Keynes, is a violation of that program (6).

Finally, Austrians criticize the use of mathematics as a tool of economics analysis and by extension, econometrics as a means of testing economic theory. All mathematics does is to take sensible verbal propositions and translate them laboriously into symbols, thereby losing meaning in the translation with no corresponding gain. And econometrics attempts the futile task of proving apodictically certain theory while searching for quantitative constants[19] in human action that simply do not exist. The proper method for Austrian (and all other good) economists to follow, according to Dolan's summary of the conference, was to engage in logical, verbal deduction of the implications of a few fundamental axioms of human experience. Just as was the case in *Human Action*, little was said here about the role of empirical research, what Mises called "history."

To show the practical application of these three methodological principles, Dolan chose three examples: Austrian theories of market processes as illustrated by Kirzner's theory of entrepreneurship, the Austrian theory of capital so recently rediscovered by Hicks, and the Mises–Hayek theory of money and inflation, which in 1974 was of immediate policy relevance.

[19] The charge that econometricians were engaged in a futile search for economics "constants" was heard more than once in Austrian circles as a criticism of econometrics. Unfortunately, too often this was no more than a slavish repetition of one of Mises' minor arguments against a misinterpretation of a particular statistical study.

In the late 1930s, Paul Douglas had intemperately praised Henry Schultz's *The Theory and Measurement of Demand* as a step toward achieving the economic equivalent of "the determination of atomic weights for the development of chemistry." Mises rightly pointed out the ephemeral nature of any elasticity measures and the utter futility of thinking of such measures as equivalent to the constants in natural science (Mises, 1963:352). However, he seemed to generalize Douglas's misguided interpretation to all forms of "quantitative economics" regardless of how carefully and circumspectly the researcher defined his objective. Many of Mises' followers then took his criticism of "constants" in human action as a sufficient criticism of all econometric work as well.

The latter two of these illustrations in light of subsequent events were not convincing evidence of an Austrian alternative paradigm. Austrian attention to human purposes led to a theory of capital that emphasized its heterogeneity and resisted attempts to aggregate its value. This same attention to human purposes also led to a theory of money creation that emphasized its path of entry into the system and posited important relative price effects. Although both of these propositions were indeed identifiably different from then-current received economic doctrine, they were also beginning to receive some attention from mainstream theorists. As Dolan himself predicted at the end of his article, the ability of an Austrian doctrine to be incorporated into the mainstream argued against its status as extraordinary science. Subsequent work on the microfoundations of macroeconomics and the investigation of relative price effects in money transmission certainly seemed to show the power of neoclassical economics to absorb critical viewpoints and to undercut Austrian claims to being able to illuminate economic problems differently.

This easy if partial incorporation of an Austrian problem into neoclassical economics was arguably not so successful with the third of Dolan's examples, the Austrian emphasis on market processes. At the time, one might have assumed exactly the contrary. The theory of market processes seemed to be a likely candidate for easy assimilation into the neoclassical corpus largely because all economics teachers found themselves "telling stories" about market adjustment processes to flesh out their graphs and equations. Clearly providing the impetus for some formalization of those stories seemed exactly the kind of contribution Austrians were always making to mainstream economics. Moreover, Kirzner's theory of entrepreneurship appeared to be just the necessary ingredient to make economist's adjustment stories a coherent part of equilibrium analysis. It was taken for granted that Austrians could provide a supplement to equilibrium conditions with accounts of market processes, a claim consistent with Rothbard's as well as with Kirzner's work. It was not suspected at the time that this very issue of the relationship between equilibrium and processes would be the center of a major and still unresolved debate within the Austrian tradition itself. Indeed, at South Royalton, the very possibility of a major debate within the new Austrian economists was not entertained.

Dolan's essay and the collected conference papers captured accurately the view among the conference speakers and participants about what was important in Austrian economics: praxeology, verbal deductive economics, no use of mathematics, limited use of econometrics, suspicion of macroeconomics, specific theories of entrepreneurship, capital and business fluctuations, and money – all attitudes and theories derived from

Mises and Rothbard. More than this, however, Dolan captured a wide-spread attitude at that conference, an attitude that Austrian economics was a completed project that had to be learned from the masters, taught to students, and communicated, it was hoped, to a misguided economics profession.

For a large subset of the participants at South Royalton, the relevant question for discussion was not so much "What does all this imply that we don't yet understand?" as it was, "What did Mises say about this?" This was certainly true of Rothbard who, at least on the subject of the use of mathematics in economics, refused even to elaborate on his pronouncements in response to a friendly question from a genuinely puzzled participant. His talk, he explained, was the final word on the subject.[20] In contrast, Kirzner seemed to be enlivened by challenging discussion, although even he gave others the impression that when all was said and done, he was confident that Mises was probably correct in most matters.[21] The only speaker who seemed to see much theoretical work still to be done in defining and developing an Austrian economics was Ludwig Lachmann.

Lachmann, professor of economics at the University of Witwatersrand, South Africa, since 1949, was in most respects the odd man out at South Royalton. A long-time laborer in the fields of subjectivist economics and author of a book and essays on the subject of capital theory, Lachmann was the only speaker of the three at this site of the Austrian revival who had not studied directly under Ludwig von Mises.

As a student, he had studied at the University of Berlin and the University of Zurich, where his interests were in the business cycle analysis of Hahn, Hawtrey, Wicksell, and Mises. Despite the hostility to Austrian economics in his German education, he had the good luck to be tutored by Emil Kauder, who stressed the importance of subjectivism in economics and introduced him to Hayek's work. During this time, Lachmann also became interested in the "causal-genetic" approach to economics advo-

20 I know for a fact that the question was friendly but puzzled since I posed it myself and was astonished by the hostility with which it was greeted. Interestingly, Rothbard's behavior in this episode served to divide the participants into camps, a division that would only intensify over the coming years. Those who were interested onlookers to the Austrian movement were repelled by Rothbard's attitude. Many more committed Austrians, I was later told, were embarrassed by Rothbard's behavior, while a few of his more ardent followers thought he was entirely justified not to waste his time answering "deviationists."

21 Interestingly, Hayek's work took a distinct back seat to Mises' at South Royalton. Although his work on business cycles and inflation was discussed and treated with respect, there was no sense that he might in any way be Ludwig von Mises' professional equal in Austrian economics. This attitude might have been a by-product of Rothbard's animosity toward what he regarded as Hayek's apostasy on questions of methodology. Rothbard's influence was great among several of the participants who took his lead in attitudes toward other economists as well as toward economic ideas.

cated by Hans Mayer and the "verstehende" method of Max Weber. In 1933, Lachmann went to England to study at the London School of Economics, where his thinking matured in a distinctly Austrian direction. He became, along with G. L. S. Shackle, a student of Hayek's and continued his research into business cycles and capital theory. During this time Lachmann also fell under the influence of the subjective cost tradition that was emerging at the London School of Economics. Unlike most other Austrians, however, he also found some merit in Keynes – or at least in Keynes's insistence on the importance of subjective expectations in *The General Theory.*

Lachmann subsequently took positions at Aberystwyth, Wales, the University of Hull, and finally Witwatersrand in South Africa, positions that separated him even more than other Austrians from the centers of academic debate. As a consequence, his economics was a more exotic mix[22] than the American Austrians were accustomed to hearing, and he injected an important element of controversy into what might have otherwise been too much a case of preaching to the choir.[23]

In his first lecture at South Royalton, he immediately articulated what was to become the Austrian claim to theoretical distinction: the theory of the market process. He argued in a Hayekian manner that in order to theorize about the market process, it was important to focus first on the question of the kinds of knowledge market participants possess and the ways in which that knowledge changes. With the problem of knowledge clearly in view, the market process then can be understood as "the outward manifestation of an unending stream of knowledge . . . [that] is continuously changing in society, a process hard to describe. Knowledge defies all attempts to treat it as a 'datum' or an object identifiable in time and space" (Lachmann 1976b:127).

Mises had emphasized that all action takes place in time, yet "as soon as we permit time to elapse, we must permit knowledge to change, and knowledge cannot be regarded as a function of anything" (128).[24] If all action takes place in time, and elapsed time always means a change in knowledge, and if knowledge cannot be a "function of anything," how then, Lachmann asked, can we theorize about a price system that tends toward equilibrium?

---

[22] As I will argue later, though exotic, the mix that Lachmann brought to the Austrian conversation was more true to the whole Mengerian tradition than the version of Austrian economics dominating in America during the 1950s and 1960s.

[23] For a short but excellent intellectual biography of Lachmann, see Grinder (1977).

[24] This phrase, which Lachmann had originally used in an essay in *Metroeconomica* (reprinted in Lachmann, 1977:81–93), was the quotation with which Shackle introduced his book *Epistemics and Economics* (1972). The link between Shackle and Lachmann was very strong, indeed.

The market is a process with no clearly defined "initial conditions" and "no end or final point of rest in sight." Instead it is a "sequence of individual interactions, each denoting the encounter (and sometimes collision) of a number of plans, which, while coherent individually and reflecting the individual equilibrium of the actor, are incoherent as a group" (131). The problem, according to Lachmann, is to figure out how to describe this never-ending, directionless process that characterized the market order without resorting to fictions like general equilibrium. Clearly, this put him at odds with virtually the entire economics profession, as well as most of the Austrians present at South Royalton. Relying more on the early chapters of *Human Action* than the later ones, on the premises more than on the integrated analysis, Lachmann concluded that Austrian economics, if it was anything, was a radical challenge to the orthodoxy. There was much work to be done.

Lachmann's message was radical, but it is not clear that many actually heard it at South Royalton. It was just too foreign to American ways of thinking to be immediately absorbed, except by Kirzner with whom he had had a lengthy correspondence and who quickly grasped the challenge Lachmann was offering. For many of the others, Lachmann may as well have been speaking a foreign language.[25] Although ultimately, Lachmann's challenge to orthodoxy, and especially to orthodox notions of equilibrium, both neoclassical and Austrian, was to shape nearly two decades of subsequent Austrian debate, at the time, Lachmann was something of a mystery even to the new Austrians.

With the exception of the three speakers, the majority of the enthusiasts for Austrian ideas at that conference were either graduate students or young assistant professors. Most young students of economics, no matter where they are educated, usually believe that they have discovered truth and their job is to carry the truth to the world around them.[26] One is

[25] Perhaps my description of Lachmann's reception is too much colored by my own recollection of South Royalton. As an assistant professor with standard economic training who was intrigued by the Austrian's political message but largely ignorant of the specifics of Austrian economic analysis, I found Lachmann to be virtually incomprehensible. He was raising problems and issues that I had never considered before or even heard considered by anyone else. I was still grappling with questions of method and technique, of entrepreneurship and competition, and with the larger question of whether the Austrians were crackpots or serious contenders for academic respectability and was not ready to begin to grasp the consequences of subjectivism of expectations and uncertainty. It took me years to start appreciating Lachmann's message. In light of many subsequent judgments I heard from Austrians about Lachmann's murkiness, I am confident I was not alone in my failure to appreciate his contributions straight off. On the other hand, my colleague Don Lavoie remembers himself and a group of his friends being "shaken up" by Lachmann right from the beginning and finding the issues he raised exciting and fun to debate (personal communication, 1992).

[26] At least, that used to be the case. After reading Klamer and Colander, *The Making of an Economist* (1990), I am not certain that graduate students have much enthusiasm at all for their subject anymore.

reminded most forcefully here of economics students educated during that era at the University of Chicago or perhaps University of California at Los Angeles. This attitude was doubly evident at South Royalton, where the young Austrians also believed their truth was being unjustifiably ignored by a mistaken and biased academic community. South Royalton was the rallying point for a crusade, a crusade to show Milton Friedman that Austrian economics is good economics.

In retrospect, a conviction that they had discovered important truths held by many of the participants at South Royalton was probably necessary in order to give these young, mostly unknown economists a reason to pursue an eccentric research program that flew in the face of received doctrine. If one is going to be unorthodox in a very orthodox academic community, one had better really believe in what one is doing. Clearly, all these bright and energetic budding economists could have been assured of at least moderately successful (and some even brilliant) careers by working within the mainstream. Instead, they were undeniably taking a huge risk with their future income streams to attempt the difficult task of developing an alternative Austrian paradigm.[27] They could never have done the work that needed to be done without the confidence that they were at least on the right track. Ironically, much in the same manner as Hayek explains the evolution of the common law, the attempt on the part of these young Austrians to "learn" the theory led them inexorably to discover new ideas and new implications of accepted doctrine.

Indeed, in the process of trying to show Milton Friedman that Austrian economics is good economics, the South Royalton Austrians discovered over time that the job was more complicated than they first suspected. The problems were more abstruse, the theories less obvious, and their implications were largely unplumbed. What started out as a crusade for Austrian economics turned into a deep and extensive examination of a core of ideas that began with Menger and that have been amended, enlarged, weeded out, and improved on by scores of scholars for over a century.

[27] Indeed, some paid the price for their heterodoxy in the form of truncated academic careers. Edwin Dolan was himself an imaginative thinker who gave up on a standard academic career after being let go from Dartmouth College. Gerald O'Driscoll is another case of someone who undoubtedly could have had a comfortable academic career had he not had the misfortune of believing an out-of-fashion doctrine. If living well is the best revenge, however, both Dolan and O'Driscoll have gotten theirs. Dolan has made his mark on academics by writing and revising the best-selling principles of economics text in the United States as a freelance author. O'Driscoll eventually became vice-president of the Federal Reserve Bank of Dallas and continues to write extensively in monetary theory.

CHAPTER 6

Defining the Austrian paradigm

If, in 1974, one had nothing but *The Foundations of Modern Austrian Economics* as one's guide to understanding the Austrian tradition, one might perhaps be forgiven for being greatly mystified by the claims made therein. It is not clear from that volume, for instance, why "action" is more useful a concept than "maximization" or why Mises' evenly rotating economy is a superior construct to Walras's general equilibrium. Why call economics "praxeology," and why is it any better to refer to an individual's scale of values than to his preference function? Why is the concept of market clearing not made more precise by mathematical formulation rather than less so? For that matter, is mathematics not an aid to systematic thinking, and why, then, should economics want to do without it? And finally, why does it matter what the market process is as long as it is tending toward equilibrium anyway?

All these questions needed to be addressed within a systematic presentation of the Austrian view in the light of modern economic theory in order to sort out the vital issues from the peripheral, the insightful contributions from the pedestrian, but to do so was not easy. Mises spent his years in America isolated from the contemporary academic community and Rothbard apparently saw little to be gained from debate with those in the economics profession who were prone to disagree with him. Yet young economists trying to make their living within an established profession could not afford the luxury of talking only to themselves. They had to find a way to articulate and explain their ideas within the accepted academic channels.

Immediately after the South Royalton Conference, the hard work of articulating and explaining the Austrian "paradigm" began in earnest. Two more conferences similar in nature to South Royalton were held over the next two years, again sponsored by the Institute for Humane Studies.[1]

---

[1] Austrians were often suspect by some of their academic colleagues because of the role that "private" funds played in bringing about the revival. It is certainly true that without the initial support of the Koch Foundation or the Institute for Humane Studies, it would have been much more difficult for the revival to have gathered sufficient momentum to keep young economists interested and participating. Similarly, without the aid of the Volker Fund, neither Mises nor Hayek would have had the opportunity to teach in the United States. The private foundations that supported the early Austrian

These conferences aimed to bring together scholars who found merit in the Austrian tradition and were willing to work at developing it in more modern dress. In this they largely succeeded. Although a conference that was held in 1975 was characterized by some acrimony between those who saw little to change in a basically sound corpus of Misesian doctrine and those who saw the Austrian tradition primarily as a framework for the development of new ideas, by 1976 at a subsequent conference, it seemed clear that if Austrian economics was to be accepted, its ideas had to be further developed. This change of attitude was captured by the title given to the conference volume by its editor, Louis Spadaro: *New Directions in Austrian Economics* (1978).

New Directions was a step forward for the new Austrians. Although it contained several articles primarily critical of neoclassical economics (Rizzo on econometrics, Littlechild on social cost, Armentano on monopoly theory),[2] those that dominated the volume were either attempts at further articulating Austrian assumptions and method (Egger, Kirzner, O'Driscoll) or at working out novel theoretical implications of the Austrian tradition (O'Driscoll on spontaneous order, Moss on interest theory, Garrison on macroeconomics, Rothbard on money).

Once again, however, it was Lachmann who sounded the note around which the rest of the orchestra was to tune. His essay "An Austrian Stocktaking" called everyone's attention to some of the important unifying themes of the Austrian tradition:

The first, and most prominent, feature of Austrian economics is a radical subjectivism, today no longer confined to human preferences but extended to expectations. . . .

Secondly, . . . [t]ime is the dimension of all change. It is impossible for time to elapse without the constellation of knowledge changing. But knowledge shapes action, and action shapes the observable human world. Hence, it is impossible for us to predict any future state of this world.

---

revival were staffed by people who had studied Mises' economics and were convinced that there was merit in what he said. Yet, the charge that the foundations were "politically" motivated seems to miss the point. Much of academic research is funded by private money through such agencies as the Ford Foundation or the Rockefeller Foundation, neither of which is somehow free of all nonacademic agendas. One also must wonder why it is taken for granted that funds that come from organizations like the National Science Foundation or the National Endowment for the Arts is less subject to ideological constraints than private monies. Austrians would be likely to point out that government monies are collected through coercive taxes and dispensed according to the agendas pursued by small groups of scholars who influence such agencies.

2 This is not meant to belittle the contribution criticism makes to the articulating of an alternative. Indeed, criticism of other's mistakes is often an indispensable aid to clarifying one's own thinking. This principle is well illustrated by the very creative contributions Rizzo and Littlechild were later to make to Austrian economics.

The third feature of Austrian economics . . . is a distrust of all those formaliza-
tions of economic experience that do not have an identifiable source in the minds
of an economic actor. (1978b:1–2)

Lachmann had initially joined Kirzner in convincing the new Austrians
that their strength lay in a theory of the market process. Now he was
offering suggestions on how to proceed with developing such a theory. By
identifying radical subjectivism, time, and methodological individualism
as the cornerstones of Austrian economics, he was in fact emphasizing
those parts of Mises that were most different from mainstream economics
and were also most faithful to the original Mengerian program. As it
turned out, by focusing on subjectivism, time, and methodological individualism, Lachmann also was inadvertently giving the new Austrians
their marching orders. Almost all subsequent writing was to be an
elaboration of some implication of these themes.

Over the next two decades, the growing ranks of the new Austrians
attempted to articulate the implications of radical subjectivism, time and
methodological individualism to a variety of different issues. Sessions on
Austrian economics increasingly were organized at professional meetings. Conferences continued to be held with great regularity.[3] A voluminous literature, often unpublished, emerged from Austrian pens. Even
more surprisingly, three formal programs in Austrian economics were
initiated within the academy, the first at New York University, where Mises
had lectured, where Kirzner was a faculty member, and where Lachmann
had a visiting appointment; the second at young but growing George
Mason University, where the Center for the Study of Market Processes was
established by four veterans of South Royalton, and at Auburn University,
where one South Royalton alumnus taught and several other faculty were
sympathetic to Austrian ideas. At George Mason University, and to a lesser
extent New York University and Auburn, graduate students could study
Austrian ideas relatively unmolested by mainstream disdain and could
hope to carve out a career by writing dissertations in areas that skirted the
borders between Austrian and neoclassical economics.[4]

[3] It would be difficult to overestimate the importance of conferences on Austrian
economics in the early days of the revival. Without some means of bringing otherwise
isolated scholars together into an intellectual community, very little conversation could
have taken place and little progress made. The rather long, intensive conferences
modeled after South Royalton were supplemented by shorter regional conferences
aimed at acquainting the audience with issues in Austrian economics. This whole
network of conferences and the interactions among the people who attended were, in
some respects, an alternative university that existed outside the official academy but
was connected to it via the participation of faculty from standard universities.

[4] Recently, George Mason students have become especially successful in publishing their
dissertations. Four books based on dissertations have been published within a two-year
period. Cordato (1992) is a thoughtful attempt to provide a theory of efficiency from

Austrian economics was, ironically, only now living up to the description Dolan had prematurely painted of it as extraordinary science. An
identifiable group of economists operating on the fringes of the mainstream increasingly behaved as a scientific community. Points of controversy of interest to that group alone were hotly discussed and debated,
but almost totally apart from the attention of conventional economists.
Most of the discussion of Austrian economics took place at conferences
and through the circulation of unpublished papers. Publications tended
to be concentrated in books and conference volumes or avowedly Austrian outlets such as the *Austrian Economics Newsletter, Market Process,* or
later, *The Review of Austrian Economics,* rather than refereed journals. And
of all the articles actually published, very few made it to the top ten
journals.

Breaking into mainstream professional journals is a major problem for
all heterodox views in economics, and the Austrian variant was no
exception. Hence, the published writings of the new Austrians in the
mainstream journals tended to fall into a few specific categories.[5] The
history of economic thought, often a safe haven for those working in out-
of-favor paradigms, became a refuge to reexamine the works of the older
Austrians. Work in the history of the Austrian school could often serve the
additional purpose of legitimating some unappreciated Austrian idea or
debate. Hence, besides journal articles on Menger (O'Driscoll, 1986;
Moss, 1978; Kirzner, 1978; Lachmann, 1978c; Vaughn, 1978), one saw
rehabilative work on Hayek (Moss and Vaughn, 1986; Garrison and
Bellante, 1988), on the socialist calculation debate (Vaughn, 1980a;
Murell, 1983), on Frank Fetter who was closely allied with the Austrians
(O'Driscoll, 1980a), on ordinal utility theory (High and Bloch, 1989), and
even on Keynes (Garrison, 1985) and Marx (Lavoie, 1983, 1986a).
Austrians were drawn to the history of economic thought because of the
importance they attributed to verbal rather than mathematical argument

---

an Austrian perspective that takes standard arguments about externalities into account.
Boettke (1990a) is a historical and theoretical account of the early years of the Soviet
Union that uses the Austrian arguments against central planning to illuminate actual
Russian experience. Prychitko (1991) analyzes from an Austrian perspective the theory
of worker self-management as it has been developed in Eastern Europe. Horwitz (1992)
provides an evolutionary account of free banking that takes a Hayekian view of social
processes.

[5] The following discussion is limited to publications that appeared in conventional
journals that were not either Austrian or associated with some other heterodox group.
Hence, the many contributions to Austrian theory that appeared in the *Cato Journal,
Journal of Libertarian Studies, Review of Austrian Economics, Austrian Economics Newsletter,
Market Process,* and *Critical Review* are excluded because they were read primarily by
Austrians or people sympathetic to Austrian ideas.

and because of the importance they saw in learning the origin of ideas to better understand the ideas themselves.

Law and economics, mercifully free of arcane mathematics and less hostage to formal modeling than other subdisciplines within economics, became an area congenial to new Austrians. For instance, new Austrians discussed the question of whether the common law is efficient from a Hayekian perspective (O'Driscoll, 1980b; Rizzo, 1980a). Rizzo was especially successful in carving out a niche in mainstream law journals for an economic approach to liability and tort law that reflected Austrian assumptions and methods of argumentation (1980c, 1981, 1982, 1987; Rizzo and Arnold, 1980). In particular, Rizzo criticized the Landes and Posner approach to law and economics that recommends that judges use efficiency as a criterion for rendering decisions (1980b).

Rizzo argued that to use efficiency as a criterion for deciding tort cases, one had to be able to define wealth and to calculate appropriate shadow prices for objects subject to litigation. Both were necessary to make it possible to know what decision would increase rather than decrease wealth (643); yet, given the limits of our knowledge, it is impossible to do either. Wealth is a subjective concept that includes many nonmeasurable elements such as moral valuations that defy objective definition (646). Further, even if it were possible to define wealth, the calculation of correct shadow prices to measure wealth is impossible outside of equilibrium (647). The theory of the second best tells us that existing market prices are not necessarily good proxies for equilibrium prices, and hence judicial decisions that use market prices as shadow prices in settling disputes may make decisions that increase inefficiency (652). Rizzo's arguments reflected Austrian themes of limitations on knowledge, subjectivity of value, and the empirical irrelevance of general equilibrium. As an alternative to using efficiency standards to make judicial decisions, Rizzo advocated a rule of strict liability that requires only the establishment of causation. This, too, demonstrates an Austrian approach, given its congruence with Hayek's preference for rules over discretion in the legal framework (Hayek, 1973).

Roger Garrison was relatively successful in publishing articles on the Austrian theory of the business cycle and Austrian macroeconomics in mainstream journals. Some were classified as history of economic thought, but some also were regarded as contemporary theory, partly because of renewed professional interest in sequential processes in contemporary cycle theory (Garrison 1984a, 1984b).

Lawrence White's work on monetary theory managed to hit mainstream journals (1984a, 1987), although his most interesting work from an Austrian perspective appeared more in specialized publications or in book form (1984b; 1989). His book *Free banking in Britain: theory, experience and debate* (1984b) explored both the history of free banking in England to show that free banking had actually worked well in Scotland in the late eighteenth and nineteenth centuries, and the theory of free banking to show its contemporary relevance to the debate over appropriate financial institutions. White's work had the advantage of being able to tie into contemporary debate over both the positive and normative effects of monetary institutions that did not rely exclusively on Austrian sources. After the inflationary debacle of the 1970s, the design of monetary institutions was an important economic issue. However, White's approach was clearly drawn from the Austrian tradition, which emphasized the role of a central banking system in destablizing an economy. Further, Hayek's essay "The Denationalization of Money" (1978b) helped to spur Austrian thinking about monetary institutions.

The Austrian view on this issue was to argue for nonregulated, free banking as a remedy to the instabilities caused by central banks and regulated fractional reserve banks. By developing an analysis of how a true free banking system could work to the benefit of the economy, White was further developing the Austrian case for the advantages of unregulated competition over managed, central banking. White's student George Selgin (1988; Selgin and White, 1987) took his argument one step further and provided an evolutionary account of how a free banking system could emerge without government direction or regulation to provide all the necessary services that one expects from a banking system. Selgin's analysis was clearly a continuation of Menger's story about the emergence of money from barter, and an illustration of Hayek's claim for the superiority of evolved rather than constructed institutions.[6]

Conspicuous by its absence from the mainstream journals were works of a constructive theoretical nature. Such works were so far outside of what was considered acceptable economic theory by the profession that they rarely survived the refereeing process.[7] What was considered theoretical debate by Austrians was more often considered methodological writing by

[6] Steven Horwitz, Selgin's student, takes the argument even further in his book *Monetary Evolution, Free Banking and Economic Order* (1992). This book, however, also shows the influence of Horwitz's other teacher, Don Lavoie, in that he provides an evolutionary theory of money that is embedded in a hermeneutical understanding of economics.

[7] There were a few exceptions to this rule. Stephen Littlechild published several papers attempting to formalize Austrian process analysis (1979a; Littlechild and Owen, 1980). However, his version of a process theory was very much a neoclassical application to a sequential process and hence not very different from familiar neoclassical models. The same can be said for High in his dissertation that later became a book (1991). They are Austrian in terms of the problem set out, but are neoclassical in terms of the method of illuminating the problem. Of course, saying this is to take a position on the debate that I describe in the next chapter.

mainstream economists. For example, during this period there was an intense debate over the qualities that defined entrepreneurship: Did alertness capture all the important aspects (Kirzner)? Should we rather focus on "imagination" (White, [1976] 1990), or judgment (High, 1982)? Was uncertainty bearing a part of entrepreneurial action (Lachmann, 1986)? Is it necessary to link entrepreneurship to resource ownership (Rothbard, 1982)? None of that debate was carried on in conventional journals. It was engaged in primarily through circulated papers and articles published in conference volumes on Austrian economics.[8]

This isn't to say that the South Royalton alumni were consciously trying to maintain an exclusive club. In fact, just the opposite was true. There was a conscious attempt to engage others who seemed sympathetic to some aspect of Austrian economics in Austrian debate. Hence, economists such as James Buchanan, Richard Wagner, Leland Yeager, Axel Leijonhufvud, and Sir John Hicks – economists with mainstream credentials but who shared some of the Austrian criticisms of the mainstream and who seemed to be on parallel roads to looking for alternatives – participated in symposia and contributed to conference volumes (Rizzo, 1979; Langlois, 1986b).

In addition, other critics of contemporary economics were eagerly sought as potential allies. Both G. L. S. Shackle (Rizzo, 1979) and Jack Wiseman were valued for their radical subjectivism, Brian Loasby for his application of subjectivism to the theory of the firm (1976). The Austrians also reached out to evolutionary theorists (Nelson and Winter, 1982), to post-Keynesians because of their similar views of the importance of time in economics, and to the Institutionalists who also criticized the ahistorical aridity of mainstream economics (Samuels, 1989).

This explicit effort to engage others outside the "club," though sometimes overly self-conscious, did much to broaden the Austrian debate and sharpen the issues that needed to be discussed. For instance, George Shackle and, more directly, Jack Wiseman (1985) helped the Austrians explore what they meant by subjectivism and pushed some toward a more subjectivist stance than they otherwise might have taken. Leland Yeager, who both admired Mises and yet was critical of his methodology, not only contributed to Austrian discussion on monetary theory as one might expect, but also held the young Austrians to high standards of clarity in exposition about issues of methodology and subjectivism (1987a, 1987b;

---

[8] In addition, as Dolan described in 1976, the new Austrians were publishing their theoretical work in books more than in articles. Consider the following by no means inclusive list: (Armentano, 1982; Boettke, 1990a; Cordato, 1992; Fink, 1982; High, 1990, 1991; Horwitz, 1992; Langlois, 1986b; Lavoie, 1985a, 1985b, 1990b; O'Driscoll, 1977; O'Driscoll and Rizzo, 1985; Prychitko, 1991; Rizzo, 1979; Selgin, 1988; White, 1984b, 1989).

see also High, 1987). Richard Wagner's work in public choice took a turn that was sympathetic to Mises' approach (1977a, 1977b, 1978, 1979; and Buchanan, 1977).[9] Axel Leijonhufvud's work on Keynes (1968) and his willingness to take process "stories" seriously helped the young Austrians articulate what they meant by a disequilibrium process (1986). In addition, his introduction of the idea of an equilibrium "corridor" suggested a possible way of understanding order in an imperfect world (1981). Although Hicks's "revitalization" of Menger's theory of capital was ultimately rejected by the new Austrians, his keen mind helped to hone the analysis of capital more completely than could have been done without him.

A special note must be made of the role James Buchanan played in the crucial years of the Austrian revival. Buchanan's Austrian sympathies were evident not only in *Cost and Choice*, but also in a variety of articles he published during the 1960s and 1970s. The most "Austrian" was his presidential address to the Southern Economic Association in 1963 (1979:17–38): "What Should Economists Do?" There he took the view that economists should stop thinking of their subject as being concerned primarily with maximization problems, but rather should regard it as the study of exchange between individuals in a catallaxy. He further called for more attention to be paid to the emergence of the rules of economic exchange as part of a competitive process. In a lecture given in 1976 (1977:82–91), "General Implications of Subjectivism," Buchanan emphasized that the principle of spontaneous order is *the* scientific principle of economics (84). While Buchanan was more prone to engage in game theoretical analysis to illuminate catallactic problems than Austrians, at this point in his career, he was walking with – or perhaps in some sense, even leading – the young Austrians.[10]

Perhaps even more important than the intellectual stimulus such eminent "fellow travelers" provided, they also helped to brace the Austrians with the realization that they were not completely alone or completely on the wrong track in following the Mengerian tradition. Other

[9] Indeed, Wagner's affinity for Mises led him to teach a graduate course in microeconomic theory at Virginia Tech using *Human Action* as one of his texts. This did not win him much approval from his colleagues.

[10] Buchanan's importance in the Austrian revival was neither limited to his written work. After his move to George Mason University in 1983, Buchanan participated in almost ·all the conferences, symposia, and special events sponsored by the Center for Study of Market Processes, often serving as speaker or commentator. In addition, until shortly after he received the Nobel prize in 1986, Buchanan taught virtually all the graduate students who came to study Austrian economics. His influence on that generation of students was immense, both substantively through his own explorations of subjectivism and its relationship to his own work, and symbolically in the luster his presence added to the students' perception of the program.

economists from other traditions were also finding merit in the ideas that formed the basis of their work.

Although the young Austrians were managing to make themselves heard in some important circles outside of their own network, being heard by the "high theorists" of economics was another story. Just as is the case for any heterodox view, publication in the "top" journals remained an elusive prize. An article accepted in the *American Economic Review*, for example, was a real cause for celebration (and not a little envy). Since it was easier to publish criticism of the neoclassical orthodoxy than constructive Austrian theory, it should come as no surprise to an economist that Austrians tended to produce more articles of a critical than a constructive nature in standard journals. This "selection process" in part explains why the young Austrians got the reputation of indulging exclusively in criticism and not offering a constructive alternative. It was also true, however, that constructive alternatives were not always clearly articulated, even within the Austrian circles.

The work of theory building went on nonetheless. Kirzner and Lachmann increasingly were regarded as the intellectual leaders of the new Austrians, and as we will see in chapter 7, the main protagonists in the debate over the nature of the new Austrian paradigm. Yet, increasingly visible at Austrian gatherings, serving as an eminent presence, was the intriguing figure of Friedrich Hayek, a man presumed to have lost interest in economics but whose post-revival noneconomics publications nevertheless had an important impact on how the Austrian paradigm came to be conceptualized.

Hayek and the reconsideration of spontaneous orders

Hayek, as we have seen, produced little writing on formal economics after 1950, when he joined the Committee on Social Thought at the University of Chicago. When he left Chicago in 1962 to accept an appointment at the University of Freiburg, his ostensible purpose was to take up again some of the economic questions he left in the 1940s (1967:251). Yet, as the two volumes of Hayek's collected essays (1967 and 1978a) that he published subsequently attest, his heart was still more in his philosophy and political theory than in his purely economic work. Within those two collections, no more than one-third and one-fourth of the books, respectively, were devoted to economic topics. The 1978 volume contained two important articles in areas for which Hayek had made his reputation in the 1930s, "Three Elucidations of the Ricardo Effect" (165–178) and "Competition as a Discovery Procedure" (179–190), but the other economic essays were by no means the most important contributions of these volumes.

More representative of Hayek's post–London School of Economics interests were *The Sensory Order* (1952), a creative work in psychology that explored how human beings conceptualized the world and were capable of learning;[11] *The Constitution of Liberty* (1960), a work in political philosophy that served as Hayek's statement of classical liberal principles; and *The Counter-Revolution in Science* (1955), a collection of essays on methodology that summarized Hayek's arguments about the misuse of science in studying human action. One might have thought that all Hayek had to contribute to economic debates had been said before 1950, yet, even within the context of Hayek's more philosophical work, he made contributions to the growing articulation of the Austrian paradigm.

In 1973, 1976, and 1979, Hayek published a three-volume treatise, *Law, Legislation and Liberty*. As its subtitle proclaimed, it was intended as "A New Statement of the Liberal Principles of Justice and Political Economy," which, along with his later volume *The Fatal Conceit* (1988), was also Hayek's final answer to socialism. Despite the avowedly political and philosophical focus of this work, it was deeply imbued with Hayek's understanding of an economic order. In fact, his entire conception of a liberal political order was founded on two ideas that he espoused during the socialist calculation debate: that market knowledge is heterogeneous and dispersed, not available apart from the operation of the market process itself (markets are discovery procedures), and that an economic system is best understood as a catallaxy rather than an economy.

Hayek's role in the calculation debate came to be well known by the new Austrians (Vaughn, 1980a), but the full implications of his comments on knowledge were only gradually discovered (Lavoie, 1985a, 1985b) and were understood partly with the aid of Hayek's further comments in *Law, Legislation and Liberty*. In the calculation debate, Hayek focused his attention on criticizing the assumption that economic knowledge was somehow "given," arguing instead that the knowledge that informs economic decision making is discovered through the actual activities of market participants, and what they discover is not abstract knowledge but specific knowledge of "time and place." In *Law, Legislation and Liberty*, however, he introduced another dimension to knowledge that in retrospect helped his case against socialism but also pointed to new features of the market process. This dimension was the "tacit" nature of much knowledge.[12]

[11] *The Sensory Order* was actually first conceived in an essay Hayek wrote in his youth before he decided to study economics. When he once again became interested in issues of mind and knowledge, he updated the research and developed it into a book-length manuscript published in 1952. Undoubtedly, the ideas that he developed in this early work contributed to his criticism of the knowledge assumptions of socialism.

[12] Although Hayek hints at the phenomenon of tacit knowledge during his debate with

Here, building on Polanyi (1958), Hayek argued that much of what we know that is important is knowledge that we either cannot articulate or have not as yet articulated. It is often knowledge of how to do something rather than knowing about something. One knows how to ride a bicycle without knowing all about the physics and mechanics of bicycle riding, for example. For the question of planned economies, the obvious implication is that for many production processes, what leads to success is often not consciously known by those in charge. At one level, this clearly undercuts the engineering model of a production function as something equally available to all producers and argues for the particularized knowledge of production techniques even in a competitive economy. There is no "given" technology, as microeconomics assumes, but only various techniques that may be known imperfectly even to the producers who employ them.

At another level, however, the introduction of tacit knowledge into our consideration of the market economy has even more radical implications. If some market-relevant knowledge is tacit, then the problem that needs to be addressed is how such tacit knowledge can be employed and communicated in a market process. How do we ever learn what the "secret of our success" is if the secret is tacit knowledge? This question points us in the direction of seeing the market process as one of trial and error where successes can only partly be grasped by outsiders and imitations are not perfect replications of the original. Where some knowledge is tacit, heterogeneity of knowledge, of techniques, of production, and of goods for sale must be widespread. Although Hayek himself did not go into detail on the implications of tacit knowledge to economic systems per se, the whole question of the role of knowledge in market economies became a major concern of the new Austrians. In fact, Hayek's work in this area became known as the "knowledge problem," both in writing and in teaching.

The second main idea derived from his economic sensibilities that served as a starting point for *Law, Legislation and Liberty* was the distinction he made between two forms of social arrangements: an organization and an order (1973:chap. 2). As Hayek argued, organizations such as business firms or households can be viewed as having a definite objective to maximize and articulatable criteria for judging success or failure. Mem-

the socialists, and although it is clear that his argument would be much strengthened by an explicit incorporation of tacit knowledge into his critique of socialism, I don't believe Hayek had actually thought of the problem in that connection until he wrote "Competition as a Discovery Procedure." It was clearly the influence of Michael Polanyi and Gilbert Ryle that made him see the missing link in his calculation arguments. Tacit knowledge thereupon became a linchpin of his argument for social evolution in *Law, Legislation and Liberty*. For a contrary view, see Lavoie (1985a) who places tacit knowledge at the center of Hayek's critique of socialism.

bers of organizations are presumed to accept the goals of the organization and to endeavor to achieve them. An order, on the other hand, is simply a system of rules established to enable individuals to achieve their own objectives. There is no objective function to maximize and there are no criteria for judging success or failure apart from the aims and purposes of the participants within the order.

Hayek argued that although all societies are made up of organizations and orders, a liberal polity as a whole had to be conceived as a social order whose sole purpose was to facilitate the achievement of the projects and plans of its citizens. Laws are to be construed as rules of a game whose sole purpose is to create a climate for peaceful, cooperative interaction among all the various actors in the order. There is no way to reconcile "national priorities" with individual liberty since that seems to require a fully shared system of values that can be ranked in an unproblematic way. Hence, in a liberal polity, there are no national objectives, and criteria for social justice that include some end-state pattern of distribution are a "mirage" (1976:62–101). Finally, to Hayek, the welfare state with its reliance on end-state criteria for setting policy and its tacit belief in social justice is a huge category mistake, an attempt to substitute an organization for an order.

There are many subtleties to Hayek's argument and some difficult problems to sort out, none of which we can address here. His political philosophy has generated a voluminous literature that is too extensive even to cite in this context. What is significant for our purposes, however, is that Hayek's model for all social orders as opposed to organizations is the market order. To underscore the significance of his classification, Hayek, inspired by Mises' use of the term "catallactics" to describe the theory of exchange, calls the market order a catallaxy and not an economy (1976:107). An economy suggests the maximization of some objective as one might do when managing a household estate. One could, for instance, imagine a social welfare function that applies to a household in which there is either a single authority figure who makes decisions for the welfare of the whole or in which there is a very strong agreement among the members of the household on the nature of the ends they will pursue. However, in a catallaxy, there is no single benevolent dictator and no one scale of values is being maximized; individuals might be modeled as maximizing their own several interests, but these interests cannot be ranked in any rational order. Hence, there can be no social welfare function[13] because social welfare is a by-product of the rule-following

---

[13] Note the similarity to the Arrow impossibility theorem (Arrow, 1963) and to the problem of cycling in majority rule that is identified in the public choice literature. (Mueller, 1989:63–65).

behavior of individuals as they strive to satisfy their own projects and plans.

In so describing the market order, Hayek was, of course, harkening back to the idea of a spontaneous order that informed Menger's work, as well as to the ideas of the Scottish Enlightenment, a source to which Hayek particularly called attention. In this literature, a spontaneous order was one that had consequences that were mutually beneficial but were nevertheless unplanned by any one person. While Hayek particularly called attention to Adam Ferguson's description of an order as the "result of human action, but not the execution of any human design" (Hayek, 1967:96), the concept was also the heart of Adam Smith's "simple system of natural liberty." Smith argued that in an order in which each person could pursue his own interests only by engaging the interests of others through mutually beneficial trade, each person would be "led by an invisible hand to promote an end which was no part of his intention" (Smith, [1776] 1981:456). The invisible hand was Smith's metaphor for describing the mutually beneficial aspect of trade in an exchange economy that emerged as the unplanned consequence of the prosecution of individual plans.[14] Obviously, the notion of spontaneous orders had been the underlying theme of Hayek's critique of socialism, although it was not until the completion of *Law, Legislation and Liberty* that he clarified the connection between the two.

There are two ways in which we can understand a spontaneous order, reflecting two different ways of conceptualizing the world. First, one can see a spontaneous order as a more or less static system of rules in which people act to achieve their goals. The specific actions they take depend upon their perception of opportunities and their own preferences, but

---

[14] Unfortunately, the metaphor of the invisible hand has been interpreted as a description of some notion of welfare maximization. Indeed, general equilibrium theorists today argue that they are providing a rigorous representation of Adam Smith's claim by showing the very stringent conditions that are necessary for the invisible hand to be beneficial. This work, they claim, points the way, really, to an examination of market failure (Hahn, 1982).

Hayek would object to such a characterization because it implies that we can define what is beneficial apart from the actual trading behavior of individuals faced with real market alternatives. Yet there is no way for an outside observer to know what the actual choice set or the actual knowledge possessed by any economic actor is in order to judge any market arrangement a "failure" as compared to an ideal. Where market "failures" lead to political remedies, moreover, there is no reason to believe that governmental agencies will have any better knowledge than market actors and hence no presumption that such failures could be corrected (see Vaughn, 1987b). On the other hand, Hayek himself can be faulted for being misunderstood (or for being himself unclear) on this issue. By describing the outcome of the market as a system that generates a result in a spontaneous manner that seems as if it were designed by a superior intelligence (Hayek, 1948:86) he does suggest that the system leads to some sort of externally identifiable optimum.

the process for taking these actions depends upon the legal and informal rule structure in which they operate, a rules structure that includes rules of business trading as well as of cultural norms and legal prescriptions. It is in this sense that Hayek thinks of the market – an orderly process of exchange within the context of a set of widely understood rules.

Second, a spontaneous order can be seen as a process of systematic, ordered change in either the formal or informal rule structures by which people attempt to achieve their purposes. In this sense, the spontaneous order is the unplanned and often unconscious changes in rules and institutions that occur as the by-product of purposive actions. Menger's story about the origin of money is the prototypical example of this kind of spontaneous order in economics, the basic structure of which, he argued, could be generalized to explaining the emergence and progress of other kinds of social institutions.

Hayek builds his political theory on this second understanding of spontaneous order. He attempts to discover where the rules of order come from, how they are changed, what function they serve in social intercourse.[15] His theory draws on the eighteenth-century discovery of the "twin concepts of evolution and the spontaneous formation of an order" (Hayek, 1973:23). He develops an evolutionary theory of cultural rules that explains how we might have evolved beneficial rules of social organization despite the limits to our knowledge and rationality. Hayek's theory of cultural evolution has proven to be the most controversial aspect of his work and has drawn criticism from friend and foe alike. Although not all of the critics have fully understood Hayek's theory, it is nevertheless fraught with difficulties and ambiguities that make for fascinating analysis. However, this is not the place to provide a critique of Hayek's theory of social evolution.[16] Instead, here we limit our focus to two important implications of his theory of spontaneous orders.

[15] Hayek's theory of political institutions has often been compared to James Buchanan's. Both see the market as giving rise to a catallaxy rather than an economy, and both understand economic activity to be carried on within the context of a set of rules. Where they differ is in their treatment of the source of rules. Hayek believes there is an intimate connection between the process by which rules emerge in a society and the nature and efficacy of those rules. Buchanan treats the historical origin of rules as irrelevant to his project of describing the conditions under which individuals can be said to have achieved a rational social contract (Buchanan, 1975).

[16] One of the most thorough investigations and critiques of Hayek's theory of the evolution of social rules is found in Vanberg (1986). Here Vanberg argues that while beneficial spontaneous orders are possible within appropriate rules structures, Hayek's account of the emergence of rules fails to supply reasons why benign rules themselves are likely to emerge from an evolutionary process. For a more sympathetic account, see (Boettke, 1990b), where he argues that Hayek's work can best be seen as an attempt to provide a nonrationalist account of how free persons can generate mutually beneficial associations.

First, by examining the emergence, evolution, and knowledge properties of all social institutions, Hayek inadvertently called Austrian attention once again to the nature of market institutions as well. This led some to explore the relationship of Austrian economics to the "new institutional economics" and to examine the role of institutions in the actions of purposeful and planful individuals (Langlois, 1986, 1986b; Boettke, 1989). Not since Menger had the Austrian literature so self-consciously asked questions about the institutional context in which individuals made economic decisions.[17]

Second, Hayek focused on such questions as how did these institutions emerge, how did they come to survive, and what can we know about their function? The evolutionary context in which Hayek placed his analysis of political and social institutions was to spark an interest in the use of evolutionary reasoning to explain economic institutions in particular. As a consequence, although not much evolutionary theory has been produced, several Austrians have at least written about the need for further research in evolutionary economics (Boettke, Horwitz, and Prychitko, 1986; Langlois, 1983; Witt, 1991; Horwitz, 1992). Although progress has been slight so far in both of these areas, there is a strong sense within Austrian circles that these are areas that require investigation. As it will be argued later, these two implications of Hayek's work may turn out to be Hayek's major contributions to Austrian economics (or economics in general), perhaps equaling in importance his identification of competition as rivalry and the knowledge problem in social order.

In sum, Hayek's critique of the knowledge requirements of a centrally planned economy led him to envision the market order as a discovery procedure, a means of inducing individuals to learn more about the opportunities available to them and to create new products and new methods of production. However, his understanding of the market discovery procedure led him to examine the origin of all social institutions from the perspective of the limitations on knowledge that constrain individual choices. This led him to develop an evolutionary theory of social institutions wherein those that survived only did so because they better helped individuals within a society to achieve their goals. However Hayek's theory will ultimately be judged by the continuing debate he has engendered, it is indisputable that his theory of social evolution helped to point Austrian economists toward the study of economic institutions and

---

[17] Ludwig Lachmann's 1971 book, *The Legacy of Max Weber,* was an exception to this rule. It was an attempt to investigate the role of institutions in social order building on Weber's earlier work. It was, however, not an evolutionary account of the origin of institutions but more an analysis of the function of and relationship among the institutions of social order.

evolutionary orders in a systematic way. As we will see in chapter 7, Hayek's theories of limited knowledge and of spontaneous orders also tended to emphasize the case made by Ludwig Lachmann that economics should largely be a study of economic institutions within a nonequilibrium context.

Controversies and deep divisions

The main tenets of Austrian economics as understood by new Austrians in the 1970s – subjectivism, the importance of processes, and methodological individualism – were of such a general nature that it would have been astounding if the attempt to flesh out and draw inferences from these foundational concepts did not lead to a divergence of opinion. As we have seen, the writings of Menger, of Mises, and of Hayek were not so obviously clear and coherent that there could be no disputes about the nature of Austrian economics. And so, disputes did arise, and often they were no more than minor differences of opinion. However, there were two developments in the literature created by the new Austrians that engendered heated and divisive controversy. The first was an innovative rethinking of Austrian methodology that appeared to challenge one of the most deeply felt of all Mises' doctrines. The second was no less than an attempt to systematize all the disparate threads of post-revival Austrianism into a coherent whole. An ambition of both was to move the Austrian program forward into new ground. Both were deeply informed by Hayek's work, both took Lachmann's strictures on subjectivism very seriously, and both served to split the new Austrians into two often acrimonious camps.

Hermeneutics and economic history

One of the most controversial developments in Austrian economics in the 1980s was Don Lavoie's work in methodology. Lavoie's methodological position emerged partly from a belief that Austrian economics had for too long concentrated on pure theory to the exclusion of empirical economics, and partly from the recognition that if Austrian economics was to make an impact on the discovery of new knowledge, it required a research agenda.

Because of Mises' (and Menger's) objections to quantitative economics, the new Austrians tended to be critical of econometrics. Austrians criticized econometrics for a number of reasons: It limited the kinds of questions that could be asked, it relied too much on aggregate data, it often misunderstood its own limitations (Rizzo, 1978). However, Lavoie, as well as his Austrian colleagues at George Mason University, believed it was self-defeating for Austrian economics to remain forever on a plane that was too theoretical (and ironically, too methodological).[18] If the insights of the Austrian tradition were to have positive payoff, they would have to illuminate reality in some powerful way. What was needed, then, was a distinctive Austrian approach to empirical economics, one that was true to Austrian notions of subjectivism and process.

To develop this approach, Lavoie reached back to the original German context of Menger's work and forward to the methodological ideas of Ludwig Lachmann (and by implication, of Max Weber and Alfred Shutz). Out of this, he and his students at George Mason University formed a workshop that groped toward a method of doing "history" that significantly broadened the kinds of arguments that would be considered admissible to explaining some historical event. Taking their cue from Mises' discussions of the relationship between theory and history, they organized an Austrian history workshop to study economic history as empirical economics. In this workshop, empirical economics was not so much a means of "testing" theoretical assumptions as it was a form of interpreting real events in the light of theory. In this view, economic history cum empirical economics is using economic theory to tell a coherent story about the unfolding of some event. True to its subjectivist roots, it is an act of discovering the meaning of the event from the perspective of both the participants in the event and the economic theorist. Good economic history is an interactive process that involves the ideas and perceptions of both the subject and the scientist. To the members of the Austrian history workshop, economic history when well done should not only look at numbers derived from quantitative models, but should also examine written records, oral histories, and data generally found in archives to fully illuminate some event in history. Indeed, this approach elevates the case study over statistical modeling techniques as the appropriate method of tapping into the meaning of historical events to the participants.

In many respects, this view of Austrian economic history is simply a rediscovery of the techniques used by good historians before the onset of cliometrics. For Lavoie, economic history is the interpretation of all of this disparate data from the perspective of the organizing principle of economic theory. Yet, if that is the case, perhaps he has gone too far in disparaging statistical model building in economic research.[19] Lavoie

---

[18] The original impetus to engage in more empirical research came from the Market Process Center founder Richard Fink, who also was one of the critics of the use of conventional equilibrium constructs in Austrian economics (see Cowen and Fink 1985).

[19] Lavoie counters that he only disparages the "exclusivity of mainstream empirical work." Perhaps so, but little work seems to have been done on how to integrate quantitative as well as qualitative sources into Austrian historical research.

would also agree that the techniques of research should be appropriate to the questions being asked. In that case, some questions (how did the price of wheat change as a consequence of the introduction of a new farming technique, or what was the rate of inflation during the interwar period in Germany, or do the jobs lost from reducing trade barriers outnumber the gains?) can only be addressed by using statistical modeling techniques. Here, the meaning to be extracted from the data depends upon the meaning that the economist brings to his definition of variables, but the variables themselves are necessarily quantitative in nature. One might argue that these are not the only relevant questions an economist can ask, or even the most important ones, but they are nevertheless questions for which case studies provide idiosyncratic answers.

Even if one were to take the position that Lavoie and his history workshop have oversold the centrality of case studies and archival research to empirical economics, it still appears that their reintroduction of more traditional historical techniques into the economist's tool box should be uncontroversial in Austrian circles. Certainly, some very good work came out of that workshop (High and Coppin, 1988; Boettke, 1990a). Yet, Lavoie's work on economic history engendered more controversy within Austrian circles than almost anyone else besides Ludwig Lachmann. Many who had otherwise praised his writings on the economics of socialism (1985a) and on national planning (1985b) were appalled by his new emphasis on applied economics, largely because of the context in which he placed it, for Lavoie argued that his approach to doing Austrian economic history was a reflection of a larger methodological program not generally associated with Austrian economics: from the Continental philosophy of hermeneutics.[20]

Hermeneutics originally was a technique of biblical exegesis, the discovery of meaning in an obscure and problematic text. Its philosophical roots were in Continental philosophy and grew out of the phenomenology of Husserl, and the philosophies of Dilthy, Heidegger and, most recently, Gadamer, who were endeavoring to find a way to understand the obscure and problematic text of human interaction.[21] (Alfred Schutz and Max Weber, two sociologists for whom Mises had great respect, were also influenced by this tradition.) Phenomenology was

---

[20] For articles favoring the hermeneutical approach to economic inquiry, see (Johnson, 1990; Palmer, 1987; Ebeling, 1986; Lavoie, 1986b, 1987, 1990a, 1990b). For arguments critical of the adoption of hermeneutics as the methodology of Austrian economics, see (Smith, 1990; Rothbard, 1989; Hoppe, 1989). The following account of the hermeneutics of Austrian economics is a distillation from Lavoie, Palmer, and Johnson. It should also be pointed out that Lachmann referred on many occasions to the "Austrian hermeneutic," and was the inspiration for Lavoie's original work.

[21] The interpretation of hermeneutics that places Husserl in the same tradition with Heidegger and Gadamer is taken from (Johnson, 1990:176–177).

launched as a challenge to the pretensions of modern science with its claim to having a monopoly on objective knowledge. It began with Husserl's rejection of the subjective/objective duality of Descartes where one could only "know" one's internal subjective state. Phenomenology was conceived as a way of confronting reality directly; one accepts reality as given (much as the text of a book is given) and concentrates on how to understand that reality.

In this tradition, "understanding" (what Weber called *verstehen*) is a function of our interpretative context, the background that we bring to our perception of reality. Contrary to what many critics claim, however, understanding does not proceed from a purely idiosyncratic, personally subjective view of the world. Our individual contexts are part of a shared context of meaning derived from language, culture, and shared experiences. In this view, we can understand one another because we share the same context. This view of understanding, then, is fundamentally historical in the sense that our context comes out of a shared history, as it were, but a history modified by personal experience and expectations. Hence, the hermeneutical tradition appears to encompass those aspects of time and subjectivity that are central to Austrian claims for uniqueness. People not only understand each other because of their mutual context; the procedures of scientists are also affected by their contexts. Austrians had long argued that the social sciences were different from the natural sciences because humans have a source of information about each other that they do not have about nonhuman entities. But of what is that information composed? Mises, taking a Kantian perspective, had argued that social scientists could have a priori knowledge of human action because of the way in which our brains are structured. Lavoie and the Austrian hermeneuticists argue instead that our scientific "understanding" of human action derives from the linguistic and experiential culture common to both subject and observer. We can speak of human purposes, for example, because we have a shared linguistic meaning of the term that describes our common "life world."

Many were initially suspicious of "Austrian" hermeneutics. To some, it smacked too much of postmodern deconstructionism, with its apparent conclusion that there is no truth, there are no unambiguous meanings to events, and since everything depends upon the perspective of the observer, anything goes. Clearly, this is not an idle worry. If we are all prisoners of our context, how are we ever able to resolve disputes of the truth of any phenomenon? As for historical interpretation, whose interpretation counts and how do we know it counts? And insofar as our current beliefs and future actions depend upon our notions of truth, is not the implication that we cannot know the truth a priori or even come to an unproblematic empirical account of the truth devastating to our ability to improve our knowledge? Indeed, what does knowledge mean in this context? Hermeneutics seems to deny any privileging of one context over another.

The hermeneuticists countered that recognizing the contextual nature of our knowledge does not mean that "anything goes" at all. Hermeneutics is a philosophy of how to study reality, not a denial of the reality that is the subject of study (Johnson, 1990:188). We simply must begin by recognizing that all facts are, as Hayek argued in several places, theory-laden. Facts, at least in the social sciences, do not exist apart from the theories that people bring to interpret them. Yet, objectively, the world exists and events happen. Hermeneutics is a philosophy of how one chooses among theories to explain real world events, recognizing that there is no way to jump out of human contextual understanding to settle which theory is the most truthful. However, this does not mean "anything goes."

Within any context, there are widely shared views as to what are convincing arguments for or against some explanation of reality despite the fact that the criteria for better or worse are not objectively given to us (McCloskey, 1985). It is simply the case that within particular communities, there are recognized standards of what kinds of arguments are more convincing than others. This is especially true in scientific communities where the rules of evidence are particularly stringent (although not identical to the rules laymen think of as the "scientific method"). All hermeneutics argues is that no one can claim to have a pipeline to the truth that trumps all other arguments; there is no "archimedean point" outside of human understanding against which all other arguments are to be judged. Especially in social science, there are no "crucial experiments" to unequivocally separate truth from falsehood since the initial conditions, design, and results of any experiment are open to dispute.

In science, as in all of human efforts to know, it is the dispute itself that is the method of arriving at a consensus about the "truth," albeit a provisional one. This further implies that any search for truth is of necessity a community endeavor, as Kuhn and Lakatos had already argued. Hence, Lavoie's brand of hermeneutics at a minimum can be viewed as part of the ongoing discussion of the sociology and actual practice of scientific communities. The history workshop can further be viewed as a plea to widen the standards for convincing arguments within the economic community.

While asserting the importance of scientific communities in theory development is largely uncontroversial, the argument that hermeneutics is not purely relativist may not be entirely convincing. The whole hermeneutics tradition might be regarded as a slippery slope to the negation of science itself. It seems particularly radical in light of Menger's and Mises' emphasis on the dichotomy between true theory and application to reality. A hermeneuticist must deny that theory can be discovered from pure a priori principles spun out of the logic of action. One important implication of Lavoie's hermeneutics seems to be that theory must be informed by empirical reality, at the very least the reality filtered through the theorist's context. Theory and history then become a two-way interaction between subject and social scientist where no sharp a priori isolation is possible. This is a direct denial of one of the cornerstones of Mises' methodology and one that cries out for further elaboration.

If theories are all contextual in nature, how do we choose theories across differing communities? Even more crucial, is there some universal substance to human nature that should transcend contexts, or is human nature itself an illusory concept? Specifically, is the action axiom itself contextual? If so, that certainly would seem to deny the cornerstone of all economic theory. On the other hand, Mises had been uncompromisingly antipositivist and had praised Max Weber and the method of "understanding." On these grounds, Lavoie claims he is developing the essential part of Mises' methodology while eliminating the inconsistencies. For Lavoie, the essence of Mises' methodology is his claim that economics aims at understanding and not at prediction.

Another apparent implication of hermeneutics is also troubling. If not only our theory and our explanations of events derive from our shared life world with our subjects, but if the subjects themselves develop their own values and understanding of events from their context, what is the status of the individual in a hermeneutical economics? Can we still speak of individuals who choose independently of one another and act unambiguously to improve their situations? If our meanings and our values are derived from our contexts, how do individuals come to differ in their understanding and their choices? Yet, again, it seems patently obvious that individuals do differ on all dimensions. What is the relationship between man the social being and man the individual chooser in hermeneutic theory?

The hermeneuticists answer that economic theory is not best thought of as the theory of Robinson Crusoe maximizing in splendid isolation. It is a theory of exchange and interaction among individuals in a cooperative endeavor.[22] Hermeneutical theory does not deny the crucial role of

---

[22] We recall that James Buchanan made exactly the same point in *What Should Economists Do?* (1979). Here he argued that the subject matter of economics should be "the propensity to truck, barter and exchange one thing for another," which Adam Smith had identified two centuries earlier, and that the adoption of a "sophisticated catallac-

individuals in economic theory; individuals still confront obstacles, still compete with one another and still make choices. Rather than banishing the valuing, planning, choosing individual from economics, hermeneutics attempts to place him or her within an interactive process, a process that involves cooperation as much as competition. In principle, it seems no violation of individualism to agree that much of what we know and think is influenced by our contexts, yet more work needs to be done to develop a useful theory of the relationship between the acting individual and his social and economic context.

The challenge of hermeneutics seems to bring us back once again to Hayek's concern with knowledge and institutions. Given the huge amounts of tacit knowledge and institutional knowledge that is characteristic of a market order, how do individuals learn and change their minds? To be true to the Austrian tradition, such an inquiry should not deny the existential reality of individuals, but simply attempt a richer explanation of individual behavior than can be achieved with economists' usual assumption of given preference function and either no, adaptive, or rational expectations.

Hermeneutics is still considered heresy by many Austrians. Some object on philosophical grounds that deny the applicability of Continental philosophy to the Austrian tradition. Others decry the loss of the possibility of theoretical certainty that hermeneutical economics engenders. Still others, I suspect, are most worried that hermeneutics makes the old arguments for the unchallenged supremacy of the free market open to challenge. If our theory is not a priori certain; if people's values, beliefs, and knowledge are contingent and contextual; if even the theorist is ultimately limited by her context – can we still claim to be certain that the free market bestows all those benefits that Mises described from his utilitarian viewpoint? For all these reasons, hermeneutics had divided the contemporary Austrian community.

The economics of time and ignorance

Controversy also erupted in Austrian circles from another quarter. The 1980s was witness to the publication of a bold attempt to develop a comprehensive restatement of the Austrian paradigm, written by two veterans of South Royalton and young faculty members at New York University, Gerald O'Driscoll and Mario Rizzo. Originally conceived as a

tics" rather than a theory of resource allocation was the appropriate approach to the discipline, the approach of Archbishop Whately, H. D. Macleod, Latham Perry, and Alfred Ammon. Lavoie would argue that hermeneutics is simply trying to provide a philosophical justification for this approach to economics.

paper to "explain" the Austrian outlook to non-Austrians,[23] their 1985 book, *The Economics of Time and Ignorance,* emerged over a several-year gestation period as a creative attempt to develop an Austrian economics that was consistent with several uniquely Austrian propositions and was a genuine alternative to neoclassical economics.

The Economics of Time and Ignorance was a major contribution to the burgeoning Austrian literature, indeed, a watershed event in the history of the Austrian revival. For the first time in print, all of the controversies and disparate observations and theoretical propositions of latter-day Austrians were examined critically in order to try to glean from them a distinctive Austrian paradigm. The authors explored the philosophical and epistemological foundations of Austrian economics, examined the coherence of many of the theoretical claims made by Austrian economists and set the ideas they examined within the context of contemporary economic theory to a degree that had not been attempted by any Austrians since Hayek. The consequence was that O'Driscoll and Rizzo managed to define the distinctive Austrian paradigm in a way that took account of many diverse strands in the Austrian literature. Although many of their propositions were the subject of controversy, after 1985, it would be impossible to think of Austrian economics as anything but the economics of time and ignorance.

From the beginning of the Austrian revival, Austrians had consistently referred to their brand of economics as "subjectivism," sometimes modified as "thoroughgoing," sometimes as "radical" subjectivism. Consequently, O'Driscoll and Rizzo begin with an explanation of what Austrians mean by subjectivism. Austrian subjectivism is "dynamic subjectivism," whereas neoclassical economics subscribes to "static subjectivism." Once again addressing the limitations of determinism in human science that had been raised by Mises and carried on by Hayek, they argued that the static subjectivism of neoclassical economics is limited to recognizing the subjectivity of preferences, and it models choice simply as constrained maximization. Hence, the outcomes of choice are fully determined within the assumptions of the models. Dynamic subjectivism on the other hand, recognizes the creativity and nondeterminate nature of human

---

[23] O'Driscoll and Rizzo's initial paper, "What Is Austrian economics?" was presented at the 1980 meetings of the American Economic Association in Denver, Colorado, in a session on Austrian economics. It was obvious from this session that interest in (or curiosity about) Austrian economics was growing in the profession at large. The audience at this session was packed with people who had come to listen and ask questions. It is undoubtedly true that some of the discussion generated at that session led O'Driscoll and Rizzo to revise and expand their paper into book form. During the years it took them to complete their project, not only the title changed, but so did their perception about what was important and coherent in the Austrian tradition.

choice (30). It was dynamic subjectivism that could account for the open-endedness of economic processes. The rest of the book is an unfolding of the meaning and assumptions of dynamic subjectivism.

Their notion of dynamic subjectivism leads them to explore the meaning of time in human action, building on Mises' abbreviated exploration of time in *Human Action* and on Mises' own inspiration here, Henri Bergson. Once again contrasting Austrian economics to neoclassical economics, they introduce the distinction between "Newtonian time," the conceptualization of time characteristic of neoclassical economics in which outcomes are completely determined by initial conditions and hence time is reduced more to space than sequence and "real time," which is unidirectional and unrepeatable and in which unpredictable change takes place. Real time is the time of human beings in which the world changes as a consequences of human action and learning takes place.

Unlike Mises, O'Driscoll and Rizzo link time inexorably to learning and to the ignorance that is the implication of changes in knowledge. Changes in knowledge are the consequence of the human experience of time, and any theory of economic processes that take place in time must be a theory of learning. Building on Hayek, they considerably broaden the analysis of knowledge in economics, drawing attention to its context, its acquisition, its place in a market economy, and its multifaceted nature (35–44). As Hayek had taught, knowledge can take many forms. For the analysis of market processes, it is important to emphasize a wide variety of characteristics of knowledge: "knowledge is (1) private, (2) empirical, (3) often tacit, (4) not all gained through price signals, and (5) often the source of surprise" (102). It is, however, never deterministic since we cannot know in advance what it is we will learn from any new experience.

Changes in knowledge through time also contribute to the fundamental problem that Mises identified. The future is always uncertain and action is always speculation. Familiar institutions and entrepreneurship reduce the discoordination that results from incomplete knowledge and uncertainty, but the discoordination can never be totally eradicated. There will always be unintended consequences to human action. Hence, O'Driscoll and Rizzo argue, the economic system is not usefully thought of as one that settles down to an equilibrium position. Indeed, market activity can be "made intelligible as a process of attempting to correct errors and coordinate behavior," but "there is no stable endpoint toward which the process must lead, nor a single path that it must follow. . . . Thus we have a process of evolution without traditional equilibria" (5).

The authors draw a number of implications about the nature of market processes from the structure of assumptions and observations about the nature of reality with which they start. Some of these implications are familiar, some not so familiar. For instance, they examine the competitive process from the perspective of the kinds of knowledge that people hold. They argue that because knowledge is often private there are no single unique solutions to individual economic problems and no outside parties can judge the "efficiency" of an action (103). Tacit knowledge implies that an observer may not be able to discern the reasons for behavior and actors themselves may not be able fully to report the reasons for their conduct to outsiders (105). Hence, it may not be possible ever to replicate the market actions of others. Similarly, the existence of private and tacit knowledge implies that nonprice signals can contain important market information (106).

All of these implications further suggest that one cannot use external end-state standards for judging market outcomes (103–109) and specific controls may interfere with unappreciated knowledge flows in markets (117). As far as individual action is concerned, they emphasize that the uncertainties people face and the pervasiveness of unintended consequences to human action explain in large measure the value of following rules rather than attempting to maximize utility at every turn.

The book is replete with fascinating insights and novel ways of tying the Austrian concerns to developments in other literatures.[24] Further, they conclude by enumerating some unanswered questions that require investigation from the Austrian perspective they present: questions of law and economics (232), money as evolved institutions (233), and nonprice information structures (234). Many of their specific deductions and suggestions could well be challenged by other Austrians, but the one area that engendered the most heated response was their attempt to develop a new definition of equilibrium that would be applicable to the kind of social world about which they were theorizing.

Where the new Austrians had almost without discussion begun employing Hayek's definition of equilibrium as "plan coordination," O'Driscoll and Rizzo objected that plan coordination still implied the kind of unachievable end-state determinateness that Austrians objected to in more conventional general equilibrium terms. What was needed was a notion of equilibrium that described an orderly process that still permitted the emergence of unexpected or undetermined behavior. Their candidate was pattern coordination, a construct that required only that typical features of human behavior such as ongoing rules or institutions

---

[24] Specifically, O'Driscoll and Rizzo show the links between Austrian views and the post-Keynesian view of time (9), they endorse fully Nelson and Winter's evolutionary approach to analyzing firm behavior (124–125), and they show the affinity of an Austrian theory of monopoly to the question of property rights (153–155).

be predictable and coordinated while unpredictable actions could occur within these regularities (85–88).

Pattern coordination (which we will turn to in greater detail in the last chapter of this book) was O'Driscoll and Rizzo's attempt to deal with an economy that had, as they described it, "no stable endpoint toward which the process must lead, nor a single path that it must follow" (5). By so characterizing the Austrian vision of the market process, O'Driscoll and Rizzo were taking sides in a debate among new Austrians about the theoretical implications of Austrian concerns with subjectivism, market process, and methodological individuals, the hallmarks of Austrian economics Lachmann had identified at South Royalton. By calling their book *The Economics of Time and Ignorance,* they were distilling the essential features of Lachmann's description and using them as the starting point for a complete revision of the Austrian conception of economic order. Although all Austrians agreed in principle that economics should not abstract from either real time or ignorance, the precise way in which either time or ignorance could be incorporated into an equilibrium theory of markets was a topic of debate.

The debate had been taking place sub rosa almost from the beginning of the revival. It certainly reared its head in the early days of the Austrian seminar that began at New York University in 1975 (Lavoie, 1978:2).[25] While it was carried on more or less as a side issue for subsequent years, the publication of *The Economics of Time and Ignorance* brought it to the fore with a vengeance. Almost simultaneous with the book's publication, there appeared side by side reviews of the book by the two main protagonists to the debate, Kirzner and Lachmann, in the journal *Market Process.*

Kirzner began his review with two paragraphs of extravagant praise of the book, calling it a "courageous, and in many respects a brilliant attempt by two distinguished Austrian scholars to re-examine the foundation of Austrian Economics" (1985b:1). The laudatory tone immediately evaporated in his even more vehement rejection of O'Driscoll and Rizzo's criticism of plan coordination as the method of equilibrium analysis. Kirzner accused them of rendering "invalid any postulation of processes of systematic market coordination that refer to the meshing of specific

[25] "Until recently Austrian economics had often matured independently in the minds of isolated readers, taking on different shades of emphasis and interpretation that had not had much chance for confrontation in the fruitful atmosphere of scientific criticism. It was in the AES [Austrian Economics Seminar] at New York University that the Austrian spectrum was revealed and the lines of disagreement drawn. Rothbard and others attacked what has affectionately come to be known as 'Lachmannia,' an allegedly nihilistic tendency associated with Keynes and Shackle. On the other hand, Lachmann and others attacked what they perceived as latent 'Ricardianism,' a mechanistic tendency allegedly implicit in some of the Austrian literature." Lavoie reporting on the first year of the AES in the *Austrian Economics Newsletter,* 1978.

activities" (4). He instead advocated a "middle-of-the road" position that postulated such an equilibrium but realized it would never in practice be attainable.[26] Lachmann, on the other hand, praised the authors for breaking new ground and only criticized them for perhaps conceding too much to predictive science by proposing that a construct such as pattern prediction might be useful in actual prediction (1985:17). Thus, Kirzner criticized them sharply for being too extreme in their willingness to abandon traditional equilibrium constructs and Lachmann gently chided them for failing to be extreme enough.

These two book reviews captured the division of opinion about the whole question of the relationship of Austrian economics to mainstream modes of reasoning. One side seemed to be suggesting that Austrian economics is simply a different set of questions (about economics processes and the limits to knowledge) that can be posed within the conventional neoclassical framework of equilibrium analysis, and on occasion answered with the aid of conventional tools (graphical analysis and/or mathematical symbols). The other side seemed to believe that the set of assumptions about reality and the set of questions Austrians address are so different that they must somehow transcend a typical neoclassical framework of analysis. The debate reflected the whole post-revival problem in a nutshell. What is Austrian economics? Is it a supplement to neoclassical economics or is it an alternative economic paradigm? Is it part of ordinary science or is it truly extraordinary science?

This debate was played out in several arenas and among a great variety of participants. The major protagonists were not surprisingly the authors of the simultaneous book reviews, two of the major figures from the South Royalton conference, and O'Driscoll and Rizzo's two senior colleagues at New York University: Israel Kirzner and Ludwig Lachmann. These two men, long-time correspondents and eventually colleagues for over a decade, epitomized a sharp conflict within the American Austrian movement, a conflict that involved one's very conceptualization of the nature of a market order. What makes this debate so important is that both claimed allegiance to Menger, Mises, and Hayek, and both shared many judgments about the importance and efficacy of the market process, yet they came to very different conclusions about the nature and future directions of Austrian economics. Only by examining their arguments can we understand the dilemma facing Austrian economists today.

[26] This was essentially the position advocated by Roger Garrison (1982). Recently, Kirzner (1992:3–4) reasserted this position again.

CHAPTER 7

Market process: the problem of order in Austrian economics

During the period from 1974 to 1986, Israel Kirzner and Ludwig Lachmann were the acknowledged leaders of the new Austrian economics in America. They had been instrumental in sparking the Austrian revival, and they were the inspiration for most of the intellectual work that was done during those years.[1] Both in the Ph.D. program and through the program of visiting appointments that Kirzner arranged at New York University, together Kirzner and Lachmann trained (and/or influenced) almost all of the younger economists who were to become identified with Austrian economics in some formal way. The New York University seminar and visiting program created an intellectual network of people who increasingly came to represent Austrian economics to the profession.[2]

During their entire professional association, Kirzner and Lachmann continually engaged in a friendly and deeply respectful rivalry about the nature and implications of Austrian economics. Although rarely stated as such in their published work, it is clear both from their writings and their exchanges at conferences during this time that their arguments were often responses to issues and ideas proposed by the other. While they agreed on many specific issues, they differed most emphatically about the degree to which Austrian economics could be made consistent with neoclassical orthodoxy. Kirzner's approach was to incorporate Austrian

---

[1] Rothbard participated in the building of the new Austrian community for several years after South Royalton, but increasingly, the difference between his project of defending his vision of Mises at all costs and the more open inquiry of those surrounding Kirzner and Lachmann led him to go off on his own. Rothbard was instrumental in founding the Ludwig von Mises Institute and the *Review of Austrian Economics,* which he edits, and is "dean" of the recently begun summer program for interested undergraduate students he calls Mises University held at Stanford University. From his base at the University of Nevada at Las Vegas, he continues to espouse his brand of Austrian economics supported by dedicated followers. However, he and his group find little to admire in the new Austrian economics I describe in these pages, insisting instead that Mises, or rather Rothbard's interpretation of Mises is, if not the last word, surely close to the last word on economic theory. Rothbard does not accept the description of Austrian economics as the economics of time and ignorance and criticizes those who suggest there may be theoretical problems in the Misesian oeuvre.

[2] In fact, either graduate training at New York University or participation in the visiting program there virtually became a defining characteristic of a new Austrian economist in the 1980s.

insights within the context of the larger neoclassical paradigm whereas Lachmann was more inclined to jettison most of the orthodoxy as excess baggage in his search for a more fruitful way to theorize about social reality. The specific debate between them, however, focused on questions of the nature and role of equilibrium analysis in economics. This debate, largely dormant since Lachmann's death in 1990, split the new Austrians into two camps that are still at odds with each other. One can only understand the current status and possible future directions of modern Austrian economics through an examination of the issues raised in this decade-long debate.

Kirzner on entrepreneurship and equilibrating processes

Although Kirzner has been a vocal critic of neoclassical orthodoxy all of his professional life, his criticisms have been more in the nature of family feuds than of all-out warfare. His stated view is that neoclassical economics started off on the right track during the marginal revolution when it explained price as the consequence of the subjective valuations of individual actors, rather than as the product of some objective criteria. It took an unfortunate turn in the middle of the twentieth century, however, when a growing preoccupation with an excessive formalism in theoretical constructs caused neoclassical economics to lose sight of its subjectivist roots. As a result, according to Kirzner, neoclassical economics developed an "excessive preoccupation with the conditions of equilibrium"[3] and thereby limited itself to the description of static states. Echoing the attitude of Carl Menger, Kirzner argues that equilibrium prices, although important, are merely epiphenomena to the real meat of economic theory, market processes (1973:6).

But how is one to theorize about a market process? For Kirzner, this means providing an explanation of how real markets can approach equilibrium. The static equilibrium theories of conventional economics with their presumptions of homogeneous knowledge and maximizing behavior can only tell us what equilibrium is implied by a set of parameters: They can never explain how partially ignorant maximizing agents act to bring about an equilibrium.[4] For that one needs a theory of a prime mover in markets, which to Kirzner means a theory of entrepreneurship.

[3] This is a paraphrase of Hayek's assessment of his opponents errors during the socialist calculation debate in the 1930s and 1940s (1948:188). It became a common Austrian criticism of neoclassical economics.

[4] Walras's auctioneer was a recognition of the importance of incorporating some process to achieve equilibrium to avoid the problem of false trading. Without some process, a system can only be thought to be instantaneously equilibrated by some omniscient being who simultaneously solves all the equations. Yet the whole problem of economics

Entrepreneurship as alertness

As we have seen, Kirzner first introduced his theory of the entrepreneur in his 1973 book, *Competition and Entrepreneurship*, in which he laid out a theoretical structure that had two purposes: to provide a systematic exposition of what he considered to be the core insights of Austrian economics and to do so in a way that would communicate with neoclassical economists. In the course of almost twenty years of subsequent explanation and clarification, Kirzner's original structure has remained essentially unchanged. One can regard all of Kirzner's work on entrepreneurship after 1973 as so many elaborations of his pathbreaking book.

To Kirzner, entrepreneurship is a particular kind of action that is distinct from maximizing behavior and without which a market process would be unexplainable. Economists generally model human action as the maximization of utility subject to constraints, a form of behavior Kirzner calls "Robbinsian maximizing" after Lionel Robbins, who defined economics as the rational allocation of scarce means among competing and unlimited ends (Robbins, [1932] 1962).[5] This definition, while useful, is incomplete. Pure "Robbinsian maximizers" can only operate within a known means–ends framework. They can never be the source of changes in the means–ends framework – a source of novelty in the economic system. In fact, they could never even be understood to bring about a general equilibrium since all they could do is to operate within the context of what they know. How would any simple "Robbinsian maximizer" come to recognize that price differentials exist? For this, Kirzner argues, one needs to invoke a kind of behavior that is not strictly maximizing yet is purposeful, motivated by the chance for gain and yet is not simply reactive to a given means–ends framework. In short, economics needs a theory of entrepreneurial action (1973:32–34).

Entrepreneurs to Kirzner are the embodiment of a quality he refers to as "alertness" (1973:35). They notice opportunities for profit that others have missed, and through their alertness to profit opportunities, they redefine the means–ends framework.

It is this feature of entrepreneurship that accounts for the orderly, equilibrating market process: entrepreneurs notice opportunities for

is how can partly ignorant individuals interact in an orderly fashion without an omniscient director? This, of course, was Hayek's main point in the calculation debate.

[5] Ironically, when Robbins wrote *The Nature and Significance of Economic Science*, he was attempting to bring Austrian insights to English economics. Robbins had traveled to Austria where he both met with faculty members at the University of Vienna and also participated in Mises' private seminar. He was a great admirer of Mises and also was instrumental in bringing Hayek to London.

profit that others miss. These profit opportunities are there for the taking, but they are not equally obvious to every purposeful human actor. In fact, entrepreneurship is only understandable as the differential perception of past error, past failure on the part of Robbinsian maximizers to recognize that an opportunity for profit is available (1973:67). Such opportunities present themselves in the form of price discrepancies between purchase price and sales price from which the entrepreneur can profit. Hence, in Kirzner's system, the entrepreneur functions as an arbitrageur, buying cheap and selling dear. As an unintended consequence of his exploiting his profit opportunity, he brings the market closer to equilibrium (1973:73).

Despite the fact that he speaks of "the entrepreneur," Kirzner is clear that he is describing a function rather than a kind of person, just as labor and capital are themselves functions in economic theory. That is, entrepreneurship represents a kind of behavior that is present in all human action (1973:31), and it provides an explanation for a source of income: Labor receives wages, capitalists receive interest, and entrepreneurs receive profit (48). However, although entrepreneurship is a function in this sense, it cannot strictly be said to be a factor of production that earns a "return." Unlike other factors of production, it cannot be invested in, searched for, or calculated within a production plan, nor does it have a price. Entrepreneurship is pure, unplanned, and unplannable alertness to opportunities that cannot be predicted in advance, cannot be hired and deployed by another, or invested in. And although it might make sense to theorize about uniform rates of return to capital investment, there is no sense in which a uniform rate of profit in equilibrium has meaning.[6]

In Kirzner's system, profit is a strictly disequilibrium phenomenon that disappears in equilibrium (7). Profit arises out of the initial exploitation of an opportunity. Once the opportunity is exploited, all subsequent efforts devoted to that opportunity, such as repeated exploitation or

---

[6] Kirzner also argues that since entrepreneurship is a pure function, entrepreneurs qua entrepreneurs need own no other resources in order to make profits. In the simple one-period case, we can imagine them buying low and selling high simultaneously, receiving their profit for no investment at all in either material resources or time. Of course, the one-period case is a fiction, but even where time elapses between purchase and sale, entrepreneurs can borrow capital and pay the interest payment out of their earnings without owning any capital themselves. Even where they own capital, one should think of them lending themselves capital as distinct from receiving entrepreneurial profit for their pure alertness. This was a direct rebuttal of the position Murray Rothbard takes in *Man, Economy and State* (1962b:chap. 8), where the analysis centers on capitalist-entrepreneurs. One might characterize the difference between the two conceptions of entrepreneurs as the difference between an abstraction (Kirzner) and an ideal type (Rothbard).

imitation by others, are simply acts of calculation on the basis of given information.

If entrepreneurship cannot be planned or predicted, does this mean that it is the result of pure luck? Kirzner argues no (1979:155). Although entrepreneurship is serendipitous discovery, it is not luck because some people are more alert than others and/or condition themselves to being in a state of alertness. People are alert in the sense that they tend to notice what is in their interests. However, since interests and particularized knowledge differ, people will notice different profit opportunities. Hence, although one cannot predict what any one or any group of people may notice, one can predict that "given the right institutions, opportunities will be noticed" (1979:170).

Interestingly, Kirzner does not in these early essays consider the possibility that entrepreneurs could be incorrect in their hunches. Error only enters Kirzner's system as the failure to notice an opportunity that is available (1979:130), not through actions based on faulty perceptions. Hence, it seems that it is impossible in Kirzner's system for an entrepreneur to be destabilizing.[7]

Kirzner on Schumpeter

Obviously, Kirzner's system differs markedly from Joseph Schumpeter's view of the entrepreneurial process, a difference Kirzner himself emphasizes (1973:7). Schumpeter was an Austrian by birth and learned his economics in Vienna, but he soon abandoned Menger and adopted a Walrasian understanding of economic order. This is evident in his early attempt to explain the capitalist process in *The Economics of Development* ([1934] 1961), where he described the entrepreneur as the disrupter of existing equilibrium. Here, the norm was a Walrasian general equilibrium position in which all markets clear. It was entrepreneurial innovation that accounted for change in an otherwise featureless repetition of economic equilibria. Entrepreneurs destroyed old patterns of behavior as they introduced their creations into the system ([1934] 1961:92). Hence, entrepreneurship was inherently innovative and therefore destabilizing (although ultimately beneficial and responsible for economics growth) in Schumpeter's view.

---

[7] Given Kirzner's definition of entrepreneurship and entrepreneurial error, the stabilizing function of entrepreneurs in Kirzner's system is definitional. Although this definition makes his system tautologically complete, it does not help us to understand the kinds of mistaken perceptions and evaluations that cause so many business enterprises to make losses or to fail every year. We will return to this point later.

It was exactly this view of the economy that Kirzner was determined to oppose with his theory of entrepreneurship. Where Schumpeter saw entrepreneurs as creators and innovators, Kirzner saw them as discovers of that which was already present to be noticed. Entrepreneurs do not destroy old equilibrium patterns nor do they create opportunities in Kirzner's system, they take advantage of existing discontinuities to bring the system closer to the true equilibrium that reflects people's preferences and opportunities (1973:72–73). Although this might seem a semantic quibble to some, for Kirzner the differing implications of the two views of entrepreneurship are significant.

At least according to Kirzner, Schumpeter's view seems to imply that an economy can function very nicely without entrepreneurs: that given any set of parameters, central planners can eventually arrive at equilibrium prices and thereby plan and control an economy. In Kirzner's view, the economy is never actually in equilibrium because there are always profit opportunities inherent in *somebody's* data that could be exploited. Indeed, without the entrepreneur, an economy would always be worse off than it could be even within the framework of the existing opportunities. Prices would be in perpetual disequilibrium without entrepreneurs to set them right. In this way, Kirzner's response to Schumpeter was another round in the economic calculation debate that had been fought thirty years before Kirzner wrote (1979:118–119).

Seen in this light, one can understand Kirzner's insistence that the entrepreneur creates nothing ex nihilo. If the entrepreneurial role were to be considered the creation of wealth ex nihilo, the implications might be drawn that an economy could function efficiently at any given level of wealth without entrepreneurs. On the other hand, if one sees the economic problem as one of coordinating existing information as well as arriving at uniform market prices, then entrepreneurship is the means of uncovering and eradicating differences in information within the system. Entrepreneurs then become guarantors of coordination rather than disrupters of economic life.[8]

---

[8] Although Schumpeter's version of entrepreneurship still seems to dominate Kirzner's, there is a sense in which Kirzner has the stronger case, especially when it is examined against the backdrop of central planning. Schumpeter's version would hold "as a matter of blueprint logic" that once equilibrium prices were arrived at by the central planners, they could be repeated ad infinitum without any loss of efficiency, albeit without economic growth either. In Kirzner's story, however, the central planners could never arrive at those equilibrium prices in the first place. The only way to approach an equilibrium is through the actions of alert entrepreneurs who "notice what is in their interests to notice" and who can profit from exploiting those interests. Central planning will have no profits and no room for entrepreneurs; hence, prices will always reflect incomplete information. Even if one somehow were able to start from what appears to be an equilibrium, however, because entrepreneurs are alert, they cannot

Kirzner's insistence on the coordinating nature of entrepreneurship is logically coherent within a timeless, static context, but it is not clear that the logic also applies to the activities of the entrepreneur in real time.

Entrepreneurship and time

Although Kirzner's obvious differences with Schumpeter's version of entrepreneurship are not surprising, his differences from his teacher, Mises, are another story. Mises, as we saw in earlier chapters, viewed the entrepreneurial function as dealing with uncertainty – "acting man in regard to the changes occurring in the data of the market" (1963:254) – and profit the reward for successfully dealing with uncertainty. The future is always uncertain, and all action takes time. Hence every entrepreneur must be a speculator. "His success or failure depends on the correctness of his anticipations of uncertain events" (1963:291). Although Kirzner never denies the fact that the world is uncertain, it is clearly not emphasized in his early works on entrepreneurship. Indeed, despite Kirzner's frequent reminders that entrepreneurs operate in time, the argument of *Competition and Entrepreneurship* is fully worked out on the assumption of a one-period world. Kirzner argues that the single-period model is perfectly generalizable to entrepreneurship through time, an argument that is by no means unchallenged.

Kirzner first addressed the issue of uncertainty and entrepreneurship in 1981[9] in a paper in which he examined to what degree his theory of entrepreneurial alertness differs from Mises' emphasis on uncertainty bearing. He argues that his understanding of entrepreneurship as alertness to opportunities for arbitrage is fully compatible with the problem of uncertainty. Although entrepreneurial activity is indeed speculative, as Mises argued, "far from being numbed by the inescapable uncertainty of our world, men act upon their judgments of what opportunities have been left unexploited by others" (1982:141).

Entrepreneurship is based on discovering error, but we can distinguish two meanings of entrepreneurship. The first is "selecting the means–ends framework." Because of the uncertainty of the "human predicament," one cannot be sure of the relevant framework for calculating, but the

help but notice ways to improve the coordination of the system, and the central plan will become less and less relevant.

[9] The occasion for the presentation was a conference Kirzner organized for Liberty Fund to honor Ludwig von Mises' one-hundredth birthday. It was already evident during that conference that a rift was developing between those who like Kirzner wanted to preserve a strong link to equilibrium economics and the Lachmannians who were willing to pursue subjectivism wherever it should lead.

entrepreneur can benefit by choosing the correct framework. The second meaning, "noticing missed opportunities," refers not to current uncertainty but to earlier error and hence is not affected by the recognition of uncertainty (1982:147–148). The entrepreneur's role here is to be "alert to the future" to make his view of the future close to the real future. The closer his view is to the real view of the future, the greater will be his chance of making profit. Hence, once again, the entrepreneur's role is to coordinate the market, but now, he coordinates over time. He will be able to accomplish this because he is "motivated" to be correct about the future (1982:149–151).

The coordinating ability of entrepreneurs over time is crucial to sustaining Kirzner's view of the market process, yet how convincing is his case? This article while appearing to deal with issues of uncertainty seems to avoid it altogether. It is as if Kirzner at this stage could not come to grips with what the passage of time really implies for human action. Having fully digested the implications of differential knowledge and consequent scope for error in economic activity, he neglected time altogether. Certainly the entrepreneur tries to choose the right means–ends framework, certainly she tries to recognize past error, certainly she tries to make her anticipation of the future "the" correct one. But what guarantee do we have that she will succeed? Certainly, being motivated to succeed does not ensure success. She simply may be mistaken in her judgment about the course of future events.

Perhaps the problem of uncertainty is not most usefully captured by referring to it as a problem of choosing the "right" means–ends framework. At one level, uncertainty can refer to the uncertainty as to whether or not the entrepreneurial hunch is correct. The entrepreneur may feel something akin to certainty, but subsequent events may well prove her wrong. Her interpretive framework may be faulty, or her information incorrect. This is a form of uncertainty that does not hinge on the passage of time, simply imperfect information despite the noncalculative character of the entrepreneurial act.

However, if .we do consider the passage of time, another kind of uncertainty comes into the picture. If we take seriously Mises' dictum that the passage of time implies changes in knowledge, then even if entrepreneurs are correct in their identification of past market errors, there is no guarantee that their ventures to exploit those errors will succeed. If the "data" are continually changing, as Mises argued (1963:245), the opportunity that entrepreneurs think they see can well disappear before they can fully exploit their vision. People's tastes may change, someone else may make a discovery that changes the potential profitability of one's venture, people may pursue their own plans in an unpredicted way. In this more realistic world, one can be alert and still be incorrect. Speculators often lose money.

Indeed, in this scenario, it seems unhelpful even to speak of entrepreneurs striving to formulate the "correct" vision of the future as if the future were something already implicit in the "data" and one's only problem is to guess correctly what that future will be. Even if, in some purely formal sense, at any moment in time there might be a future inherent in "the data," the actual future that emerges is surely the product of the unpredictable discoveries of Kirzner's entrepreneurs. Given that all opportunities cannot be expected to be discovered in some predictable pattern, nor even discovered at all, each actual discovery, in Kirzner's system, should change the future in totally unpredictable ways. And again, what was an opportunity at one moment in time could turn into a failure in the next. In such a world, what could possibly be the "correct" anticipation of the future except in a purely ex post sense?

Kirzner's treatment of uncertainty at this stage is troubling because he fails to consider those aspects of uncertainty that would challenge his system. If entrepreneurs can be wrong, not in the simple sense of missing opportunities but in the far more important sense of using resources in ways that lead to losses, how can they be seen as the unequivocal driving force bringing the system toward equilibrium? If they can be wrong, perhaps they can be a destabilizing influence on the market and perhaps that instability can persist for long periods of time. This was, after all Keynes's argument. Certainly it requires some answer other than calling on the fact that entrepreneurs will be motivated to be correct.

One might argue that the problem here is one of emphasis. Kirzner in part is saying that without entrepreneurs, it is unlikely that there will be any intertemporal coordination at all. Someone has to make the judgments about the future and take risks on the basis of those judgments. One cannot avoid dealing with uncertainty, one can only change who it is that will bear the consequences. Entrepreneurs who specialize in bearing risk will tend to be more successful than those who accept risk by default. Entrepreneurial action, then, need not be perfect, only on net more correct than an economic system without markets and entrepreneurs. The problem with this argument, however, is that it fails to supply arguments about why entrepreneurs in an uncertain world should on net be correct enough to drive the system toward equilibrium. If the data are constantly changing, what does equilibrium mean, anyway?

There are signs that for a time, at least, Kirzner himself was troubled by the introduction of uncertainty into his model. In an article published in 1983, he described the market as "a sequential, systematic process of continual adjustment, incessantly buffeted and redirected by exogenous changes" (1985a:156). There, he identifies two kinds of discoordination: the first with respect to information already known and the second with respect to future discoveries. He argues that "current market activities may be fully coordinated with each other, yet be very imperfectly coordinated with future activities *as these will turn out to be informed by as yet undiscovered truths*" (159). Although even here entrepreneurs are identified as "correctly perceiving elements to be calculated" (157), instead of bringing about equilibrium, they are responsible for bringing about whatever "allocative balance" exists in the market (162). The implication here seems to be the more modest one that entrepreneurs are necessary not to guarantee coordination, but only to bring about whatever approximation to equilibrium is possible in the real world of time and ignorance.

In an even later article (1985a:84–85), Kirzner distinguishes among three types of entrepreneurship: arbitrage, speculation, and innovation, all of which, he argues, are adequately described by his term, "alertness," although in another place (1985a:116) he suggests that each of these may be a product of a completely different thought process. One might, from these articles, conclude that Kirzner, reacting to the influence of Lachmann and, indirectly through Lachmann, of Shackle, was beginning to rethink some of his earlier ideas on equilibrium and entrepreneurship, and was perhaps ready to question more closely the relationship of Austrian economics to the neoclassical mainstream. However, in the introduction to *Discovery and the Capitalist Process* (1985a), he reasserted with full vigor his position of 1973. He argued that his work was a reaction to the "stark options" in which entrepreneurship is regarded either as an automatic response to market demand (as in neoclassical economics) or as originative, spontaneous, and unexplained (as in the writings of Shackle).

Kirzner's aim was to show that through the concept of "alertness" one can "incorporate entrepreneurship into the analysis without surrendering the heart of microeconomic theory" (11). Indeed, microeconomics needs his conception of the entrepreneur in order to be complete. He rejects once again the notion that entrepreneurs create anything ex nihilo, instead arguing that by discovering opportunities already "there" to be discovered, they are introducing genuine novelty into the system. He reasserts that "human alertness at all times furnishes agents with the propensity to discover information that will be useful to them" (12), and this will result in a continuous discovery process that "in the absence of external changes in underlying conditions, fuels a tendency toward equilibrium." His parting shot is aimed directly at the Shackelians: To accept the view that ignorance is an "indelible feature of the situation is to give up systematic market processes" (13). Entrepreneurs must eliminate ignorance untainted by their own error in order for market processes to be systematically explainable.

Nor has Kirzner's position undergone any recent change. In the introduction to his most recent collection of essays (Kirzner, 1992), Kirzner faces head on the claim by the "radical subjectivists" that the unknowability of the future makes his claim that entrepreneurs always coordinate economic activity unsupported. He once again argues for the Austrian "middle ground," which neither assumes economies are always in equilibrium, as neoclassical supporters do, nor that they are completely chaotic, as radical subjectivists do. Instead, Austrians insist on "the existence of important processes of equilibration" in markets (34). He argues that even when entrepreneurial error occurs, the reaction of other entrepreneurs serves to coordinate markets nevertheless. However, entrepreneurial error here is still simply the failure to notice some profitable opportunity. He gives an example in which entrepreneurs fail to notice the demand for one commodity and produce a less valued one instead. He argues that further market actions to react to the provision of the less valued good are nevertheless coordinating because these entrepreneurs are operating according to the reality they now face. History has changed and the original opportunity set no longer applies.

Kirzner's example is convincing as far as it goes, but he still does not examine the consequences of the kind of entrepreneurial error that leads to losses and the waste of resources in ventures undesired by consumers. These are the kind of actions that make some people worse off than they were before. In what sense is this equilibrating? Although there are seeds of an answer to this question here (one might point to the importance of decentralized entrepreneurial behavior limiting and partly correcting the damage done by previous mistakes, for example), Kirzner's approach will continue to fall short until he accounts for the systematic effects of entrepreneurial mistakes, with "discoordinating" actions of entrepreneurs. To do so does not necessarily lead to the abandonment of a theory of orderly markets; it simply changes the way in which we explain the order that is, as Kirzner points out, readily observed in real life.

Kirzner appears to have largely succeeded in his goal to provide a theory of the entrepreneur that accounts for the missing link in neoclassical price theory: He inserts an element of undetermined action in an otherwise fully determinate model of price adjustment. Indeed, at one level, he has simply formalized a set of verbal stories countless economics professors tell their introductory students as they try to explain how some particular market reaches equilibrium. This is in itself no small accomplishment since, as we have seen, it also permits him to reinterpret the neoclassical notion of competition and monopoly in a way that brings more congruence between neoclassical and Austrian theory. Competition is rivalry and implies rivalrous practices omitted from perfect competition theory. Monopoly only makes sense as exclusive resource ownership since downward-sloping demand curves are ubiquitous and in no way interfere with rivalrous behavior. Yet, Kirzner seems to have succeeded by taking inadequate account of a significant aspect of the Austrian research program. By incompletely examining the implications of the passage of time in the world, he has improved upon a model of market behavior that still fails to capture the central problem of human action.

Lachmann and the kaleidic world

Although both agree on many of the important presuppositions of Austrian economics and especially on the central importance of market processes in economic theory, Ludwig Lachmann's writings present a stark contrast to Kirzner's. Where Kirzner can be seen as attempting some reconciliation between Mises and conventional microeconomic theory, Lachmann's work is more concerned with reconciling some of Mises' insights with those of his other intellectual influences: Max Weber, John Maynard Keynes, and George Shackle. And Mises plus Weber, Keynes, and Shackle is very different economics from Mises plus neoclassical price theory.

Whereas Kirzner approached a theory of the market process through the phenomenon of the arbitraging entrepreneur, Lachmann's way in was through capital theory. Or rather, through the theory of capital, which Lachmann argued was a completely different thing. Conventional capital theory after Keynes had come to mean a theory of interest, but for Lachmann a theory of capital should rather examine how individuals choose to create particular kinds of intermediate goods at particular times and how these intermediate goods lead to the eventual production of consumer goods. He thus saw himself as carrying forth Hayek's program of examining "what type of equipment it will be most profitable to create under various conditions, and how the equipment existing at any moment will be used, rather than to explain the factors which determined the value of a given stock of productive equipment and of the income that will be derived from it" (1978a:vii).

Obviously, Lachmann, like both Menger and Hayek before him, saw capital as a collection of heterogeneous goods whose structure and alternative uses were fundamental to describing the contours of a market economy. Capital was the outcome of conscious plans of entrepreneurs to construct equipment that would only yield a return in the future. Hence the decision to invest in any particular kind of capital equipment is a consequence of an entrepreneur's assessment of current economic conditions and his expectations about the future. One can readily appreciate how his work in capital theory would draw his attention to problems of time and futurity in economics.

Lachmann was also fascinated with the fact that the existing capital stock is continuously reshuffled and reused (cf. Mises, 1963:502–505). Entrepreneurs make production plans, but these plans often are impossible to complete because of mistaken expectations about the plans of others. Where people have differing expectations about the future, it is impossible for them all to be correct. Hence, a certain incompatibility of plans is natural to the market process. Some investments will turn out to have been mistaken from the perspective of the investor. Nevertheless, investment, good or bad, leads to the creation of material objects that exist regardless of the success or failure of the plan. These objects, "fossils of former projects" (1986:61) or "tracks of history," are ultimately used for purposes other than those they were originally constructed to serve. Although such reshuffling of the capital stock into alternative occupations is a testament to the flexibility of the market process, it nevertheless inevitably results in some "discoordination" in the system (1976c:149–150). Such considerations made Lachmann mindful of the problem of disequilibrating tendencies in market economies as well as equilibrating ones.[10] Considerations both of time and disequilibrating tendencies figure prominently in his scattered attempts to develop an alternative economic paradigm to the static equilibrium framework of contemporary economic theory.

To Lachmann, the nature of the market process is such that it makes no sense to attempt to describe equilibrium states for the market as a whole. This was a method appropriate, perhaps, to the classical school that saw value as a real phenomenon where prices could be imagined to converge to a "center of gravity," but once value is understood as a consequence of utility, the economist's job is to assess the mental acts of multitudes of consumers, and the notion of a center of gravity ceases to be helpful (1986:14). Instead, the market is better understood as "a particular kind of process, a continuous process without beginning or end, propelled by

---

[10] Obviously, Lachmann sides with Hayek in maintaining that it is unhelpful to think of capital as the source of a continuous income stream, as Frank Knight argued in his debates with Hayek. For capital to produce any income at all requires acts of judgment based upon assessment of the current situation and expectations of the future. It is just as easy for capital to generate losses as profit for any individual producer. Although one might focus as Knight did on the potential permanence of income producible by the capital stock for some kinds of questions, Lachmann would argue that it is misleading to abstract from the human actions that use capital to produce income for most questions of economic theory and policy.

the interaction between the forces of equilibrium and the forces of change" (1976a:60). In fact, rather than a mechanical resolution of forces that equilibrium conjures up, a better metaphor for the market is Shackle's "kaleidic society," a notion that may seem alien to Austrians at first but is completely consistent with their assumptions (1976a:61). That is, the kaleidic society captures the implications of human action within the context of real time and heterogeneous and imperfect knowledge.

Individual action in real time

Like Shackle, Lachmann regards the future as undetermined, the unpredictable consequence of creative and undetermined choices to pursue ends within the constraints of means and obstacles in the present. Hence, one can never "see" into the future; one can only imagine and conjecture, interpret the present, and form expectations about the future. As Lachmann repeats many times in his writing, "The future is unknowable, but not unimaginable" (1976a:55). Although the undetermined nature of the future makes it unknowable, the reason it is not unimaginable is that there is some consistency in human action that makes some futures more likely to emerge than others. However, it is impossible for either the actor or the social scientist to predict which of the many possible futures one could imagine will actually occur. Hence, uncertainty is a fact of life, and all expectations are subjective estimations of possible futures.

But why is human action undetermined or unpredictable? Kirzner, while arguing forcefully for a kind of undetermined action in his theory of entrepreneurship, is willing to accept fully determined Robbinsian maximizing as a theoretical proposition once a means–ends framework is established. Lachmann is less willing to go even this far toward rapproachment with neoclassical modeling. As a true student of Shackle, he emphasizes that all action except "routine action" is undetermined creative choice.[11] Shackle emphasizes the importance of imagination in choice where choice is an undetermined cut between past and future. Lachmann accepts this view but goes further than Shackle by providing an explanation for the indeterminate nature of choice rooted in a theory

[11] It is not clear to what extent Lachmann's "routine" overlaps with Kirzner's Robbinsian maximizing. On the one hand, in the context of Lachmann's discussion, "routine" seems to suggest unthinking repetition, as in brushing one's teeth or driving a car while Kirzner's Robbinsian maximizing covers all those fully conscious rational economic calculations of neoclassical economic theory. If this interpretation is correct, Lachmann would seem to deny the possibility of determinate calculation in Kirzner's sense. On the other hand, Lachmann might simply be stressing Kirzner's notion of undetermined entrepreneurial behavior to a greater degree than Kirzner did.

of mind that is reminiscent of Hayek's work on the sensory order (Hayek, 1952; see also Hayek, 1978a:35–49).

The reason that choice can never be fully predicted, Lachmann would argue, is that no two minds are alike; neither in the bits of knowledge they contain nor in their method of interpreting the information they receive. The world does not present itself to the human mind in an unproblematic way. Sensory data must be interpreted and this interpretation process is subjective and never exactly duplicated from one mind to another. Hence, the means–ends framework and the obstacles that individuals perceive are themselves subjective in that the same "information" will invoke differing interpretations among different human beings (1971:39).

Although human action is not determinate, neither is it arbitrary. Lachmann sees human action as "free within an area bounded by constraints" (1971:37). Since the purpose of economic theory in Lachmann's view is to make the world intelligible in terms of human action, it would seem to be imperative to develop a theory of action that specifies the areas of freedom as well as the constraints. To Lachmann, the way forward is not to focus on momentary acts of choice or the solution to maximizing problems. Rather, he reinterprets praxeology, the study of how human beings use means to achieve ends, in the Hayekian manner as the study of how human beings devise and act upon plans to use means to achieve ends. Whereas the simpler Misesian formulation could be construed in a static timeless manner, the notion of devising and acting upon plans focuses us squarely on the importance of acting in time.[12]

The notion of a plan, Lachmann argues, is particularly congenial to praxeology since it is a human phenomenon that has no counterpart in nature. Inanimate objects do not plan,[13] whereas human action can only be understood in terms of the plan of which it is a part. People carry an image of what it is they want in their minds. Action is the carrying out of the project designed to bring about imagined ends. Indeed, concepts like success and failure only make sense as the outcomes of some plan (1971:29–30).

[12] Not surprisingly, it is also more consistent with Mises' notion of subjective time as the "real present," time as actually experienced by people and as relevant to their plans or expectations about change. See chapter 4.

[13] Lachmann does not address the question of whether animals can be said to plan, although his identification of planning as distinctively human seems to indicate that he would place animal behavior in the deterministic category. However, his argument does not require that all animals except man be considered reactors rather than planners. One might be able to develop a praxeology of ape behavior that might have similarities to humans, although the behaviorists would deny this. Of course, behaviorists might deny that humans plan creatively as well.

Although people formulate and act upon plans, as Lachmann emphasized in his theory of capital, this does not mean that plans can always be carried out smoothly and without adjustment to new circumstances. Plans are, after all, carried out in time, and the passage of time implies that knowledge and circumstances will change. Lachmann especially emphasizes the degree to which knowledge is affected by the passage of time. Problems of time and knowledge are inseparable to Lachmann, as they were in principle to Mises. Lachmann repeats often the dictum that "as soon as we permit time to elapse we must permit knowledge to change, and knowledge cannot be regarded as a function of anything else" (1976b:127–128). The passage of time (and presumably action in time), means that people will learn more about both their ends and means, and more about the plans that other people are undertaking. This will imply that initial plans must be revised, often many times in the light of new knowledge. Revision of plans, then, is the norm rather than the exception in human action. In such a world, it would be extremely unlikely that all plans would ever be "coordinated." It is for this reason that Lachmann describes the market as "a sequence of individual interactions, each denoting the encounter (and sometimes collision) of a number of plans, which, while coherent individually and reflecting the individual equilibrium of the actor, are incoherent as a group. The process would not go on otherwise" (1976b:131). For Lachmann, it seems this process is such that we cannot even predict the direction of change.

Lachmann's view about the market process, stated so baldly, seems to contradict the very notion of order that informs economic analysis. Without a tendency toward equilibrium, how can we theorize about the market process at all? What can we say about it other than that change happens? So ingrained are familiar notions of equilibrium in the economics profession, that Lachmann's arguments have led others, both within and without Austrian circles, to charge him with nihilism; with denying the possibility of theory altogether. Yet Lachmann claims that he does not deny theory, simply the wrong kind of theory.[14] In several places (1971, 1986) he gives us clues to his view of an alternative theory of the market process. Whether these clues lead to a solution is an open question.

---

[14] "As regards 'nihilism,' this appears to be a term more appropriate to describing the mentality of those who, blind to the variegated activity of human minds when engaged in the formation of expectations, are frantically searching for links of mechanical causation where there are none, than to that of those who do their best to draw the attention of their colleagues to the problems we all face" (Lachmann, 1986:140).

Lachmann's theory of institutions

Unfortunately, Lachmann never wrote a systematic treatise on the order of *Human Action*. Those interested in Lachmann's positive program for economics must attempt to piece together a system from several sources. Primary among them are *The Legacy of Max Weber* (1971) and his last book, *The Market as an Economic Process* (1986). Although there are some real differences in Lachmann's sentiments as expressed in these two books, there is enough continuity to get a glimpse of what he thinks a viable alternative to neoclassical economics would look like.

The Legacy of Max Weber is an undeservedly neglected book. As the title indicates, it is not so much an explication of Weber's thought as it is an attempt to build upon some aspects of Weber's work that pertain to economic theory. Specifically, Lachmann wishes to ground Weber's use of ideal types in a theory of human action based on the notion of the plan and hence render ideal types more a theoretical than strictly historical construct. More important for our purposes, Lachmann intended to bring some coherence to Weber's widespread remarks about institutions by outlining a general theory of institutions; how they evolve and what function they serve in human social life. Lachmann's theory of institutions developed in chapter two of *The Legacy of Max Weber* provides one basis for Lachmann's claim that his view of the market process is not nihilistic, that order can be explained without recourse to general equilibrium constructs.

Lachmann begins here with his notion of "the plan" as the basic unit of analysis of human action with all of its implications for unpredictability, failure, and revision. However, within this world of the unpredictable unfolding of a multitude of human plans, Lachmann sees institutions serving as "points of orientation." Institutions are "recurrent patterns of conduct" (75) that "coordinate activities to a common signpost" (49). They enable us to predict some actions of others with a fair amount of confidence. As such, they help to reduce the potential chaos that might ensue in an undetermined world.

Lachmann illustrates his point by referring to Menger's theory of institutions. Specifically, the price system is an institution that provides a sufficient level of predictability of action and interpretation to allow people to pursue their plans with some possibility of success. In addition, the price system allows enough flexibility of action to permit useful market institutions to emerge. Within markets, "profits . . . are sign posts of entrepreneurial success. In symbolic form they convey knowledge" (1977:102).

The price system works because "some men realize that it is possible to pursue their interests more effectively than they have done so far and that an existing situation offers opportunities not so far exploited. In concert with others, they do exploit them. If they are successful their example will find ready imitators, at first a few, later on many." In this way, successful plans "gradually crystallize into institutions."[15] The mechanism for such crystallization is imitation, "the most important form by which the ways of the elite become the property of the masses. Once an idea originally grasped by an eager mind has been 'tested' and found successful, it can be safely employed as a means to success by minds less eager and lacking in originality. Institutions are the relics of the pioneering efforts of former generations from which we are still drawing benefit" (1971:68).

None of this implies either perfection in outcome or unqualified "efficiency" in markets, however. Market processes are not clockworks. The price system may offer "points of orientation," but it does not guarantee any particular outcome. What the price system does offer is a method for carrying out plans in an orderly, coherent process; a method for detecting error; and the flexibility to adapt to errors when they are perceived.

The price system is one kind of institution in society that allows the generation of other, subsidiary market institutions like firms, financial intermediaries, wholesalers, stock markets, and so on. Similarly, the price system operates within the context of other social institutions such as families and, most important, the legal structure. Neoclassical economists define order and efficiency with respect to the price system as the achievement of general equilibrium, a construct that Lachmann finds fantastic for all his previously articulated reasons of subjectivity, knowledge, and time. Markets can be orderly without tending toward or achieving general equilibrium. However, he addresses the problem of coordination and order that neoclassical economics tries to solve with a theory of general equilibrium, but at a different level of social organization. Although individual plans and actions will never be completely coordinated as is required in general equilibrium theory, it is legitimate to question the coherence and coordination of the social institutions that people take as signposts for their actions (1971:70).

Lachmann envisions the social world as a series of nested institutions all of which affect human plans and projects. In a world of uncertainty and

---

[15] Notice that this implicitly assumes that success is sufficiently observable to permit close imitation. Yet the recognition that knowledge is sometimes tacit implies that imitation is not always perfect or even certain to occur. This opens up a set of questions about the circumstances under which learning can be successfully transmitted from entrepreneur to entrepreneur. It also suggests a stronger theoretical case for the existence and necessity of diversity in production techniques and products in a market order.

change, institutions face two challenges: They must be permanent enough to serve their function as points of orientation for human plans, but they also must be flexible enough to change with changed circumstances. No society can function with continual flux in its institutional structure, but a society that never permits its institutional structure to change will suffer increasing inefficiencies (89). Further, in order to enable individuals to act with efficacy, the institutional structure must be compatible within itself. For society to flourish, finally, Lachmann argues that it must possess a few fundamental institutions like political and legal structures and perhaps certain social structures such as family relationships that change infrequently and provide the firm outer structure of society, but it must also possess wide scope for freedom of contract to allow the emergence of new institutions to serve new problems (90).

Lachmann is addressing several problems at once with his discussion of institutions. He alludes to questions of how an institutional structure emerges (both as the unintended by-product of purposeful human action as in Menger and through conscious design [69]), he describes potential characteristics of an institutional structure, and he posits a set of characteristics for a well-functioning set of related institutions. Yet no clearly articulated theory of institutions emerges from all of this, at least no theory that translates easily into analysis and policy.

In the end, Lachmann says many tantalizing things about institutions without developing a theory of the relationship between action and institutions that generates confidence in the relative beneficence and coherence of the market order. We have learned something of the importance of institutions, but we have no account of how institutional permanence, coherence, and flexibility might arise. Lachmann still has not solved his problem of order. He has just moved it to another level of social interaction.

The market as an economic process

In his last book, *The Market as an Economic Process* (1986), Lachmann tries again to give us a coherent alternative to conventional economic theory. Here he draws together most of his earlier themes: the unknowability of the future; the concomitant uncertainty within which everyone acts; the unpredictability of choice and the inability of economics to be a predictive science; the subjectivity of knowledge, interpretation, and expectations; the inappropriateness of equilibrium theorizing. Instead of continuing his promising program of developing a theory of institutions, however, in this book he lets the role of institutions recede into the background. It forms an indispensable presence, but is not a conscious focus.

Ironically, in this last book, Lachmann once again invokes the legacy of Max Weber, but from a different and less self-conscious perspective. Whereas in the *Legacy*, Lachmann had criticized Weber's use of the ideal type as being insufficiently sensitive to the causes of human action, here, he argues that the appropriate way to theorize about economic phenomena is to employ the construct of the ideal type (1986:34).

An ideal type, according to Lachmann, is not a pure abstraction or generic concept such as "horse" or "father" that abstracts from all particular horses or fathers. Rather, it is a construct that accentuates "certain properties found either in reality, or in our imagination, even though we also have to abstract from other properties found there." Since this may not be a perfectly pellucid definition, an example might help. A financial intermediary is an ideal type in that it is an abstract notion that nevertheless is only useful in certain historical instances. The ideal type of "financial intermediary" would make no sense in a noncredit economy, for example. Hence, an ideal type is a "foil against which to hold real events so as to bring out particular properties of the latter by comparison" (34). There needs to be some grounding in a real phenomenon and some comparison to reality possible in order for a construct to be an ideal type. In this sense, homoeconomicus is not an ideal type, but a pure abstraction.[16]

An example of an ideal type used in neoclassical economics, according to Lachmann, is the model of perfect competition (35). It takes certain properties of some real markets such as price taking, widespread knowledge, and shared technical information and exaggerates them into an ideal type. Unfortunately, neoclassical economics does not know what to do from there. The proper procedure is to use the ideal type to examine the deviations from it in the real world (cf. Mises, 1963:246–247). Hence, when Jevons introduced recontracting and Walras the auctioneer, they

---

[16] Lachmann appreciated the role that ideal types were meant to play in Weber's view of social science. According to Lachmann, Weber wanted ideal types to be useful as ordering devices in understanding social phenomena, "measuring rods" to allow us to gain knowledge of reality by understanding the distance between the ideal type and the real phenomenon under investigation (1971:26–27). However, he thought Weber's use of the ideal type was far too broad to make it useful for analytic purposes, as it encompassed rational schemes of action (of which Lachmann approved), irrational schemes, historical generalizations, actions, and ideas. Lachmann argued that Weber's concept had to be narrowed to be useful and suggested that at least some distinction needed to be made between rational schemes of action (Lachmann's plans) and historical generalizations. In *The Market as an Economic Process* (1986), Lachmann carried this through by distinguishing between abstractions (figments of imagination), ideal types that had to have some grounding in historical reality, and real types that were generalizations from reality.

were identifying a problem that was solved in some fashion or other by real types. The ideal type of the auctioneer should have started a research effort to learn what the real life counterpart was to this ideal type (39–40). (And, had this been done, neoclassical economics might have immediately focused on the importance of explaining market processes rather than limiting its fire power to equilibrium states.)

Ideal types are empirically relevant constructs. Hence, the usefulness of an ideal type depends on the events one wants to study. As we have seen, the ideal type of a financial intermediary is only useful, for example, in a credit economy. But when it is empirically relevant, the ideal type allows us to identify real counterparts or "real types." So, for example, a financial intermediary is an ideal type that allows us to identify the Victorian merchant banker as a real type (36). Such reliance on the empirical grounding of ideal types and the historical relevance of real types, Lachmann implies, will permit economics to perform its legitimate function, providing classificatory and theoretical schema for historical research. Economics cannot predict the future, but it can help to explain the past. Hence, our theoretical constructs are best thought of as aids to the interpretation of the history.

In the rest of the book, and especially in his chapter on markets and the market, Lachmann pursues his program of disaggregating typical economic concepts from abstractions to ideal types. In particular, he implicitly argues, instead of examining the world through the lens of the abstraction called "the market," we need to develop ideal types of particular kinds of markets: asset markets versus production markets, fix-price markets or flex-price markets, markets dominated by merchants versus markets dominated by salesmen. Such distinctions will make a difference as to how markets adjust to change. Austrians, he claims, should be interested not in questions of price determination, but in questions of price formation. What prices emerge in a market is less interesting than how prices emerge: Who sets the price, what information does she have, to what signals does she respond? Rather than focusing on the empirically irrelevant case of equilibrium prices, it is far more important to ask what are the consequences of particular kinds of price setting over time (128).

Lachmann addresses some of his questions and in the course of his book says some interesting things about particular markets. For instance, as he wrote several times before, asset markets are more volatile than production markets because in asset markets value depends purely on expectations, and owners can "change sides" at will as bulls become bears and vice versa. The function of the price system in these markets is to divide the bulls and the bears, which perhaps means to allow people to hold the assets they wish to hold on the basis of their expectations about the future and thus to generate prices that reflect a consensus view of future outcomes. In such a setting, one side or the other will be correct and thus be prepared for further market activity in the future.

Where markets are characterized by fix price rather than flex price, he further argues, quantity adjustments will be the norm. (He makes the unsupported claim that almost all markets are fix-price markets now, a belief he shared with the post-Keynesians.) Where markets are dominated by salesmen, prices will be more rigid than where they are dominated by merchants, once again, because merchants can change sides (133–134).

But where does this leave us with respect to the problem of order in society? Is there anything we can say about the market process that allows us to assert its fundamental coherence and order? Does it permit us to see markets as useful tools for carrying out individual projects and plans with a reasonable assurance of success? Even more to the point, under Lachmann's framework are we justified in viewing unmolested markets as in any way better than markets minutely controlled by political decision making? Can we still argue that decentralized decision making in a regime of property rights is superior to central planning? If we are not to speak of "equilibrium" can we still speak, then, as did Adam Smith, of a "simple system of natural liberty" in which the invisible hand, any invisible hand, is operative? Or are we forced to conclude that the market system is simply one institutional order among many in society that may or may not be coherent on its own, and may or may not be compatible with the other institutions of society? In a reversion to neoclassical language, Lachmann tells us that markets are subject to both disequilibrating and equilibrating tendencies (37), but he takes no position on which kinds of tendencies dominate the system.

In the end, as with *The Legacy of Max Weber,* the reader is left frustrated and dissatisfied. One can agree with Lachmann on all aspects of his description of the human condition, one can follow his criticism of the conventional orthodoxy and be eager to follow him in his pursuit of examining real markets, but ultimately one cannot help but feel that he has taken a tour of individual trees and missed the forest. Lachmann leaves us with a detailed understanding of some market processes, but no overall theory of the market process itself.

Conclusion

Neither Kirzner nor Lachmann has been successful in explaining market order without abstracting from time and ignorance. Kirzner, in an attempt to inject entrepreneurship into an equilibrium model of markets, is successful in accounting for and explaining the implications of a special kind of heterogeneity in knowledge among market participants, but the cost has been to ignore the consequences of the passage of real time. Lachmann, in an attempt to take radical subjectivism and real time seriously in his interpretation of economic action, tries to devise an alternative to equilibrium theorizing but fails to produce the kind of overall theoretical structure that would seriously challenge neoclassical hegemony. Perhaps the new Austrian economics has taken on an impossible task. But if Austrian economics fails to satisfy, then neoclassical economics is in even worse shape since the same conditions of human existence that undercut Kirzner's neat reconciliation and leave Lachmann without a comprehensive theory also threaten the foundation of neoclassical economics. Perhaps the very recognition of time and ignorance in human action plays havoc with any theory of self-ordering market processes.

Before we give in to this genuine form of nihilism, however, we must also recognize that there is *something* "out there" that economists have been trying to describe for anywhere from two hundred to two thousand years, depending upon the depth of one's historical perspective. The world is sufficiently orderly and comprehensible for us to say, for example, that Americans are wealthier than Pakistanis on average, or that there is more capital equipment available to create new goods now than there was in 1600, or that Europe has a more "rational" and productive economy than the former Soviet Union. Moreover, the world is also sufficiently orderly for us to live most of our catallactic lives with some sense of continuity and predictability.

Neoclassical economics has attempted to capture and theorize about this perceived order using constructs borrowed from physics and statical mechanics. Austrians criticize neoclassicals for this approach, but so far have not come up with a fully articulated alternative. Yet, there are clear indications within the Austrian tradition that suggest alternatives to conventional equilibrium theorizing. It is to these possible alternatives that we now turn.

CHAPTER 8

Austrian economics: which way forward?

I began this project to discover whether there is or could be a distinctive and separate approach to economics that follows naturally from the Austrian tradition. I approached this question by examining the origin and development of the modern Austrian school, since by understanding the history of the debates we could better understand the current literature and its place within the discipline of economics as a whole. During the course of this narrative, several persistent themes in the Austrian literature from Menger to the present argued for, at a minimum, an Austrian perspective and a set of Austrian questions: themes such as the importance of dynamic growth and development, the generation and function of knowledge in economic action, the uncertainties associated with processes in time, and the pivotal importance of diversity and heterogeneity in economic life. These themes suggested that Austrian economics cannot usefully be considered merely a variation on the economics of rationality and constrained maximization.

Despite these common themes, the division within current Austrian circles as typified by the debate between Kirzner and Lachmann presented in chapter 7, demonstrates that there is some deep disagreement among Austrian economists concerning the implications of those themes. There is not one, but at least two recognized approaches to doing Austrian economics, both sharing the same ancestors from Menger to the present, but differing greatly on the implications of the ideas of those ancestors. These two approaches differ most over the relationship between Austrian and neoclassical economics.

As we have seen, all Austrians have criticized neoclassical economics for various reasons: for its "excessive preoccupation" with equilibrium states, for its high level of formalism, its too extensive level of aggregation, for the mechanistic way in which limited analysis is often translated into policy.

Austrians are not only united in their criticisms of neoclassical economics, however; we have also seen that they hold some commonly shared beliefs about the nature of human action and the circumstances of economic reality. O'Driscoll and Rizzo claim that what distinguishes Austrian from neoclassical economics is a different set of beginning assumptions about the nature of the conditions under which human action takes place. Austrians agree with neoclassical economics that human beings attempt to act rationally to achieve their purposes. However, because human action always takes place in time and always under conditions of partial ignorance about the present and total ignorance about the future, a theory of market processes can be neither static in nature nor based on the assumption of perfect knowledge. Nor is rational ignorance a promising assumption for Austrians who deny that all the relevant future states of the world are listable by the choosing agent. Subjectivism is not only a characteristic of preferences, but also of knowledge and expectations.

All Austrians agree that this "dynamic subjectivism," as O'Driscoll and Rizzo call it, requires some adjustment in the way economists understand human action in the real world. But whether the adjustment should take the form of arguing for changes in the use of the equilibrium–maximization framework of neoclassical economic theory to better reflect Austrian insights, or whether it should strive to overturn that theory and replace it whole cloth with another is very much an open question.

Despite some of the more intemperate claims of a few Austrians critical of Lachmann, it should also be pointed out that this debate is not a disagreement over whether markets should be conceived of as being part of some orderly process. No one, including Lachmann, advocates abandoning all theory and turning instead to exhaustive descriptions of reality. As Menger, Mises, and Hayek continually emphasized, one cannot even develop categories of description without some theoretical structure to organize raw observation. The Lachmannians are not nihilists; they simply find fault with the currently dominant organizing principle of economics and strive to develop an alternative.[1]

Economics is a social science that by definition is concerned with understanding order in human society. As human beings we recognize many recurring patterns of behavior that result in orderly social processes – customs, manners, laws, institutions, and relationships. In addition, often what seems disorderly or chaotic at first glance, upon further investigation, can be shown to reflect some deeper unsuspected

---

[1] O'Driscoll and Rizzo argue that a genuine process analysis in the Austrian tradition will have to have some concept of equilibrium since equilibrium theorizing is simply "a type of causal reasoning" (1985:118). But this definition of equilibrium is so broad that it applies to any mode of theorizing that follows standard rules of logic. Surely, if we are to be true to the etymology of the word, to call something "equilibrium" requires that it explain a balance or a state of rest. Although I agree with O'Driscoll and Rizzo that Austrians are also trying to find a metaphor that explains some sort of balance in the social world, to use the term "equilibrium" given its present connotations can only confuse debate.

principles of order, usually some purposeful response to perceived constraints.

It was the recognition and attempt to begin to explain these hidden principles of social order that first led to the development of the discipline of economics in the seventeenth century. Without some coherent theoretical explanation of social order that goes beyond the obvious and well-recognized regularities of everyday life, there is no economic science. The question is, how do we explain this social order that goes beyond our immediate perceptions while remaining true to our recognition that humans act not only to make themselves better off, but that they do so in a world of limited resources, incomplete knowledge, and radical uncertainty? And how is that to be done in a manner that is at some deep level more satisfying than the neoclassical orthodoxy?

Neoclassical economics has provided a largely coherent and convincing explanation of economic order that allows us to classify and explain a wide variety of human social actions. Its use of equilibrium constructs as the resolution of opposing forces provides convenient slots in which to place real-world events and a method of interpretation that simplifies an often confusing reality. Without too much mental gymnastics, most real economic events can be analyzed within the categories of supply or demand, production or distribution, consumption or production, preferences or constraints. The equilibrium solutions can be taken either to be characteristic of the real world, as Reder (1982) has argued is the hallmark of the Chicago School; as a statement about the possibility of simultaneous maximization of preferences and profits throughout the system, as general equilibrium theory takes it; or as the end point of some largely undefined process in the market, as most practicing economists assume. Whatever its logical status, equilibrium theory provides categories of meaning that give us fixed points in a changing world.

Neoclassical economics is successful because it takes plausible statements about human action (human beings want to maximize the satisfaction of their preferences and do so in a rational manner within the constraints they face) and makes simplifying assumptions about reality (they have perfect – or adequate – knowledge about their own preferences and constraints and real time does not pass) to enable one to come up with unequivocal (although often unrealized) predictions about the future state of the world.

We have seen that Austrian economists have identified many shortcomings in neoclassical economics: in addition to their obvious criticisms concerning the lack of theories of adjustment processes to equilibrium positions and the artificiality of either the perfect knowledge or the rational ignorance assumptions, they have also criticized what they see as the misperception of the importance of heterogeneity in both inputs and products in market economies, and the criteria for judging economic performance, to name just a few of their objections. Yet, despite all the shortcomings that Austrian economists and others have identified in neoclassical economics, neoclassical economics refuses to be dislodged from its position of preeminence in economic discourse largely because it has proven useful enough to illuminate many important features of markets and market economies. It is obviously not enough for Austrian economists to criticize the assumptions and theories of neoclassical economics. Austrians must show either that their criticisms can help improve the nature of neoclassical economics to expand its range of explanation or they must describe an alternative theoretical structure that explains economic order better than neoclassical economics.

A supplement to neoclassical economics

In many respects, the Austrians have already done much to accomplish the first goal. Austrian critiques of neoclassical economics have often been incorporated into conventional theory. We have seen how Mises' emphasis on the importance of market prices caused a revolution in the neoclassical theories of central planning. Further, Hayek's work on knowledge, for example, was partly responsible for the development of information theory, just as his critique of the incentive structures of central planning led eventually to the investigation of incentive-compatible central-planning models. Kirzner's (and earlier, Schumpeter's) work on entrepreneurship was an important addition to neoclassical theories of markets. And the Austrian emphasis on the limits of government intervention added to a growing revisionism in antitrust economics and monopoly theory. In regard to many of these issues, Austrians were not alone in their attempts to reform some aspects of current economic theory, but their voices were significant.

Although the Austrian tradition of providing insights to or reinterpretations of conventional theory is long and rich, in chapter 7, doubts were raised about the integrity of grafting Austrian insights onto a basically neoclassical framework of analysis. Certainly that was a question raised about Kirzner's theory of entrepreneurship, an issue so rich that it can virtually serve as the prototype of all Austrian concerns.

We argued that Kirzner was quite right to insist neoclassical economics requires some analysis of process to explain how markets might reach equilibrium. Kirzner hypothesized an alert entrepreneur who learns what others do not know – who notices opportunities that others miss and acts upon that knowledge to bring markets closer to equilibrium. Clearly,

without the entrepreneur or some such undetermined agent to bring
about change, neoclassical economics has no explanation for how anything happens. But, the catch is that once real time and its concomitant
feature of genuine uncertainty are introduced in entrepreneurial activity,
there is no longer an a priori reason for expecting entrepreneurial action
to be necessarily equilibrating in the neoclassical sense. Entrepreneurs
make mistakes as well as enjoy successes. Hence, Kirzner's analysis shows
that entrepreneurs are necessary but not sufficient for bringing about
market-clearing prices. There is no explanation in the Kirznerian (or the
Misesean) oeuvre to convince us that entrepreneurial successes will
necessarily outweigh their failures and hence lead the economy toward
greater equilibration.

Yet, despite the pessimism of chapter 7, this may not be a crushing
criticism of either Kirzner or the line of argument he represents. If we are
willing to accept Hayek's claim that the tendency toward equilibrium is an
empirical proposition (a position Kirzner rejects [1979:29–31]), the
Austrian-economics-as-supplement-to-neoclassical economics project has
much to recommend it. Austrians can simply claim that they are describing a crushingly obvious, empirically relevant route by which an economic
system normally approaches equilibrium. By introducing problems of
incomplete knowledge and real time, they may undercut a priori arguments for full market clearing, but by positing the existence of alert
entrepreneurs, they at least partly save the day.

Once this step is taken, Austrian ideas can well supplement the rather
arid formalism of much neoclassical argument. And, by hooking into
familiar language and established metaphor, Austrians can perhaps
communicate insights and critiques that would be totally dismissed if
expressed in terms that were too foreign to the recipients. To say that
entrepreneurs are the agents that bring about equilibrium communicates
the importance of nondetermined discovery to neoclassical economists in
a way that high flown discourse on the nature of unending, nondirection-
al processes does not.

Borrowing the language and equilibrium metaphor of neoclassical
economics also makes it possible to provide useful interpretations of what
neoclassical economics means as applied to the real world. Take, for
example, the issue of product differentiation that Kirzner raised in
Competition and Entrepreneurship. There he argued effectively that rather
than being monopolistic elements, product variation is often a symptom
of entrepreneurial discovery that is still subject to competitive forces.
Product variation is an entrepreneurial discovery that is actually equilibrating in the sense that it brings consumers more of what they really
want. One might quibble that Kirzner must be using "equilibrating"

differently here from neoclassical economists, but nevertheless, his point is better understood in this language than if he had invented a whole new way of speaking about the consequences of entrepreneurial action.

One can think of other examples. Explanations of advertising, business mergers, resale price maintenance as fundamentally competitive rather than noncompetitive actions can be accomplished by reinterpreting categories within the neoclassical paradigm. One can accept much of the formal structure of the perfectly competitive model, for example, yet argue that it does not go "far enough." Competition should be thought of as rivalry; production functions should not be conceived of as equally evident to every producer; knowledge is limited and specialized so that entrepreneurship is necessary to bring about equilibrium; the subjective nature of costs renders cost–benefit analysis in public policy formation elusive. At this level, the Austrian contribution to contemporary economics is one of interpretation. How do economic models really apply to the real world, and what are the limitations to their application? Remember, Hayek criticized the socialists not for starting with equilibrium theories but for displaying an "excessive preoccupation" with equilibrium.

As important as this contribution to economics may be – and I regard it as very important, indeed – if Austrians confine themselves to working and thinking within the dominant neoclassical paradigm, they may well find themselves serving more as critics than as constructive contributors to economic science. Their theoretical contributions, moreover, will likely continue to be regarded as sources of economic "intuitions" that require "formalization" to be fully respectable. Even more likely, they could be relegated to the role of philosophical conscience of the economics profession. This may not be a bad thing; Lord knows, economics needs some kind of conscience, but it is also true that most people are not particularly fond of having a conscience, despite the fact that they may be better off with one than without. Perhaps this explains the attitude of partial admiration and partial ridicule that Austrians often face from their neoclassical colleagues.

There are pitfalls other than being marginalized that go along with serving in the role of critics, interpreters, and conscience of neoclassical economics. One is that some important Austrian insights may not adapt well to neoclassical language. What is of great significance in one system of thought can seem trivial or beside the point in another. To say, for example, that economic growth is not simply a function of more investment but of the kinds of capital goods produced, the ways in which production is organized, and the scope for entrepreneurial alertness is of real significance with important policy implications to Austrians who hold that the details of the economic order are important to understanding the overall patterns that emerge. To a neoclassical economist, it is simply a truism, and a trivial one at that, that does not touch the heart of their inquiry. In addition, subtleties of analysis or interpretation that are difficult to articulate can easily be dismissed as "mere words" or "hand waving." This was, we remember, the fate of Hayek's analysis of the role of managers in socialist firms – an analysis that even Schumpeter dismissed as merely a problem of practical implementation of a theoretically unassailable plan. It was also the fate of many of Mises' redefinitions of familiar terms to make them more consonant with his understanding of economics; the evenly rotating economy as general equilibrium and his definition of inflation are examples. Expressing new concepts in familiar language seems to be no more successful than putting new wine in old bottles.

In sum, an Austrian economics that borrows the conventional metaphor and language of neoclassical economics clearly can contribute to economic discourse, but its service is more in the nature of an interpretive obligato than a dominant theme. Such an interpretive framework is certainly useful, but not revolutionary and perhaps not even much noted.

Were this all that could be drawn from the Austrian tradition, one might be honored to be of some service to the cause of economic science even if the service were largely unappreciated. But a case can be made that such peripheral status is an undervaluing of the implications of the Austrian tradition. It represents the *least* that Austrian economists might accomplish rather than the most, but it takes an almost foolhardy boldness to reach for the most.

An alternative conception of order

To explore fully the implications of the Austrians' "alternative starting place," the recognition of heterogeneous and incomplete knowledge and of the passage of real time, it is necessary to eschew the easy assimilation to neoclassical economics offered by adopting both its metaphor and language and to strike out on a new path to economic explanation. Clearly, this was Lachmannn's clarion call. Yet, new paths that lead to a desirable destination are not easily blazed, as Lachmann himself inadvertently demonstrated. In science as in business, entrepreneurial ventures are fraught with pitfalls and losses may be more common than gains. And once the equilibrating metaphor is deeply ingrained in our habits of reasoning, how do we break away to formulate a new concept of order? Even Lachmann, who made the most cogent case for departing from the well-traveled route of standard equilibrium analysis, gave us few clues as to how to conceptualize the order we wish to describe. His descriptions of market processes emphasized the open-endedness and ongoingness of economic life, but how do we conceptualize an ongoing and open-ended process? In a world of limitless possibilities, how do we put theoretical limits on the possible futures that can emerge? Are there alternatives to neoclassical equilibrium theorizing that capture the market phenomena in more fruitful ways? Lachmann's image of the kaleidoscope does not get us very far.

One route that has been tried in the Austrian literature has been to redefine the meaning of equilibrium to make it more consistent with the Austrian understanding of human action. We noted that during the calculation debate, Hayek mused that instead of thinking of equilibrium purely as a set of market-clearing prices, it might more profitably be considered a state in which individual plans were coordinated. This, apparently in an attempt to incorporate time-consuming processes into the conceptualization, would allow for the possibility that an economy could be on a path toward equilibrium without actually having all markets clear. People would be acting in a way that was mutually consistent and reinforcing over time. Later, Austrians picked up on this definition and started routinely referring to equilibrium as plan coordination. Kirzner uses the term extensively in his work, as do White, Fink, High, Lavoie, Garrison, and others.

It is not clear, however, that plan coordination escapes the difficulties Austrians identify in Walrasian equilibrium. In particular, even the Hayekian version of plan coordination is still a description of a determinate system in which nothing new is learned and no changes are endogenously brought about. Yet a concept of order that truly incorporates time and ignorance would have to account for learning and endogenous but unpredictable change.

As we saw earlier, O'Driscoll and Rizzo note this difficulty with Hayek's notion of plan coordination and offer an alternative that attempts to incorporate endogenous, unpredictable change in our understanding of economic order. They argue that the order one observes in a market economy is better thought of as "pattern coordination" rather than "plan coordination." Although they are maddeningly terse in their development of the concept, it does appear to meet some of the objections that Austrians have had to conventional equilibrium notions. Their notion of pattern coordination is both open-ended and consistent with ongoing, describable processes.

According to O'Driscoll and Rizzo, the actions of individuals display both "typical" features, features that are more or less repeated and predictable, and "unique" features, features that depend upon the circumstances and are unpredictable. Typical features are unchanging within the model and can only be altered through exogenous shocks. Unique features involve learning and change with the passage of time and hence are endogenous features of the model. All pattern coordination requires is that individual actions "are coordinated with respect to their typical features, even if their unique aspects fail to mesh" (1985:85). Hence, individuals may plan to engage in patterns of actions that are regular and predictable while the specific content of the actions can entail learning and change. Out of this an order emerges that is recognizable because of its typical features, but not predictable because of the learning that takes place in its unique features. This notion of order encompasses both stability and ordered change as a feature of the model.[2]

O'Driscoll and Rizzo emphasize that the kind of new knowledge that arises from the unique features of their model through the passage of time is the Hayekian nontheoretical "knowledge of the particular circumstances of time and place" (Hayek, 1948: 521), and they identify the acquisition of this knowledge as solely an entrepreneurial activity:

Although such knowledge cannot be anticipated in either an exact or a probabilistic sense, the essence of entrepreneurship is to attempt to "see" these developments in advance. Because this aspect of the future is, by definition, time-dependent, no logically sufficient basis can be given for any particular prediction. Therefore, the entrepreneurial predictions will appear to be creative or intuitive rather than strict implications of a model. The goal of the economist, therefore, must be to render entrepreneurial prediction and its derivative behavior "intelligible." (1985:87)

That is, such behavior must be "intelligible" rather than predictable within the confines of the model.[3]

It is a merit of O'Driscoll and Rizzo's redefinition of equilibrium as pattern coordination that they incorporate aspects both of stability and change into their construct. It seems eminently consistent with Austrian

---

[2] For example, you may plan to do your weekly grocery shopping at a specific supermarket at a specific time in full confidence that the store will be open and have sufficient food for sale to meet your needs. However, you will not know exactly what selection will be available this week nor what the exact quality will be, nor do you know in perfect detail what you are likely to buy because those kinds of decisions will depend upon the circumstances of that time and that place. Even you, as the consumer, will not be able to predict the unique features of your transaction (exactly what you buy) although the typical features (that you will go shopping, that the store will be open and have an array of goods for sale) are easily predicted by you and by observant outsiders. Further, your unique and unpredicted actions will affect the future array of specific goods available for sale, but will not immediately affect the stable features of the transaction, the viability of the store itself.

[3] In terms of our supermarket example, one would have to call the specific decisions about what array of goods to purchase "entrepreneurial," to follow O'Driscoll and Rizzo exactly. Although this may be unconventional, it is certainly admissible, I should think.

assumptions to explain human action as a mixture of repeated patterns of behavior and unpredictable entrepreneurial discovery. But having said that, where do we go from here? The immediate implication O'Driscoll and Rizzo draw is that pattern coordination can make entrepreneurial action "intelligible" within the confines of their model rather than something exogenous to it, an improvement over models with no ability to account for unpredictable discovery except as exogenous shocks. Yet, although their formulation of pattern coordination is descriptively satisfying (we recognize a familiar world in their construct), it is not clear what other purpose pattern coordination can serve. O'Driscoll and Rizzo admit that they have not formalized a method of explaining indeterminate open-ended processes and they regard this as an urgent task for Austrian economics (1985:87). Before it can be formalized, we need to be clear about what work we want pattern coordination to perform (and what we mean by formalization).

O'Driscoll and Rizzo begin on the right track by distinguishing between typical patterns and unique behavior, but they make the functional separation between the two far too stark. A useful concept of order in human affairs should not only present both typical and unique aspects of human action, but should also show the important links between them. To see this better, we need to return for a moment to Lachmann's suggestions for a theory of institutions.

People carry out their projects and plans within a variety of social institutions, all of which have both tacit and explicit rules of behavior. These institutions vary from the formal systems of law to conventions of social behavior, to the explicit and implicit cultures of business organization. Indeed, an agreement between two people to engage in a recurrent pattern of behavior vis à vis each other is also a form of "institution" or typical behavior. What is common to all social institutions is that they place limits on our expectations about the future and in fact make the carrying out of our daily lives orderly rather than chaotic. Portions of the future become relatively predictable so that our plans have some hope of being realized. This is the truth that Lachmann was trying to capture in his discussions of *The Legacy of Max Weber*. Institutions, to Lachmann, were "points of orientation" for human beings. Creative or entrepreneurial action, according to Lachmann, takes place in the "interstices" of institutions: in the areas of freedom not bound by rigid rules of social order. This seems to dictate an analysis that explains entrepreneurial action within the confines of the institutional barriers, as O'Driscoll and Rizzo recommend. So far, we have no quarrel with O'Driscoll and Rizzo. One natural ambition within the Austrian tradition should obviously be to make particular nondeterministic entrepreneurial acts intelligible in its social context. However, we can go even further than this. As Lachmann pointed out, the institutions of society are not themselves unchanging. This seems to suggest the need to develop a theory of institutional change that is related to the entrepreneurial discoveries that introduce novelty into the system. O'Driscoll and Rizzo want to explain the changes in institutions as the product of exogenous shocks, yet an integrated theory of the market process would seem to require that the process of institutional change be itself endogenous (or at least *some* institutional changes should be explained endogenously). Changes in market institutions, for example, must at least some of the time be a consequence of human responses to new knowledge, even if the consequences are unintended.[4]

This is not exactly a new idea in the Austrian tradition. Menger's adaptation of the eighteenth century concept of a spontaneous order as an order that emerges as the product of human action but not of human design, an unintended consequence of individual purposeful action, is a way of explaining the emergence of social institutions as the product of learning that occurs in the particulars of time and place. And Menger's theory clearly contained the germ of Hayek's theory of the evolution of social institutions in *Law, Legislation and Liberty.*

Menger's story about spontaneous orders was one that relied on the discovery of some particular features of reality that proves profitable to the individual discoverer who is then imitated by others. Discovery and imitation and consequent institutional change are clearly part of an entrepreneurial market process. Where Menger can be criticized, however, is for concentrating too much on the successful outcomes of spontaneous orders, and for neglecting the importance of error and failure in the generation of new knowledge. Menger's theory of spontaneous order and of economic progress was one of continual improvement in knowledge and action over time, but this improvement is as much a product of failure as success.

To be sure, Menger portrayed human beings as having limited information and foresight, but he did not fully appreciate the implications of these limitations. People were at any moment in time ignorant of the capabilities of resources to satisfy their wants, but over time, they would become less ignorant and hence more wealthy. Yet the process of learning is never the product of success alone. All new knowledge comes about through some process of trial and error, the glimpse of a new idea and the

---

[4] Since all institutions are the product of human action, either intended or unintended, it is difficult to imagine a theory of human action that explained institutions as exogenously caused. Even the occurrence of fires, floods, earthquakes, and locust require that human beings adjust to new circumstances in novel ways that are not predictable in advance. A theory of human action should be able to account for such adjustments.

testing of this idea against the appropriate reality. In the marketplace, the learning that takes place is at least as much the consequence of entrepreneurial failure as of entrepreneurial success. Hence, the market process itself is a process of trial and error, of experimentation that may lead to success or failure, but always leads to the discovery of new knowledge, as Hayek suggested when he described the market as a discovery procedure. It seems obvious that this metaphor of trial and error and discovery should dictate the way in which Austrians frame their analysis of the market process.

This, too is not a new idea. Virtually every Austrian from Menger on has taken the trial-and-error process of market experimentation for granted as the background to their theorizing. Indeed, some notion of trial and error seems to be taken for granted by neoclassical economics, too, at least at the level of the stories it tells about the real world. Certainly, when we teach beginning students about price determination in markets, we cannot do so convincingly without some story of entrepreneurial alertness and imitation to flesh out our graphs.

Despite the shared acceptance of trial-and-error processes in both Austrian and neoclassical explanations of the market process, one would expect to find real differences between the two in their interpretation of the phenomenon. These "mere stories" of market adjustments are not considered scientific by the upper echelons of the neoclassical orthodoxy, whereas for Austrians, they are the heart of what economics should be explaining. Economics to an Austrian is about unidirectional and undetermined processes of change where the "stories" are the interpretive substance of the analysis. More interestingly, however, whereas within the context of neoclassical economics the "error" part of trial-and-error processes can only be understood as waste or market failure, to an Austrian, the error that constitutes part of the market process should be construed as both integral and beneficial. And clearly, it is unavoidable.

Austrians have not played this aspect of market discovery up as much as they should. As Hayek pointed out, the proper perspective on the market is not why does it ever fail, but why should it ever succeed. And the proper approach to learning is not how can we eliminate the mistakes but how can mistakes and error be channeled into productive knowledge. Looked at in this way, Kirzner's attempt to finesse the question of entrepreneurial error is unnecessary.[5] Entrepreneurial error is only worrisome within the

---

[5] We remember that Kirzner defines entrepreneurial error as the failure to perceive the appropriate means–ends framework. A more productive definition would be the acting on incorrect "hunches" so that entrepreneurial plans fail to be realized. A concomitant feature of this kind of failure is that because the conception, execution, and consequences of an entrepreneurial endeavor are not simultaneous events, entrepreneurial mistakes may initially communicate misinformation to others who then also act inap-

context of neoclassical equilibrium analysis, where the achievement of an artificially defined state of perfection is the goal of the model.[6] In the more "pattern-coordinated" world suggested by O'Driscoll and Rizzo, all entrepreneurial action leads to new knowledge that can either be useful or not depending upon the institutional rules or the "typical features" of the world in which entrepreneurs operate. The question, then, is how do the institutional structures of the marketplace permit the use of new knowledge in human action?[7]

Clearly, it seems a promising route to travel to bring the metaphor of experimentation to the foreground of market analysis. The market process of trial and error, of experimentation and learning, leads to the creation of new products, new production techniques, just as in neoclassical economics, but in addition, it points to the creation of new modes of human interaction. New forms of business, new techniques of marketing, new routines within a business culture can all be explained as the product of trial and error and experimentation. But all processes of experimentation, selection, and change are also subsets of another scientific metaphor, that of evolutionary biology. It seems unavoidable that an analysis of economic processes should borrow to some extent the language and structure of biological evolution.

Once again, this is not a new idea in Austrian circles. We remember that Menger was more influenced by Darwin than by Newton in his understanding of economic reality and in his emphasis on growth and change. Hayek also eventually used evolutionary reasoning in his work, although he applied it to the whole problem of the emergence and persistence of cultures rather than to specifically economic categories. Economists outside the Austrian tradition have also attempted to adapt evolutionary reasoning to economic processes. Armen Alchian (1950) and Jack Hirshleifer (1982), for example, have theorized about how trial-and-error processes and consumer selection can guarantee the achievement of standard equilibrium outcomes. More recently, Nelson and Winter

propriately. Rather than being considered waste, however, it might be the case that learning takes more than one observation to be effective. People might need the example of repeated failures at some endeavor before the message is clear that the project itself is faulty.

[6] It is one of the strengths of Kirzner's most recent attempt to deal with entrepreneurial error and uncertainty (1992) that he argues this point so effectively. What is important about entrepreneurs is that they act within the context of the current "underlying realities" in which the notion of perfect coordination is irrelevant.

[7] This is exactly the question Thomas Sowell arrived at in his important but underrated book, *Knowledge and Decisions* (1980). Whether action is efficient from the point of view of maximization is an irrelevant question. What is important is how do the institutional environments in which people act permit the generation, correction, and use of knowledge to achieve individual ends.

(1982) have argued for an evolutionary account of firm behavior and development. Evolution is the natural language of process and change.

There are several reasons why evolutionary language is particularly appropriate for Austrian economics. Biological evolution must explain both stability and change – the existence of identifiable species along with their evolution and extinction. It is also a theory about the development of an open-ended system in which the future is "unknowable but not unimaginable" and in which the focus of attention is on explaining the emergence of the present from the past rather than predicting the future. We remember that originally evolution was thought of as natural history. It is a theory, further, that explains the texture of the present as a consequence of the details of the past. Details and the accidents that operate upon them are responsible for the introduction of novel forms, the selection of those forms that are adaptive to their environments, and the proliferation of the selected novelty through replication or imitation. Biological evolution, moreover, does not posit any kind of tight notion of efficiency in the emergence of biological forms, but only an ability to get along. There is no notion of efficiency external to the fact of survival.

The similarities between these features of evolutionary theory and the Austrian perception of the nature of economic reality are obvious. What is not obvious is the exact way to adapt the evolutionary paradigm to economic uses. Some have begun to attempt the translation (Witt, 1991; Horwitz, 1992), but there is much work to be done. What, if anything, is the economic analogue to genes, reproduction, genetic crossovers, mutations, organisms, species, selection, adaptation? Is there even any reason to carry the translation of biological terms into economic categories to such a level of detail? How does the fact that humans communicate verbally (and nonverbally) and that they have purposes, intentions, and plans and control their actions through thought processes affect the evolution of their rules and artifacts?[8] In sum, what is the role of individual acting human beings in the origination, transmission, and selection of economic phenomena?

One approach to this question might be to think of economics as explaining not the "origin of species," but the origin, persistence, or failure of human institutions, those regular, observable patterns of action that lend stability and predictability to human life. A fruitful line of inquiry here would perhaps locate the source of novelty in the structure of the human brain that Hayek posits in *The Sensory Order*, where creativity is

---

[8] Lachmann believed the fact that humans were conscious planning agents was so unique a feature of their makeup that study of human action required a methodology "sui generis" (1977:88), and he specifically rejected biological metaphors as a model (1971:42).

the by-product of applying rules and abstractions to new configurations of reality. The trial-and-error process within the human brain leads to spontaneous and undetermined discovery that is reinforced through a process of trial and error in action that allows people to alter their habits incrementally to better adapt to their purposes and plans.[9] Yet, this is just the beginning of the road to creating an evolutionary economics along Austrian lines. Such a project would change dramatically our notions of efficiency and our understanding of the interrelationship of all the parts of the economic process.

Hayek and others argue convincingly that the economy should be thought of as a catallaxy: a system of overlapping sets of rules and institutions in which individuals pursue their projects and plans. The internal coherence of these rules and institutions and the coherence with the entrepreneurial pursuits then become a study of open-ended catallactic processes that have no one destination (although there will be as many destinations as there are individual participants), but nevertheless exhibit ordered change.

These are just tentative suggestions that may or may not prove fruitful as they are actually worked out. However, what seems certain is that a progressing, healthy Austrian research program will have to change the organizing metaphor of economic analysis to allow it to focus on its own questions rather than someone else's. These questions will concern the way in which purposeful individuals go about making a living in a world of limited but potentially increasing knowledge and radical uncertainty about the contours of the future. The answers will involve a penetrating analysis of the interaction of creative human intelligence and the routines and institutions of human life that will require not only new theories of human action, but a total rethinking of economic policy from the perspective of pattern coordination.

Austrian economics has long been associated with free market advocacy, either because of the many benefits the Austrians believe the free market confers on its participants (Mises), because of a prior commitment to freedom and property rights (Rothbard), because it holds up well by comparison to central planning (Hayek), or a combination of all three. Yet, two circumstances call for a rethinking of the usual free market message. The first is that the collapse of central planning as a viable option removes the old Austrian adversary from contention. One no longer must argue that decentralized markets are better than central planning; that is now a given. The question now is rather what is the

---

[9] For some explorations about the links between evolutionary theory and theories of the human mind and learning that take a somewhat Hayekian approach, see Bartley and Radnitzky (1987).

proper interaction between markets (human relationships based on property and contract) and government (human relationships based on making and enforcing through coercive means rules of interaction). The topic of the day is no longer socialism but "interventionism," and it is not always clear what constitutes an intervention.

Second, the economics of time and ignorance has not yet examined the full contours of a regime of property and contract sufficiently to be able to judge unequivocally that government action is always worse than private economic action. In order to do that, questions such as the stability of decentralized systems, the effects of government on those systems, the relative properties of markets and governments with respect to the creation and the dispersion of learning, and the efficacy with which plans can be achieved need to be recast. The problem of externalities and a genuine Austrian welfare economics needs to be explored.[10] This does not imply that there are no longer good arguments for the value of free markets to the achievement of human plans. Indeed, I suspect a recasting of the Austrian arguments in light of the recognition of time and ignorance will strengthen the arguments for decentralized markets rather than centralized government in economic affairs. However, work must be done to articulate and integrate these arguments once again.

Conclusion

A final note on the nature of an Austrian research program. I make no claim that my reading of the history and current debate within Austrian circles allows me to dictate "the" future of Austrian economics, or even to have supplied the definitive meaning of Austrian economics. If there are readers who wish to claim that my reading of the literature is not really Austrian, or is not orthodox Austrian, so be it. I claim merely that there are important ideas within the Austrian tradition – ideas about processes, subjectivism, learning, and time – that suggest new ways of theorizing about human beings as they go about pursuing their projects and plans using concrete resources. In many cases, the ideas I find important are not unique to the Austrian literature, nor are all the important advances in developing these ideas even found within Austrian literature.[11]

---

[10] This is already beginning to happen. See the recent book by Roy Cordato, *Efficiency and Externalities in an Open Ended Universe: A Modern Austrian Alternative* (1992), in which he argues that typical economic inefficiency is ineradicable in markets, but that one can define a notion of catallactic efficiency as the property of the institutional setting in which economic exchange takes place.

[11] Indeed, the overlap with the emerging field of constitutional political economy with its roots in the public choice literature is a case in point. The concern there with distinguishing between the choice of rules and action within rules has strong parallels

The Austrians have played an important role in keeping a set of ideas alive in the face of a sometimes hostile mainstream. Any progress forward, however, need not, indeed should not, be a further continuance of an isolated "Austrian" economics. The already noted links between law and economics, property rights theory, post-Keynesian theory, institutionalists, and evolutionary theorists, not to mention the still strong affinities with portions of mainstream microeconomic and monetary theory guarantee that genuine progress will come from some more heterodox community. This is all to the good. In fact, it seems indisputable that scientific understanding would be much improved if at some point in the future we could genuinely and intelligently say, along with Milton Friedman, there is no such thing as Austrian economics, only good economics and bad economics. But this time we would mean that good economics was an economics not only of preferences and constraints, but also an economics of time and ignorance.

with Hayek, although Buchanan has argued firmly against an evolutionary approach to understanding the formation of appropriate rules. For some classic statements of Buchanan's constitutional perspective, see Buchanan (1977). For an approach to choice of rules that is more influenced by an evolutionary perspective, see Vanberg (1993).

References

Alchian, A. A. 1950. "Uncertainty, evolution and economic theory." *Journal of Political Economy* 58(3):211–221.

Alter, Max. 1990. *Carl Menger and the origins of Austrian economics.* Boulder, Colo.: Westfield Press.

Armentano, Dominick. 1982. *Antitrust and monopoly: anatomy of a policy failure.* New York: Wiley and Sons.

Arrow, Kenneth. 1963. *Social choice and individual values.* New Haven: Yale University Press.

Barone, Enrico. [1908] 1935. "The ministry of production in the collectivist state." In F. A. Hayek, ed. *Collectivist economic planning,* 245–290. London: George Routledge and Son.

Bartley, W. W., and Gerard Radnitzky, eds. 1987. *Evolutionary Epistemology.* LaSalle, Ill.: Open Court.

Baumol, William, J. H. Panzar, and R. D. Willig. 1982. *Contestable markets and the theory of industry structure.* New York: Harcourt, Brace, Jovanovich.

Bergson, Abram. 1948. "Socialist economics." In Howard S. Ellis, ed., *A survey of contemporary economics,* 1:412–448. Homewood, Ill.: Richard D. Irwin.

Boettke, Peter. 1989. "Evolution and economics: Austrians as institutionalists." *Researches in the history of economic thought and methodology* 6:73–90.

1990a. *The political economy of Soviet socialism: The formative years, 1918–1928.* Dordrecht: Kluwer Academic.

1990b. "The theory of spontaneous order and cultural evolution in the social theory of F. A. Hayek." *Cultural dynamics.* III, 1.

Boettke, Peter, Steven Horwitz, and David Prychitko. 1986. "Beyond equilibrium economics." *Market process* 4(2): 6–9, 20.

Bohm-Bawerk, Eugen von. [1888] 1959. *The positive theory of capital.* Translated by George Huncke. South Holland, Ill.: Libertarian Press.

[1896] 1949. *Karl Marx and the close of his system.* New York: Augustus M. Kelley.

Bostaph, Samuel. 1978. "The methodological debate between Carl Menger and the German historicists." *Atlantic economic journal* 6(3):3–16.

Buchanan, James M. 1958. *Public principles of public debt.* Homewood, Ill.: Richard D. Irwin.

1969. *Cost and choice: an inquiry into economic theory.* Chicago: University of Chicago Press.

1975. *Limits of liberty: between anarchy and leviathan.* Chicago: University of Chicago Press.

1977. *Freedom in constitutional contract.* College Station: Texas A&M University Press.

1979. *What should economists do?.* Indianapolis: Liberty Press.

Buchanan, James M., and G. F. Thirlby, eds. 1973. *LSE essays on cost.* London: Weidenfeld and Nicolson.

Buchanan, James M., and Gordon Tullock. 1962. *The calculus of consent.* Ann Arbor: University of Michigan Press.

Buchanan, James M., and Richard Wagner. 1979. *Democracy in deficit: the political legacy of Lord Keynes.* New York: Academic Press.

Bukharin, Nikolai. [1919] 1970. *The economic theory of the leisure class.* New York: Augustus M. Kelley.

Burmeister, Edwin. 1974. "Neo-austrian and alternative approaches to capital theory." *Journal of economic literature* 12(2:)413–456.

Caldwell, Bruce J. 1988. "Hayek's transformation." *History of political economy* 20(4):513–542.

ed. 1990 *Carl Menger and his legacy in economics.* Annual supplement to volume 22, *History of political economy.* Durham, N.C.: Duke University Press.

Cordato, Roy E. 1992. *Welfare economics and externalities in an open ended universe: a modern Austrian perspective.* The Netherlands: Kluwer Academic.

Cornuelle, Richard. 1992. "The power and poverty of libertarian thought." *Critical Review* 6(1):1–10.

Cowen, Tyler, and Richard Fink. 1985. "Inconsistent equilibrium constructs: the evenly rotating economy of Mises and Rothbard." *American economic review* 75(4):866–869.

Craver, Earlene. 1986. "The emigration of the Austrian economists." *History of political economy* 18(1):1–32.

Dickinson, H. D. 1933. "Price formation in a Socialist community." *Economic journal* 43:237–250.

Dolan, Edwin G. ed. 1976. *The foundations of modern Austrian economics.* Kansas City: Sheed and Ward.

Dugger, William M. 1989. "Austrians vs. institutionalists: who are the real dissenters?" *Researches in the history of economic thought and methodology* 6:115–124.

Ebeling, Richard. 1986. "Toward a hermeneutical economics: expectations, prices and the role of interpretation in a theory of the market process." In Israel Kirzner, ed., *Subjectivism, intelligibility and economic understanding,* 39–55. New York: New York University Press.

Ferguson, Adam. [1767] 1980. *An essay on the history of civil society.* New Brunswick and London: Transaction Books.

Fink, Richard, ed. 1982. *Supply-side economics: a critical appraisal.* Frederick, Md.: University Publications of America.

Friedman, Milton. 1966. "Methodology of positive economics." In *Essays in positive economics.* Chicago: University of Chicago Press.

Friedman, Milton, and Anna Swartz. 1963. *A monetary history of the United States: 1857–1960.* Princeton, N.J.: Princeton University Press.

Galbraith, John Kenneth. 1949. "In defense of laissez-faire: review of Ludwig von Mises, *Human Action.*" *New York Times,* October 30, sec. vii: 45.

Garrison, Roger. 1982. "Austrian economics as the middle ground: comment on Loasby." In Israel Kirzner, *Method, process and Austrian economics,* 131–138. Lexington, Mass.: D. C. Heath.

   1984a. "Time and money: the universals of macroeconomic theorizing." *Journal of macroeconomics* 6(2):197–213.

   1984b. "Deficits and inflation: a comment." *Economic inquiry.* 25(4):593–596.

   1985. "Intertemporal coordination and the invisible hand: an Austrian perspective on the Keynesian vision." *History of political economy* 17(2):309–321.

Garrison, Roger, and Don Bellante. 1988. "Phillips curves and Hayekian triangles: two perspectives on monetary dynamics." *History of political economy* 20:207–234.

Greaves, Percy. 1963. "Review of *America's great depression* by Murray Rothbard." *The Freeman* (November 1963):60–64.

Grinder, Walter. 1977. "In pursuit of the subjectivist paradigm." Introduction to Ludwig Lachmann. *Capital, expectations and the market process* 3–24. Kansas City: Sheed, Andrews, and McMeel.

Haberler, Gottfried. 1937. *Prosperity and depression.* London: George Allen and Unwin.

Hahn, Frank. 1982. "Reflections on the invisible hand." *Lloyd's bank review* 144(April):1–21.

Harris, Seymour E. 1949. "Capitalist manifesto: review of Ludwig von Mises, *Human Action.*" *Saturday review of literature* (September 24): 31:32.

Hayek, Friedrich. 1931. *Prices and production.* London: George Routledge and Sons.

   [1933] 1966. *Monetary theory and the trade cycle.* New York: Augustus M. Kelley.

   1935. *Collectivist economic planning.* London: George Routledge and Sons.

   [1939] 1975. *Profits, interest and investment.* Clifton, N.J.:Augustus M. Kelley.

   1941. *The pure theory of capital.* Chicago: University of Chicago Press.

   1944. *The road to serfdom.* Chicago: University of Chicago Press.

   1948. *Individualism and economic order.* Chicago: University of Chicago Press.

   1952. *The sensory order.* London: Routledge and Kegan Paul.

   1955. *The counter-revolution of science.* Glencoe, Ill.: Free Press.

   1960. *The constitution of liberty.* Chicago: University of Chicago Press.

   1964. "Hayek on Menger." In Henry Spiegel, ed., *The development of economic thought,* 342–368. New York: John Wiley and Sons.

   1967. *Studies in philosophy, politics and economics.* Chicago: University of Chicago Press.

   1973. *Law, legislation and liberty: rules and order.* Vol. 1. Chicago: University of Chicago Press.

   1976. *Law, legislation and liberty: the mirage of social justice.* Vol. 2. Chicago: University of Chicago Press.

   1978a. *New studies in philosophy, economics and the history of ideas.* Chicago: University of Chicago Press.

1978b. *The denationalization of money – the argument refined: an analysis of the theory and practice of concurrent currencies.* 2d ed. London: Institute of Economics Affairs.

1979. *Law, legislation and liberty: the political order of a free society.* Vol. 3. Chicago: University of Chicago Press.

1988. *The fatal conceit: the errors of socialism.* Chicago: University of Chicago Press.

1992. *The fortunes of liberalism.* Vol. 4. of *The collected works of F. A. Hayek.* Edited by Stephen Kresge. Chicago: University of Chicago Press.

Hazlitt, Henry. [1946] 1979. *Economics in one lesson.* New York: Crown.

1959. *The failure of the new economics.* Princeton: D. Van Nostrand.

Heiner, Ron. 1983. "The origin of predictable behavior." *American economic review* 73:560–595.

Hennings, Klaus. 1987. "Eugen von Bohm-Bawerk." In J. Eatwell, M. Milgate, and P. Newman, eds., *The new Palgrave: a dictionary of economics,* 254–259. London: Macmillan.

Hicks, J. R. 1967. *Critical essays in monetary theory.* Oxford, Clarendon Press.

1973. *Capital and time: a neo-Austrian theory.* Oxford: Clarendon Press.

Hicks, J. R., and W. Weber, eds. 1973. *Carl Menger and the Austrian school of economics.* Oxford: Clarendon Press.

High, Jack. 1982. "Alertness and judgment: comment on Kirzner." In Israel Kirzner, ed., *Method, process and Austrian economics: essays in honor of Ludwig von Mises.* Lexington, Mass.: D. C. Heath.

1987. "A note on the cost controversy." *Market process* 5(1):8–10, 26–27.

1990. *Maximizing, action and market adjustment: an inquiry into the theory of economic disequilibrium.* Munich: Philosophia Verlag.

High, Jack, and Howard Bloch. 1989. "On the history of ordinal utility theory: 1900–1932." *History of political economy* 21(2):351–365.

High, Jack, and Clayton Coppin. 1988. "Wiley, whiskey and strategic behavior: an analysis of the passage of the Pure Food Act." *Business History Review* 62:286–309.

1991. *Regulation: economic theory and history.* Ann Arbor: University of Michigan Press.

Hirshleifer, Jack. 1982. "Evolutionary models in economics and law." *Research in law and economics* 4:1–60.

Hoppe, Hans-Hermann. 1989. "In defense of extreme rationalism: thoughts on Donald McCloskey's *The rhetoric of economics.*" *Review of Austrian economics* 3:179–214.

Horwitz, Steven. 1992. *Monetary evolution, free banking and economic order.* Boulder, San Francisco, Oxford: Westfield Press.

Hurwicz, Leonid. 1973. "The design of mechanisms for resource allocation." *American economic review* 63:1–30.

Hutchison, T. W. 1966. *A review of economic doctrines: 1870–1929.* Oxford: Clarendon Press.

Jaffe, William. 1975. "Menger, Jevons and Walras dehomogenized." *Economic inquiry* 14(4):511–524.

Johnson, Gregory R. 1990. "Hermeneutics: a protreptic." *Critical review* 4(1-2):173–211.

Keynes, John Maynard. [1936] 1964. *The general theory of employment, interest and money.* New York: Harcourt, Brace and World.

Kirzner, Israel M. [1960] 1976. *The economic point of view.* Kansas City: Sheed and Ward.

1963. *Market theory and the price system.* Princeton: D. Van Nostrand.

1966. *An Essay on capital.* New York: Augustus M. Kelley.

1973. *Competition and entrepreneurship.* Chicago: University of Chicago Press.

1976. "Ludwig von Mises and the theory of capital and interest." In Laurence S. Moss, ed., *The economics of Ludwig von Mises: toward a critical reappraisal.* Kansas City: Sheed and Ward.

1978. "The entrepreneurial role in Menger's system." *Atlantic economic journal* 6(3):31–45.

1979. *Perception, opportunity and profit.* Chicago: University of Chicago Press.

ed. 1982. *Method, process, and Austrian economics: essays in honor of Ludwig von Mises.* Lexington, Mass.: D. C.Heath.

1984. "Prices, the communication of knowledge and the discovery process." In K. Leube and A. Zlabinger, eds., *The political economy of freedom: essays in honor of F. A. Hayek,* 193–206. Munchen and Wien: Philosophia Verlag.

1985a. *Discovery and the capitalist process.* Chicago: University of Chicago Press.

1985b. "The economics of time and ignorance: review essay." *Market process* 3(2):1–4, 17–18.

ed. 1986. *Subjectivism, intelligibility and economic understanding: essays in honor of Ludwig M. Lachmann on his eightieth birthday.* New York: New York University Press.

1988. "The economic calculation debate: lessons for Austrians." *Review of Austrian economics* 2:1–18.

1992. "Market process theory: in defence of the Austrian middle ground." In *The meaning of the market process: essays in the development of modern Austrian economics.* London and New York: Routledge.

Klamer, Arjo, and David Colander. 1990. *The making of an economist.* Boulder, Colo.: Westview Press.

Knight, Frank. 1950. "'Introduction' to Carl Menger." *Principles of economics.* Glencoe, Ill.: Free Press.

Kuhn, T. S. 1970. *The structure of scientific revolution.* Chicago: University of Chicago Press.

Lachmann, Ludwig. 1971. *The legacy of Max Weber.* Berkeley: Glendessary Press.

1976a. "From Mises to Shackle: an essay." *Journal of economic literature* 14:54–62.

1976b. "On the central concept of Austrian economics: the market process." In E. Dolan, ed., *The foundations of modern Austrian economics,* 126–132. Kansas City: Sheed and Ward.

1976c. "On Austrian capital theory." In E. Dolan, ed., *The foundations of modern Austrian economics,* 145–151. Kansas City: Sheed and Ward.

1977. *Capital, expectations and the market process.* Edited with an introduction by Walter Grinder. Kansas City: Sheed, Andrews, and McMeel.

[1956] 1978a. *Capital and its structure.* Kansas City: Sheed, Andrews, and McMeel.

1978b. "An Austrian stocktaking: unsettled questions and tentative answers." In L. Spadaro, ed., *New directions in Austrian economics,* 1–18. Kansas City: Sheed, Andrews, and McMeel.

1978c. "Carl Menger and the incomplete revolution of subjectivism." *Atlantic economic journal* 6(3):57–59.

1985. "Review essay of *The economics of time and ignorance* by Gerald O'Driscoll and Mario Rizzo." *Market process* 3(2):1–4, 17–18.

1986. *The market as an economic process.* Oxford: Basil Blackwell.

Lakatos, Imre. 1970. "Falsification and methodology of scientific research programmes." In I. Lakatos and A. Musgrave, eds., *Criticism and the growth of knowledge.* Cambridge: Cambridge University Press.

Lange, Oscar. 1962. *Problems of political economy of socialism.* New Delhi: People's.

Lange, Oscar, and Fred M. Taylor. 1938. *On the economic theory of socialism.* New York: McGraw-Hill.

Langlois, Richard N. 1983. "The market process: an evolutionary view." *Market Process* 1:2.

1986a. "Coherence and flexibility: social institutions in a world of radical uncertainty." In Israel Kirzner, *Subjectivism, intelligibility and economic understanding,* 171–191. New York: New York University Press.

ed. 1986b. *Economics as a process: essays in the new institutional economics.* Cambridge: Cambridge University Press.

Lavoie, Don. 1978. "Austrian economics seminar, part I: 1975–76." *Austrian economics newsletter* 1(2):2, 4, 6, 8, 12.

1983. "Some strengths in Marx's disequilibrium theory of money." *Cambridge journal of economics* 7(1):55–68.

1985a. *Rivalry and central planning: the socialist calculation debate reconsidered.* Cambridge: Cambridge University Press.

1985b. *National economic planning: what is left?* Cambridge, Mass.: Ballinger.

1986a. "Marx, the quantity theory and the theory of money." *History of political economy* 18(1):155–170.

1986b. "Euclideanism versus hermeneutics: a reinterpretation of Misesian apriorism." In Israel Kirzner, ed., *Subjectivism, intelligibility and economic understanding,* 192–210. New York: New York University Press.

1987. "The accounting of interpretation and the interpretation of accounting." *Accounting organizations and society* 12(6):579–604.

1990a. "Understanding differently: hermeneutics and the spontaneous order of communicative processes." *History of political economy.* Annual supplement to volume 22:359–378.

1990b. "Introduction." In Don Lavoie, ed., *Economics and hermeneutics,* 1–15. London and New York: Routledge.

Leijonhufvud, Axel. 1968. *On Keynesian economics and the economics of Keynes.* New York: Oxford University Press.

1981. "Effective demand failures." In *Information and coordination,* 103–129. Oxford: Oxford University Press.

1986. "Capitalism and the factory system," in Richard N. Langlois, ed., *Economics as a process: essays in the new institutional economics.* Cambridge: Cambridge University Press.

Lerner, Abba. 1937. "Statics and dynamics in socialist economics." *Economic journal* 47:251–270.

Littlechild, Stephen. 1979a. "An Entrepreneurial theory of games." *Metroeconomica* 31:145–165.

1979b. *The fallacy of the mixed economy: an Austrian critique of conventional economics and government policy.* San Francisco: Cato Institute.

Littlechild, Stephen, and G. Owen. 1980. "An Austrian model of the entrepreneurial market process." *Economic journal* 91: 348–363.

Loasby, Brian. 1976. *Choice, complexity and ignorance.* Cambridge: Cambridge University Press.

1982. "Economics of dispersed and incomplete information." In Israel Kirzner, ed., *Method, process and Austrian economics: essays in honor of Ludwig von Mises.* Lexington, Mass.: D. C. Heath.

Machlup, Fritz. 1962. *The production and distribution of knowledge in the United States.* Princeton, N.J.: Princeton University Press.

1980. "An interview with Prof. Fritz Machlup." *Austrian economics newsletter* 3(1):1, 9–12.

McCloskey, Donald. 1985. *The rhetoric of economics.* Madison: University of Wisconsin Press.

Menger, Carl. [1871] 1981. *Principles of economics.* Translated by James Dingwall and Bert F. Hoselitz. New York: New York University Press.

[1883] 1985. *Investigations into the method of the social sciences with special reference to economics.* Translated by Francis J. Nock. Edited by Lawrence White. New York: New York University Press.

Mirowski, Philip. 1989. *More heat than light: economics as social physics: physics as nature's economics.* Cambridge: Cambridge University Press.

Mises, Ludwig. [1912] 1980. *The theory of money and credit.* Translated by H. E. Bateson. Indianapolis: Liberty Classics.

[1920] 1935. "Economic calculation in the socialist commonwealth." In F. A. Hayek, ed., *Collectivist economic planning,* 87–103. London: George Routledge and Sons.

[1922] 1981. *Socialism.* Indianapolis: Liberty Classics.

[1927] 1985. *Liberalism in the classical tradition.* Irvington-on-Hudson, New York: Foundation for Economic Education.

[1944] 1962. *Bureaucracy.* New Haven, Conn.: Yale University Press.

[1949] 1963. *Human action: a treatise on economics.* New Haven, Conn.: Yale University Press.

[1953] 1977. "Comments about the mathematical treatment of economic problems." *Journal of libertarian studies* 1(2):97–100.

[1962] 1978. *The ultimate foundations of economic science: an essay on method.* Kansas City: Sheed, Andrews, and McMeel.

1963. *Theory and history: an interpretation of social and economic evolution.* New Rochelle, N.Y.: Arlington House.

[1969] 1984. *The historical setting of the Austrian School of economics.* Auburn: Ludwig von Mises Institute.

1978. *Notes and recollections.* Translated by Hans F. Sennholz. South Holland, Ill.: Libertarian Press.

1979. *Economics policy: thoughts for today and tomorrow.* South Bend, Ind.: Regnery/ Gateway.

1981. *Epistemological problems of economics.* Translated by George Riesman. New York and London: New York University Press.

1990. *Money, method and the market process.* Edited by Richard Ebeling. Dordrecht: Kluwer Academic.

Mises, Margit von. 1984. *My years with Ludwig von Mises.* Cedar Falls, Iowa: Center for Futures Education.

Morgenstern, Oskar, and J. von Neumann. 1944. *The theory of games and economic behavior.* Princeton, N.J.: Princeton University Press.

Moss, Laurence S., ed. 1976 *The economics of Ludwig von Mises: toward a critical reappraisal.* Kansas City: Sheed and Ward.

1978. "Carl Menger's theory of exchange." *Atlantic economic journal* 6:17–29.

Moss, Laurence S., and Karen I. Vaughn. 1986. "Hayek's Ricardo effect: a second look." *History of political economy* 18(4):545–565.

Mueller, Dennis. 1989. *Public choice: II.* Cambridge: Cambridge University Press.

Murrell, Peter. 1983. "Did the theory of market socialism answer the challenge of Ludwig von Mises? A reinterpretation of the socialist controversy." *History of political economy* 15(1):92–105.

Nelson, Richard R., and Sidney G. Winter. 1982. *An evolutionary theory of economic change.* Cambridge, Mass.: Harvard University Press.

O'Driscoll, Gerald P. 1977. *Economics as a coordination problem: the contributions of Friedrich Hayek.* Kansas City: Sheed, Andrews, and McMeel.

1980a. "Frank Fetter and 'Austrian' business cycle theory." *History of political economy* 12(4):542–557.

1980b. "Justice, efficiency, and the economic analysis of law: comment on Fried." *Journal of legal studies* 9(2):355–366.

1986. "Money: Menger's evolutionary theory." *History of political economy* 18(4):601–616.

O'Driscoll, Gerald P., and Mario J. Rizzo. 1985. *The economics of time and ignorance.* Oxford: Basil Blackwell.

Palmer, Tom. 1987. "Gadamer's hermeneutics and social theory." *Critical review* 1(3):91–108.

Pierson, N. G. [1902] 1935. "The problem of value in the socialist community." In F. A. Hayek, ed., *Collectivist economic planning*. London: George Routledge and Sons.

Pigou, A. C. 1920. *The economics of welfare*. London: Macmillan.

Polanyi, Michael. 1958. *Personal knowledge: towards a post-critical philosophy*. Chicago: University of Chicago Press.

Prychitko, David. 1991. *Marxism and workers' self-management: the essential tension*. New York: Greenwood Press.

Reder, M. 1982. "Chicago economics: permanence and change." *Journal of economic literature* 20:1–38.

Rima, Ingrid. 1986. *Development of economic analysis*. Homewood, Ill.: Irwin.

Rizzo, Mario. 1978. "Praxeology and econometrics: A critique of positivist economics." In Louis M. Spadaro, ed., *New directions in Austrian economics*. Kansas City: Sheed, Andrews, and McMeel.

——— ed. 1979. *Time, uncertainty and disequilibrium: exploration of Austrian themes*. Lexington, Mass.: Lexington Books.

——— 1980a. "Can there be a principle of explanation in common law decisions – comment on Priest." *Journal of legal studies* 9(2):423–427.

——— 1980b. "The Mirage of Efficiency." *Hofstra law review* 8:641–658.

——— 1980c. "Law amid flux – the economics of negligence and strict liability." *Journal of legal studies* 9(2):291–318.

——— 1981. "The imputation theory of proximate cause: an economic framework." *Georgia law review* 15:1007–1038.

——— 1982. "A theory of economic loss in the law of torts." *Journal of legal studies* 11(2):281–310.

——— 1987. "Fundamentals of causation." *Chicago-Kent law review* 63(3):397–406.

Rizzo, Mario, and F. S. Arnold. 1980. "Causal apportionment in the law of torts – an economic theory." *Columbia law review* 80(7):1399–1429.

Robbins, Lionel. [1932] 1962. *An essay on the nature and significance of economic science*. London: Macmillan.

Robinson, Joan. 1933. *The economics of imperfect competition*. London: Macmillan.

Roll, Eric. 1974. *A history of economic thought*. Homewood, Ill.: Irwin.

Rothbard, Murray N. 1956. "Toward a reconstruction of utility theory." In Mary Sennholz, ed. *On freedom and free enterprise: essays in honor of Ludwig von Mises*, 224–262. Princeton, N.J.: D. Van Nostrand Company.

——— 1957. "In defense of extreme a priorism." *Southern economic journal* (January):214–220.

——— 1962a. *The panic of 1819*. Princeton, N.J.: D. Van Nostrand.

——— 1962b. *Man, economy and state*. 2 vols. Princeton, N.J.: D. Van Nostrand.

——— 1963. *America's great depression*. Princeton, N.J.: D. Van Nostrand Company.

——— 1970. *Power and market: government and the economy*. Menlo Park, Calif.: Institute for Humane Studies.

——— 1973. "Praxeology as the method of economics." In M. Natanson, ed., *Phenomenology and the social sciences*. Evanston, Ill.: Northwestern University Press.

1982. "Professor Hebert on entrepreneurship." *Journal of libertarian studies.*

1989. "The hermeneutical invasion of philosophy and economics." *The review of Austrian economics* 3:45–60.

Samuels, Warren J. 1989. "Austrian and institutional economics: some common elements." *Researches in the history of economic thought and methodology* 6:53–72.

Schmoller, Gustav. [1883] 1968. "Die Schriften von K. Menger und W. Dilthey, pur methodologie der staats- und Sozial-Wissenschaften" (K. Menger's and W. Dilthey's writings on the methodology of the political and social sciences). Bibliography & Reference Series 169. New York: Burt Franklin.

Schuller, George. 1950 "Review of *Human Action.*" *American economic review* 40:418–422.

Schumpeter, Joseph A. [1934] 1961: *The theory of economic development.* New York/ Oxford: Oxford University Press.

[1939] 1964. *Business cycles: a theoretical, historical and statistical analysis of the capitalist process.* New York: McGraw-Hill.

[1942] 1962. *Capitalism, socialism and democracy.* New York: Harper Torchbooks.

1954. *History of economic analysis.* New York: Oxford University Press.

Selgin, George. 1988. *The Theory of Free Banking.* Totowa, N.J.: Rowman and Littlefield and the Cato Institute.

Sennholz, Mary, ed. 1956. *On freedom and free enterprise: essays in honor of Ludwig von Mises.* Princeton, N.J.: D. Van Nostrand Co. Inc.

Shackle, G. L. S. [1958] 1967. *Time in economics.* Amsterdam: North Holland.

[1961] 1969. *Decision, order and time in human affairs.* Cambridge: Cambridge University Press.

1972. *Epistemics and economics: a critique of economic doctrines.* Cambridge: Cambridge University Press.

1979. "Imagination, formalism and choice." In Mario Rizzo, ed. *Time, uncertainty and disequilibrium,* 19–31. Lexington, Mass.: Lexington Books.

Shearmur, Jeremy. 1990. "From Hayek to Menger: biology, subjectivism and welfare." *History of political economy.* Annual supplement to vol. 22: 189–214.

Smith, Adam. [1759] 1982. *The theory of moral sentiments.* Indianapolis: Liberty Classics.

[1776] 1981. *An inquiry into the nature and causes of the wealth of nations.* Indianapolis: Liberty Classics.

Smith, Barry. 1990. "On the Austrianness of Austrian economics." *Critical review* 4(1-2):212–238.

Smolensky, Eugene. 1964. "Review of *America's great depression* by Murray Rothbard." *Business history review* 38:278–280.

Sowell, Thomas. 1980. *Knowledge and decisions.* New York: Basic Books.

Spadaro, Louis M., ed. 1978. *New directions in Austrian economics.* Kansas City: Sheed, Andrews, and McMeel.

Speigel, Henry, ed. 1964. *The development of economic thought.* New York: John Wiley and Sons.

Sraffa, Piero. 1926. "The law of returns under competitive conditions." *Economic journal* 36:535–550.

Streissler, Erich, 1972. "To what extent was the Austrian school marginalist?" *History of Political Economy* 4(2):426–441.

———. 1987. "Friedrich von Wieser." In *The new Palgrave: a dictionary of economics*. London: Macmillan.

———. 1990. "Carl Menger on economic policy: the lectures to Crown Prince Rudolf." *History of political economy*. Annual supplement to vol. 22:107–132.

Stigler, George. 1941. "Carl Menger." In *Production and distribution theories*, 134–157. New York: Macmillan.

Stigler, George, and Gary Becker. 1977. "De Gustibus non est disputandum." *American Economic Review* 67:76–90.

Vanberg, Viktor. 1986. "Spontaneous Market Order and Social Rules: A Critical Examination of F. A. Hayek's theory of Cultural Evolution." *Economics and Philosophy* 2(1):75–100.

———. 1993. "Rational choice, rule-following and institutions: An evolutionary perspective." In B. Gustafsson, C. Knudsen, and U. Maki, eds., *Rationality, Institutions and Economic Methodology*. London: Routledge.

Vaughn, Karen I. 1978. "The reinterpretation of Carl Menger: some notes on recent scholarship." *Atlantic economic journal* 6(3):62–64.

———. 1980a. "Economic calculation under socialism: the Austrian contribution." *Economic inquiry* 18:535–554.

———. 1980b. "Does it matter that costs are subjective?" *Southern economic journal* 46(3):702–715.

———. 1987a. "Carl Menger." In John Eatwell, Murray Milgate, and Peter Newman, eds., *The new Palgrave: a dictionary of economics*, 438–444. London: Macmillan.

———. 1987b. "The invisible hand." In John Eatwell, Murray Milgate, and Peter Newman, eds., *The new Palgrave: a dictionary of economics*, 997–999. London: Macmillan.

———. 1990. "The Mengerian roots of the Austrian revival." *History of political economy*. Annual supplement to volume 22:379–407.

———. 1992. "The problem of order in Austrian economics: Kirzner vs. Lachmann." *Review of political economy* 4:251–274.

Veblen, Thorstein. 1919. *The place of science in modern civilization and other essays*. New York: Huebsch Press.

Wagner, R. E. 1977a. *Inheritance and the State: Tax Principles for a Free and Prosperous Commonwealth*. Washington, D.C.: American Enterprise Institute.

———. 1977b. "Economic manipulation for political profit: macroeconomic consequences and constitutional implications." *Kyklos* 30:395–410.

———. 1978. "Carl Menger's contribution to economics: introduction and final remarks." *Atlantic economic journal* 6(3):1–2, 65–69.

———. 1979. "Comment: politics, monetary control, and economic performance." In Mario J. Rizzo, ed., *Time, uncertainty and disequilibrium*, 177–186. Lexington, Mass.: Lexington Books.

White, Lawrence. [1976] 1990. "Entrepreneurship, imagination and the question of equilibration." In Stephen Littlechild, ed., *Austrian economics*. Vol. 3. Hants, England: Edward Elgar.

1984a. "Competitive payments systems and the unit of account." *American economic review* 74:699–712.

1984b. *Free banking in Britain: theory, experience and debate, 1800–1845*. Cambridge: Cambridge University Press.

1987. "Accounting for non-interest-bearing currency: a critique of the legal restrictions theory of money," *Journal of Money Credit and Banking* 19(4).

1989. *Competition and currency: essays on free banking and money*. New York: New York University Press.

White, Lawrence, and George Selgin. 1987. "The evolution of a free banking system." *Economic inquiry* 25(3):439–457.

Weiser, Friedrich von. [1893] 1971. *Natural value*. New York: Augustus M. Kelley. [1927] 1967. *Social economics*. New York: Augustus M. Kelley.

Will, Robert. 1962. "Review of *Man, economy and state* by Murray Rothbard." *Library journal.* 87:2541.

Wiseman, Jack. 1985. "Economics, subjectivism and public choice." *Market process* 3(2):14–15.

Witt, Ulrich. 1991. "Evolutionary theory – the direction Austrian economics should take?. In B. Caldwell and S. Boehm, eds., *Austrian economics: tensions and new developments*. Dodrecht/Boston: Kluwer Academic.

Wright, David McCord. 1950. "Review of *Human action*," *The annals of the American academy of political and social science* 268:229–30.

Yeager, Leland. 1987a. "Why subjectivism?" *Review of Austrian economics* 1:5–31. 1987b. "The cost controversy." *Market process* 5(2):25, 27.

Index

191

Made in the USA
Lexington, KY
29 August 2013